SHANE WARNE
My Autobiography

KT-432-398

SHANE WARNE

My Autobiography

Shane Warne

with
Richard Hobson

CORONET BOOKS
Hodder & Stoughton

Copyright © 2001 by Shane Warne

First published in paperback in Great Britain in 2002
by Hodder and Stoughton
A division of Hodder Headline PLC

The right of Shane Warne to be identified as the Author of
the Work has been asserted by him in accordance with the
Copyright, Designs and Patents Act 1988.

A Coronet paperback

6 8 10 9 7

All rights reserved. No part of this publication may be
reproduced, stored in a retrieval system, or transmitted,
in any form or by any means without the prior written
permission of the publisher, nor be otherwise circulated
in any form of binding or cover other than that in which
it is published and without a similar condition being
imposed on the subsequent purchaser.

A CIP catalogue record for this title is available
from the British Library

ISBN 0 340 769987 4

Typeset in Linotype Berling by
Rowland Phototypesetting Ltd,
Bury St Edmunds, Suffolk
Printed and bound in Great Britain by
Mackays of Chatham plc, Chatham, Kent

Hodder and Stoughton
A division of Hodder Headline PLC
338 Euston Road
London NW1 3BH

PHOTOGRAPHIC ACKNOWLEDGEMENTS

The author and publisher would like to thank the following
for permission to reproduce photographs:

David Allen, AllSport, Associated Press, Richard Binns, Philip
Brown, Colorsport, Patrick Eagar, East Sandringham Boys Club,
Empics, Hawthorn Football Club, Tom Jenkins, *Lancashire
Evening Telegraph*, Mentone Grammar, Popperfoto, Press
Association, Reuters, St Kilda Football Club, Col Whelan.

All other photographs are from private collections.

I would like to dedicate this book to my family for being there for me day in, day out and for putting up with so much. Thank you.

To my Mum and Dad for everything you have done and continue to do for me throughout my life.

To Jason, my brother and friend. You are a star and without you beside me as we grew up my competitive spirit would never have emerged. Thanks, mate.

To Simone, Brooke, Jackson and Summer. You are my life. You mean the world to me and I thank you for the wonderful joy you bring to me every day.

Acknowledgement

I would like to thank Richard Hobson, the *Times* cricket writer, for his invaluable help in putting down my recollections in a readable form. It has been an excellent partnership.

Shane Warne

CONTENTS

FOREWORD

by Ian Botham

I WAS FLATTERED to be asked to write this foreword – not only because Shane Warne is such a great cricketer, but because he's an Aussie. Everybody knows about the Ashes rivalry and being accepted by the old enemy is one of the biggest compliments I can imagine.

One of my regrets is that I couldn't hang around for long enough to play against Warney in the big arena. I would love to have taken him on in his pomp and I dare say he would have relished the challenge as well. We've exchanged plenty of friendly banter about it down the years. I'd have tried to hit him over the top – easier said than done. Let's just say the contest would have been worth watching.

At his best, he is quite simply the greatest spin bowler the game has ever seen. If he stays fit I'm sure he can reach 500 Test wickets and pass the magnificent record set by Courtney Walsh. Not many players in the game today can even think about that, but then Warney is a genuine match winner.

He has done more for the game than simply made life a misery for batsmen. Few players have been better ambassadors. Sometimes we forget that we're part of the entertainment industry, but not Warney. His charisma and emotion shine through and I don't think it's an exaggeration to say that he has single-handedly inspired tens of thousands of kids to pick up bat and ball. You only have to look at the number of them flipping leg-breaks to each other on the outfields at lunch and tea.

What about Shane Warne the man? Well, I can give you one tip straight away. Don't take him along to a restaurant if you fancy a good meal. Unless toasted cheese sandwiches or ham and pineapple pizza are on the menu, he won't be interested.

Despite our culinary differences, Warney has become a really good friend over the years. And the fact that's he's always good for a few quid on the golf course doesn't influence my judgement one bit! Away from the spotlight and among people he trusts he is one of the lads. He enjoys a beer, a laugh and a good time as much as the next man. But he's also one of the warmest, most loyal and generous people I've been lucky enough to come across. We've had some good nights down the years and I dare say a few sore heads the next morning.

So it's always good news to find out that Warney is in town, with his lovely wife and family. He's been a credit to the game. Long may he keep on twirling away.

Ian Botham

SHANE WARNE CHRONOLOGY

Compiled by Richard Hobson

Born Ferntree Gully, 13 September 1969

1990–91

Attends Cricket Academy at the Australian Institute of Sport. Makes first-class debut for Victoria.

1991–92

Makes Test debut against India at Sydney. Ravi Shastri becomes first Test wicket.

1992–93

Tours Sri Lanka and takes 7–52 against West Indies at Melbourne. Then tours New Zealand, making his one-day international debut at Wellington.

1993

Tours England and takes the wicket of Mike Gatting with his first ball in Ashes cricket.

1993–94

Match figures of 12–128 against South Africa at Sydney. Takes his 100th Test wicket (Brian McMillan) in 23rd game. Tours South Africa and plays in Sharjah. Named International Cricketer of the Year.

1994

Named Wisden Cricketer of the Year.

1994–95

Tours Sri Lanka, Pakistan and New Zealand. Career best figures of 8–71 against England at Brisbane and hat-trick (Philip DeFreitas, Darren Gough and Devon Malcolm) in the next Test at Melbourne. Then tours West Indies.

1995–96

Helps Australia to reach the World Cup final in India and Pakistan, losing to Sri Lanka. Claims 200th Test wicket (Chaminda Vaas) in 42nd match. Undergoes operation on spinning finger.

1996–97

Tours South Africa. Made captain of Victoria.

1997

Tours England and passes Richie Benaud's record of 248 Test wickets to become most successful leg-spinner in international history.

1997–98

Takes 300th Test wicket (Jacques Kallis) in 63rd game. Tours India and plays in Sharjah. Stands in for Steve Waugh to captain

Australia in a one-day international. International Cricketer of the Year for a second time. Becomes most successful spinner in the history of cricket, overtaking Lance Gibbs' haul of 309 wickets.

1998–99

Undergoes shoulder operation but takes the wicket of Mark Butcher in his first over back for Australia. Tours West Indies. Captains his country in ten one-day internationals.

1999

Helps Australia to win the World Cup as joint leading wicket taker in the tournament (20 at 18.05). Man of the match in semi-final and final.

1999–2000

Tours Sri Lanka, Zimbabwe, New Zealand and South Africa. Takes 356th Test wicket (Paul Wiseman) to overtake Dennis Lillee's Australian record.

2000

Plays county cricket in England, for Hampshire. Named one of the Cricketers of the Century by Wisden Cricketers' Almanack (along with Sir Donald Bradman, Sir Garfield Sobers, Sir Vivian Richards, Sir Jack Hobbs). Selected in Australian Team of the Century.

2000–01

Breaks finger while fielding for Victoria. Recovers to tour India. Tours England and claims 31 wickets as Australia retain the Ashes. Takes 400th wicket (Alec Stewart) in 92nd game, the first Australian bowler and sixth ever to reach the landmark.

1

EARLY DAYS

S OMETIMES I wonder how different my life might have been
if I was a few inches taller and a bit quicker, like in the
film *Sliding Doors*. The chances are I might not have played
professional cricket. As a child I had one and only one ambition
– to be an Australian Rules footballer. I wanted to be another
Dermott Brereton or Trevor Barker, two of the kings of the
sport in the Melbourne area at the time. While I did play a bit
of cricket in the summer it was only because my mates did.
Temperatures are pretty high in Australia and being on the
beach was more fun than the thought of racing around a cricket
field all afternoon. It was only when I reached the age of nineteen and was deemed surplus to the requirements of my
beloved St Kilda Aussie Rules club that I even thought of
cricket as a possible livelihood. Unbelievably, some three years
later I was making my Test debut.

I genuinely thought I had a chance of making the grade
at Aussie Rules, right up to the day when that heartbreaking
letter of rejection landed on the doormat. It seemed that,
despite the hundreds of hours of practice I put in over a
number of years, I just didn't have the goods required at
that level in the late 1980s. My favourite position had
always been full forward, which I filled quite successfully at
school and in the junior levels. My strengths were that I was

1

quick over short distances, had decent hands and a good kick.

Once I started to play against adults, though, I was just too short, and then when I moved to half-forward I wasn't fast enough to cover the ground. The people who mattered decided I was almost good enough in two positions, but not quite there in either. The truth hurts sometimes. In my opinion I just wasn't good enough.

Setbacks like that had been rare in my childhood and youth. I was really happy both at home and school – more so than I realised at the time where school is concerned. I was very fortunate to have a mum and dad who were helpful and supportive of everything my brother and I wanted to do. They encouraged me to try everything that came my way but without pushing or forcing me to do something I didn't fancy. They were always there with lifts to and from activities. Now, when a parent asks me when I think their child will be old enough to start cricket, I tell them they should let him try all sports, not just concentrate on one. Kids fall naturally into what they really like and if that happens to be tennis or soccer rather than cricket, then so be it. The important thing is to let them taste as much variety as possible. I even gave up a year of football to play competitive tennis.

My mum, Brigitte, and dad, Keith, were both sporty at heart. Like all good Australians they loved the outdoor life. Mum played basketball and tennis, she was a natural athlete and very fit. She was born in Germany but emigrated with her parents at a very young age. With my dad also extremely keen on tennis, as well as football, they were obviously a match waiting to happen.

Jason, my younger brother, was happy to spend hours with me in the backyard playing Aussie Rules, tennis and cricket, as we imitated the stars of the day. Mum and dad moved around the Melbourne area a fair bit, from Ferntree Gully, then

Hampton, and have settled in Black Rock by the sea. Even at an early age I realised that life doesn't come much better than relaxing on the beach as the sun beats down. It's great fun on the beach.

As a schoolboy I could hardly describe myself as academic. A lot of time I would be a lesson behind. If the lesson was English, I would be doing my Maths homework from the previous night ready for the next lesson. Then in Maths, I might be copying somebody's History essay. Somehow the work usually got done and I managed to scrape through. Now I realise how easy and how much fun those days really were, but at the time I just thought school was a pain in the neck, something that was stopping me from being on the beach or playing sport. I had a lot of luck at cards against one particular person and stopped in at his family shop and accepted cigarettes and chips as payments. I was lucky in my involvement with the cricket and football teams. I had a lot of friends at school.

Perhaps I should have taken lessons more seriously. I liked to see the funny side in everything. I was mischievous rather than nasty, especially on camps and field trips where we could escape from the teacher's attention. Inevitably this made me more familiar with the headmaster's study than I would have liked. 'Bend over, Warne, it's time to practise my golf swing,' the head would say on more occasions than I care to remember, before swishing the cane across my backside and sending me running towards the toilets to check the blood marks. If only I'd engaged my brain before my mouth, school would have been a much less painful experience.

I began at Sandringham Primary, then Hampton High for years seven, eight and nine, before winning a sports scholarship to go to Mentone Grammar, an all-boys establishment which, much to my approval, recognised the importance of sport on the curriculum. Of the academic subjects my favourite was

3

book-keeping and accounting. I even enrolled in a course for six months or so when I left but lost complete interest when we started to learn contract law. After fifteen years in classrooms I decided that enough was probably enough. I was a pretty ordinary student whose desires lay elsewhere. English was possibly my least favourite lesson. I can honestly say I have never read a complete book in my life. I've started a few but tend to lose concentration and forget what has happened in the previous pages. Sometimes now I will have a quick look at the pictures if I see one of Steve Waugh's diaries or another cricket book in the dressing room, but that's about all.

Growing up in the days of Lillee and Thomson, it was inevitable that most kids my age wanted to bowl as fast as we could. I was no different, except that I suppose I had a more curious mind than some of my mates. My first club was East Sandringham. I played for them until I moved to Mentone Grammar, where I played for the school at weekends. After junior practice I would sometimes stay behind to watch the grown-ups in the nets. I became fascinated at the way they could make the ball spin either way without my being able to spot the difference.

Much has been written about my earliest days as a spinner, but in truth I don't believe I was discovered as such by one person. There is no single defining moment when I saw the light and thought this was what I wanted to do for the next twenty years. I vaguely remember Ron Cantlon, a coach at East Sandringham, showing me the basic leg-spinner's grip and talking to me about spin bowling. Kim Pitt, the club captain, was another who gave me encouragement and is still a very good cricketer and friend.

But I genuinely believe that wrist-spinners have an innate natural ability. It is not a skill that can be taught from scratch because it is so unusual, and even those who are fortunate enough to have the aptitude need to put in hours and hours of hard work to develop accuracy and learn the basics. Perhaps more than any other aspect of cricket, I really think there is a craft to wrist-spin.

I was lucky that I could always spin the ball. That was the ability I had been given, but it took a long time to be able to put in on the right spot and in games I tended to mix it up with some medium pace – or fast as I liked to consider it – until probably my mid-teens. Away from matches, I would still practise and talk to as many people who were prepared to give me a few minutes about ways of improving. One thing I am good at is listening, which you need to be, especially as a leg-spinner. Basically, I taught myself as a kid, and along the way made some refinements. I had a good temperament as a youngster which has helped me in my international career.

I was fifteen when I managed to break in to the 1st XI at Mentone. We had a South African coach, John Mason, who encouraged and built up the spin bowling which had become my stock. I always got a great thrill when I captured a wicket. Not much has changed. I went on to captain the Associated Grammar Schools and to get some games for Victoria under-19s. It was through a teacher at Mentone Grammar called Andrew Lynch, a decent opening batsman with St Kilda CC, that I initially went down there while I was finishing my school days.

I spent some time with Brighton CC at sub-district level. The standard was not so high but the atmosphere seemed very relaxed. Most important, my best mates from school also played for them. Ole Mortensen, the Danish seam bowler who enjoyed success in England with Derbyshire, was player-coach. Once I finished school I left Brighton and went to St Kilda. As now, I liked to hit the ball hard, although my scores were somewhat better in junior cricket and I even managed to score the odd hundred, something that has eluded me in the first-class game (a first-class century: dreams are free!).

Games were always competitive at St Kilda CC, but I soon noticed the great camaraderie between our players and the opposition. They would always stay for a drink afterwards and I could see how the game forged so many friendships. My own beginnings could not have been much lower key. Shaun Graf, the player-coach, who also appeared for Victoria, started me in the 3rd XI. In fact, it was only when I reached the 2nd XI that people really thought I might be able to make a half-decent leggie. That was in 1988, by which time I was out of school and about to suffer the biggest disappointment of my brief life.

I'm not exactly sure what originally attracted me to Aussie Rules. I think it was the aggression, the camaraderie, getting dirty and taking that 'speccy' – the spectacular mark. It is a much quicker, more physical game than cricket and happens to be especially strong in the Melbourne area. Living just around the corner from the old Saints ground in Moorabbin, it seemed natural to support St Kilda and particularly Trevor Barker, one of the all time greats. Barker was the guy who first gave me the nickname 'Hollywood' when we had to introduce ourselves at the club. It was a great thrill to get to know people down at the club and I'm still friends with a lot of them but to get to know Barks was something I will always treasure. We became good friends until, tragically, he died a few years ago. Sometimes it's hard to see why things happen and why bad things happen to good people. Since then I have tried to help with the Trevor Barker Foundation which was set up in his memory and honour. I still wear my St Kilda jumper with a mixture of pride and regret today.

One player I liked watching because of his aggressiveness was Dermott Brereton, of nearby Hawthorn, a real flamboyant character with a great sense of fun who gave no quarter on the field. He was a rough diamond, but a diamond nonetheless. He wore an earring, dyed his hair peroxide blond and drove a Ferrari. Sound familiar? People don't believe me when I try to explain that I haven't consciously modelled myself on Brereton. How could I? His hair is long and bushy, mine has always been short or spiky. My brother Jason and I always played games in our backyard, footy or cricket. The footy always became more heated. We would try to imitate the brash and flamboyant way he made his marks.

I spent two years at St Kilda football club. The pay cheque of $30 seemed like a fortune at the time. I had been doing pretty well for the under-19s and was placed on emergency for the reserves for something like eight games without being required. With the season drawing to an end I started to wonder whether my big chance would ever come. During this particular week I had been struck down with a virus and had been sweating and shivering in bed – the classic symptoms of flu – and as the illness showed no sign of clearing by the weekend I decided to ring the club and tell them I was unavailable for the next under-19 game.

By a fateful coincidence, the phone rang before I could pick up the receiver and tap in the club number. It just happened to be Gary Colling, the reserves coach, breaking the good news that my chance to play for the reserves had finally dawned. Someone else had pulled out due to illness. There were seconds to make a decision. In the end, I thought it was the opportunity I had been waiting for. It could be my only chance and I had to take it. I overlooked all the evidence to convince myself I might have something of a recovery. If not, I would surely be able to get through the game, against Carlton, on adrenalin, passion, aggression, hunger. I couldn't have been more wrong.

By the day of the game I was no better, the ground was really wet and muddy and my marker happened to be one of the biggest, intimidating figures you could imagine. I was on and off the field, too weak to make any impression. I was trying to find something extra, dig deep, but I couldn't physically do it. My funniest memory comes from the last five minutes, when the ground was filling up before the senior game and I won a free kick right on the goal square. That was to prove the one chance of my life to kick a goal in front of a big crowd – but instead they played advantage. I think when the club officials came to discuss the playing staff for the 1989 season that listless performance counted against me, but who knows, it's something I might find out one day.

Life can be very strange. I don't know what might have happened if the opportunity had come the following week, when I was fit and raring to go again. As I keep saying, everything happens for a reason, and maybe this was a way of nudging me towards the other sport – cricket. Be that as it may, I know that my experience of Aussie Rules stood me in good stead for the future. Cricket is a team game but Aussie Rules is completely team-orientated, more run-through-brick-walls stuff, one for all and all for one. I learnt the importance of thinking about the whole picture rather than my own little corner, and whatever criticism is levelled against me as a cricketer, I don't think I can be described as selfish.

The letter of rejection came like a bolt out of the blue. I really thought I was close to a breakthrough. Being so near, at least in my own mind, made it even worse. A lot of sport at the highest level is about handling pressure and throughout my subsequent career in cricket I have invariably done well on the big occasion. Anyway, there I was, about to hit the age of twenty with my one ambition down the pan and nothing on which I could fall back. When Rick Gough, a mate from St Kilda CC suggested going to England with him for the winter to play cricket, I saw it as a way of having some fun and delaying my entry into the real world while I contemplated what to do next.

I had taken a month out after leaving school to travel around England and Europe in 1988. This was a fun trip as we went to Los Angeles, Rome, Florence, Venice, Innsbruck, Munich, London, then finished on Hawaii. It was a hell of a tour, it was fantastic. Some of us knew each other, some didn't, but we got along really well and had a ball. Unfortunately, we haven't seen much of each other since then but one day we all might get back together and share a drink over old times.

When I played I was as committed as anybody. Even after cementing a place in the 2nd XI at St Kilda CC (or so I thought) during the 1988–89 season, I did not know whether I would be able to make the next step up. But playing that summer in England kindled my enthusiasm and, as well as enjoying life to the full, I thought I'd made a number of significant improvements. One of the worst things to happen was that I put on nearly three stone and my dad didn't even recognise me when he came to meet me at the airport. Imagine my dismay when I came back to be dispatched immediately back down to the thirds. You could have got long odds then on me playing for Australia two years later, and even with my love for a bet I'm not sure I would have taken them.

In truth, my demotion was a warning to get back in shape after lording and larding it up in England rather than a reflection of my ability. I took heed of the message and with encouragement from Graf, the Fuhrer as he was known, a hard taskmaster but a fair man, and with injuries to a number of players, including the senior leggie at the club, Jamie Hascomb, I managed to reclaim my place in the seconds and then break into the firsts within two months. It turned out to be a very good season. I responded to Graf's faith in my bowling and managed to give the ball a good rip. We even reached the final of the competition and needed 18 runs to win when I joined Graf as the last man, only to finish 3 runs short when the captain lost his wicket, having ordered me to block at the other end. I was instructed not to play any shots, not even my favourite cut.

The next season Graf recommended me to the Victorian state selectors and I decided not to take up an offer to play Aussie Rules for Old Mentonians to concentrate on cricket. For the first time I felt a real momentum about my cricket. I had passion and determination and was ready to give it a real go. It also seemed that I was coming through at exactly the right time. The Academy of the Australian Institute of Sport was up and running and, unknown to me, the Australian selectors were on the lookout for leg-spinners as potentially the best way to end West Indies' domination of the world game. The Academy was where I was to end up and I went on a youth tour to the West Indies with some success in 1990.

It is hard to imagine what I might have done without cricket. In my late teens and early twenties I held a few jobs and I guess I might have continued to go from one position to another. I worked as a delivery boy for a local pizza shop – a labour of love but not really career-orientated, and hardly a great way to keep in trim. And no, there weren't bite-sized marks in any of the pizzas when I handed them over! Then I worked delivering beds for a company called Forty Winks which was owned by a family friend. It was great fun setting off in the truck and I worked with some good people and I invite anybody who thinks it is easy to try and manoeuvre a queen-sized mattress up three flights of stairs and then into a back room single-handed. Unfortunately, I didn't endear myself to the boss when I hit a garage trying to reverse one of the company trucks. Then there was the occasion when I tried to set up a waterbed the wrong way and had to call him out at 11 pm to help rectify the situation. Perhaps it was best to start looking for alternative employment after that. I also worked in a jewellery factory – once again owned by family friends – which was fun and interesting but a little bit too precise and laborious for my character.

Yes, taking all things into consideration I think I stumbled into the right career eventually.

2

CRICKET ACADEMY

MORE THAN TEN YEARS after leaving the Cricket Academy at the Australian Institute of Sport my period in Adelaide continues to be the subject of confusion. For some reason people still think that I was expelled. That is far from the truth. I left entirely of my own volition. I am not saying that the powers of the time lost much sleep at my departure, but I was certainly not kicked out. The Academy was very quick to claim me as the first of their protégés to go on to play Test cricket and put my photograph up on the wall there when I made my debut for Australia in 1991–92, little more than twelve months after leaving.

The facts of the matter are well known, but I make no apology for repeating the story here. The Academy team was in Sri Lanka but they had decided that I shouldn't tour because of a pool prank. Problems then came to a head when they wanted me to train with South Australia, whereas I always wanted to play for Victoria, my home state. I joined in with the state side in Adelaide a couple of times, but never felt I was being used as anything more than a net bowler. I thought that the idea of the Academy was to provide tuition for young cricketers, but at that stage I was not receiving any help. If I was going to train with a state squad I would rather train with the Vics. In the end I wrote a letter saying that I thought it was best for the Academy and myself if I left to try to get in the Victoria team. Without speaking to anybody in authority, I handed the note to Brendon Flynn who was in charge, packed the car and settled myself for the drive back to Melbourne. Simple as that. Sorry no gory stories, just facts.

What happened over the next year suggests that I made the right decision. Indeed, it was only a week or so later on 15 February 1991 that I made my full debut against Western Australia who included Damien Martyn, also at the Academy that year. Looking back objectively, I think that more than anything I was frustrated that my expectations of the Academy did not materialise. I did not think that I was handled particularly well, but I would like to stress that, for all the disagreements and disappointments, I do not harbour a grudge against anybody.

I am not going to pretend that I was an angel. Having said that, if all the stories about my behaviour were true then I would probably not have left alive. Some of the tales have been exaggerated for whatever motive, but nor was I ever a model pupil. I did not like the way that we seemed to be treated more like school children than young adults. There was an occasion, for example, when I was made to swim in a heavily chlorinated pool without goggles because I was not allowed to borrow a pair, having forgotten my own. Admittedly it was not my first transgression, and the problem this time stemmed from the fact that I had stayed out all night and was unable to return to the digs to pick up my gear for the 7 a.m. start – but my eyes burnt for days afterwards. That was more like medieval torture than a just punishment and it made me even more resentful towards authority. But I didn't forget my goggles again.

I ought to put my time at the Academy into context. I had already spent a winter playing in Bristol in England and had travelled around Europe with a few mates, so I was more streetwise about the ways of the world than a lot of lads my age. You could have described me as a typical youngster who loved the game of cricket but also liked a good time. As a group we stayed either in a pub or St Mark's College in Adelaide, but none of us was allowed to drink in that pub. So all we did was walk a couple of yards down the road to drink in another bar. The landlord was only too pleased to see a group of young lads looking to enjoy themselves. To be honest, I suppose it was schoolboy stuff on both sides, but it typifies the way the Academy was run back then. Peter O'Brien, who ran the pub, was a very nice man and so were his family. I remember a few times when I and one of my good friends, Stephen Cotterell, had a couple with Pete at the bar! Shh!

Maybe I did not realise how big an opportunity it was to learn the game. At that stage I just wanted to spin the ball as much as I could and hit the ball as far as it would travel. I mucked around a little bit too often, but I defy any twenty-year-old to be on his best behaviour all of the time. An environment of total discipline is not conducive for a bunch of lads living away from home, in my opinion anyway. I was just a bit of a lad. I was certainly a bit too direct in my criticism at times, and could also be a little disruptive. It might even be fair to suggest that I was a bit of an idiot. But there was never any nastiness in my behaviour.

I believed that certain things were best done in certain ways, and didn't agree with the methods of Barry Causby, one of the coaches. For example, I did not see the point in running laps of the outfield at the end of a day's play. When you have just bowled, batted and fielded for three or four hours maybe a stretch and a rest. There did not always seem to be a great deal of thought going in to some of the routines. I thought I was picked with the intention of doing everything I could to improve my cricket and undertook all of the exercises devotedly, but that enthusiasm gradually wore off for a lot of us, not just me. Maybe I'm the only one saying it in public.

Of the coaches, I thought that Jack Potter was fantastic, but unfortunately I had a personality clash with Peter Spence. We never really hit it off together – I felt he was too inflexible – and when there was a fall-out between Potter and Spence the wrong guy to my mind resigned and left. Worse followed for me when Andrew Sincock and Causby took over on a temporary basis. Sincock was not too bad, but I continued to disagree with Causby's methods. Having played a few times for South Australia, he went off to work in a bank and when it came to coaching in my view he turned out to be pretty ordinary. Even if he knew the game, I thought he was a poor communicator and he couldn't seem to make anything clear. He might have been better coaching the under-12s at the local park.

Understandably, Spence didn't like me either because I took the micky out of him in front of the others. He, after all, was the man who had sent one of the group to see a doctor for his bowels to be checked because he farted too much on the minibus to and from training! Heaven knows what he would have made of Merv Hughes's wake-up calls when you were rooming with him. Poor old Merv would have been in and out of the clinic through revolving doors. As I have suggested, Spence was probably entitled to have the odd word. Some of the mischief was out of order on probably more than the odd occasion.

Potter was the head coach when I arrived in April 1990 and he is largely responsible for teaching me to bowl the flipper. I had already tried to learn that particular delivery at St Kilda, my club side, when Shaun Graf put me on to Jim Higgs, the former Australia wrist-spinner. Unfortunately I could not get it to work and in the end the slight change of grip necessary affected my ability to bowl the stock leg-break. Potter pointed out that when I was running in to bowl I carried too many thoughts in my head. He made me go back to basics by bowling blindfold in the nets and hitting a regular spot with my leg-break routinely before starting to think about the flipper again. Keeping an uncluttered mind when I run in to bowl is some of the best advice I have received. We clicked and we were on the same wavelength, as Jack was with all the other guys.

It would be wrong, then, to think that all of my time at the Academy was wasted. My personal coach and mentor, Terry Jenner, was the best thing that happened to me there. In August 1990 I was chosen for a Young Australia trip to the West Indies under the captaincy of Jamie Cox. The side included Damien Fleming, Michael Bevan, Brendon Julian and Craig White, later to play for England, Damien Martyn, Darren Berry and a few others. The other highlight was playing in two games against the 1990–91 touring England side at St Peter's College, Adelaide. Allan Lamb captained England while Graham Gooch was injured, and we were heavily beaten both times. However, I top-scored in one match and claimed the wicket of Robin Smith, later to be my captain at Hampshire.

These experiences gave me the taste for playing international cricket, but by the time the Academy squad was due to tour Sri Lanka late in 1990 I was considered such a liability by the coaches that they refused to take me. Because they had also stopped my allowance, I was effectively on my own. That is when they told me to attend nets with South Australia, and the beginning of the end. When Jim Higgs rang from Victoria to find out how I was progressing I could not contain my frustration and let him know exactly what I thought of all and sundry. If he had not convinced me to hang in there and give the situation a few more weeks to improve I would have left earlier.

In those days lads at the Academy could be chosen to play for South Australia even though they came from other states. The possibility that I might make a first-class debut through impressing in the nets at least gave me something to aim for, even though my heart was still with Victoria, especially when I heard through the grapevine that I was being considered to play for South Australia against New South Wales. However, that opportunity did not materialise. With my buddies still in Sri Lanka I felt lonely, homesick and unappreciated. It was time to go home.

By far the best part of my eight months or so at the Academy was meeting Terry Jenner soon after returning from the West Indies trip. Our first chat proved to be the beginning of a friendship and mutual respect that has blossomed through the years. Without doubt, TJ has grown to become the biggest coaching influence on my career. I think I immediately recognised a kindred spirit. At that time he had recently left prison after serving eighteen months for embezzlement. He liked a beer and a good time, as I would soon discover during the course of several long nights chatting, but what struck me immediately was his knowledge of wrist-spin and I think in a funny sort of way it helped him through a tough time as well.

When he said something I listened, which was not always the case with the other coaches at the Academy. Everybody knows the trouble with do-this, do-that. When you are being told what to do all the time it becomes hard and sometimes you rebel. It helped that Jenner was capable of doing everything that he suggested to me. Suggested is an important word, because he never ever presented his way as the only way. In what I found to be an over-strict regime it was refreshing to meet somebody who did not impose his methods on me. He would plant an idea in my mind, but never complain if I couldn't do it. It was always 'Keep going, try harder, you'll get there' – and encouragement like that picks you up.

Setting aside my own problems, I think the Academy today provides a tremendous opportunity for young players to develop into potential Test stars. It cannot be coincidence that of the present Australia team, Michael Slater, Greg Blewett, Matthew Hayden, Justin Langer, Ricky Ponting, Adam Gilchrist, Brett Lee, Glenn McGrath and Damien Martyn all attended, as well as myself. That is some rate, and it is entirely down to the respect accorded to the man who took it over, Rod Marsh. It is mainly down to Marsh that the Academy is now the envy of the rest of the world for the conveyor belt of talent it supplies.

Five of my year have gone on to play at the highest level, including Jason Gallian, who has made three appearances for England. Some of my best mates then and still now were Damien Martyn and Stephen Cotterell. Damien had a similar outlook in life and we would often cover for each other if one of us stayed out too late the night before. He was a great looking batsman who became the second lad from the Academy to play for Australia, after myself. With more luck he could have scored a mountain of Test runs by now, but he has plenty of time.

It needs a certain amount of ability in the first place, but with the right attitude I do not see how anybody can fail to learn from listening to Marsh. Unlike the coaches when I was in Adelaide, he commands respect because he has seen everything in the game. With the likes of Dennis Lillee, Ian Chappell and Jenner also involved on a part-time basis, the brightest young players in Australia are now being exposed to the best coaching on offer. Kids today could not have better teachers.

The course now embraces everything imaginable. On reflection I suppose it was inevitable there would be a few teething problems in the early months. It was just unfortunate that they coincided with my own attendance, but that's the way it goes and, looking back, it has helped. These days it could hardly be more comprehensive, taking in not only the skills of the game, but areas like history and tradition, fitness skills, advice on diet and psychology. But I would guess the best of it is the casual chats with Marsh in the dressing room during and after games. The sort of knowledge a man like that can pass on is priceless and not likely to be found in any text book. It has to be right that Australia is using his brains for the good of our game in the longer term.

I also like the way that ex-players go in to give special presentations and established men can return for the occasional piece of fine-tuning. In 1995–96 I went back for three or four days before the West Indies toured Australia when Ian Chappell put on a course about playing short-pitched bowling. At that time I was concerned that my finger would be exposed to some short-pitched bouncers and all spinners are concerned about our fingers. Chappell has become a good friend since and I can understand with his vast knowledge and competitiveness what made him a great captain of Australia. In the same way, I have gone along on the odd occasion to work with a young spinner. The only real concern though is with other countries sending young players to our Academy. I'm all for helping other countries but, for instance, before the last series against the West Indies their young batsmen were exposed to our training and tuition. Maybe looking at the way they played they weren't listening too carefully or Rod Marsh sold them a dummy. We just have to be careful and make sure that none of our own young players are missing out.

One criticism that used to be levelled at graduates was the way that some of them came out of the Academy with a superiority complex. They thought that they left as the finished article and were ready for international cricket, even moaning if they stayed in their state 2nd XI for more than a few weeks. There is nothing wrong with confidence and self-belief, but senior players deserve respect from those who are still to achieve anything in the game. I think that word got back to the Academy and Marsh has made sure that today's kids know what they have to do to build on the excellent foundation he has given to them.

3

WARNE OF AUSTRALIA

A S A YOUNG PLAYER coming into the team in 1991–92 I
could not have wished for a better role model than Allan
Border. Although he was coming towards the end of his career,
Border was still among the best batsmen in the world at the
time and was already guaranteed a place in history. The enormous authority he carried grew through his achievements and
for everything he embodied about Australian life. He came
into the side during a terrible period and never forgot the taste
of those early defeats, really enjoying the turnaround in performances which started with the 1987 World Cup and 1989
Ashes series. From there he and Australia went on from
strength to strength.

I had met Border only once, at a Prime Minister's XI game
in December 1991, before joining up with the squad at the
Parkroyal Hotel in Sydney for my Test debut against India on
2nd January 1992. There was to be no dream start as I took
1 for 150 from 45 overs and dropped Ravi Shastri off my own
bowling when he was on 66 and heading towards a double-
century. I ended up batting to save the game with AB and after
he gave me some words of encouragement as I arrived at the
crease – 'Come on, dig in and don't get out, you're playing for
Australia' – I think I was too frightened to play a shot and lose

my wicket. In truth, he was a hugely reassuring presence. The dressing room always believed that with AB still in we were never out of it.

As I discovered even before the end of my second Test, the penultimate of the India series at the Adelaide Oval, he was an immensely loyal guy with bags of determination. On the final morning we discovered that Geoff Marsh – who had taken me under his wing in Sydney – and Mark Waugh would be dropped for the last game in Perth. AB missed the start of the day's play to telephone Laurie Sawle, the chairman of selectors, wanting to know why the changes were made. As Marsh led us on to the field I remember thinking that Test cricket was certainly an interesting game and, re-assembling at Perth, where I was to be named twelfth man, none of us knew whether AB would turn up or not before the game. He did, of course, and we trounced India with Mike Whitney taking 7 for 27 in the second innings. Fortunately for Australian cricket he decided to continue after making his point to Sawle – I imagine very firmly indeed.

My own career went through a brief lull when I returned to Victoria to find myself left out of a Sheffield Shield game against Queensland. I had made an inauspicious start to Test cricket to put it mildly. Deep down I did not think I was good enough to play in such elevated company and at that level.

When I made my Test debut I weighed in at a tubby 97 kg – the heaviest I have ever been. It said much about my ambivalence towards fitness that I should be so heavy when Australia called the first time. I remember watching the 1991–92 Melbourne Test with Dean Waugh, the brother of Steve and Mark, with my hands full of pie and beer when I bumped into Bobby Simpson, the national coach, and Ian McDonald, Australian team manager. The reason I recall the conversation is because McDonald told me I had a chance of playing in the next Test.

I thought it was his idea of a joke and didn't worry about it until the next day when he called me at home to say I was in the twelve for Sydney and required at the ACB next day to be measured for training gear.

I had played Aussie Rules at under-19 and reserves level and trained with the seniors at St Kilda, so I had an understanding of fitness and discipline. The opportunity to play in England in 1989 arose through Shaun Graf, an all-rounder with St Kilda and Victoria who had gone to Bristol in the late-70s. For my flatmate Rick Gough and me those were some very happy times. Looking back I'm not even sure how I managed to survive. I had been given the flick by St Kilda Football Club and, having set my heart on a career, I didn't have a clue what to do next. Rick was a mate from St Kilda CC who was going to Bristol anyway, so when he asked if I fancied joining him I just thought of it as an opportunity for some fun and games away from home while I pondered my future. I certainly didn't think of it as a chance to delve deeper in to the mysteries of wrist-spin. We played at least three days a week, the two of us had a ball, and I had hardly shed any of the weight I put on when Test cricket called that first time.

I had drunk alcohol before, but never in the quantities I consumed that summer. Having been used to small glasses in Australia, it was daunting at first to have the beer served in huge pint pots. They felt like we were drinking jugs. On the very first night it was an effort just to keep up with the people who would become some of my best mates. When I said I was beginning to feel queasy they suggested I move on to a cider drink called Diamond White on the basis that it would ease my stomach. I must have had the word 'mug' plastered on my forehead – plastered being the operative word. Half-a-dozen stubbies later I can honestly say I felt more drunk than I believed was possible. The next morning I felt as though somebody was ripping through my stomach with scissors when I was vomiting. To this day I have never known a worse hangover.

If that taught me to stay off Diamond White, then it didn't take away my taste for lager. Towards the end of the season we were drinking machines. I still remember a place called Busby's, which served pints at 20p each on a Monday night. Every hour was happy hour in there. On Tuesday we used to take it easy – perhaps just have a bite to eat in the beautiful pub called the George. It was owned by some of the nicest people I've ever met. They treated me like a son, they were like my parents away from home. I love going back to England to see Mike and Pat, Merv and Maureen and Simon and Judy. On Wednesdays we would frequent a place called Town's Talk. Thursday to Sunday were just drinkathons. It helped that Gough and I were staying in the cricket pavilion at the ground.

When I was first picked for Australia I couldn't believe it and didn't feel like I was ready or good enough at that level, but it was a very proud moment, still my proudest to this day. It was also an opportunity. I wanted to give it my best shot and enjoy the experience, but didn't feel confident enough to think that I would play more than one or two matches. Even playing for Victoria was more than I expected. The jump from a youth tour to the West Indies and the full Australia side happened in sixteen months. I suppose that being given a place in the Academy and the desire to see a leg-spinner come through should have told me I had a chance. I strongly believe it was a case of being in the right place at the right time.

I did not have the craft to succeed at Test level and my body certainly wasn't prepared to compete against the best in the world. Having taken only one wicket in two games against India it was a surprise to be chosen for the tour of Sri Lanka. In between, I had a long think about what I really wanted to achieve. Brief though it was, I had had a taste of playing for Australia and realised that was what I wanted to do. The selectors had shown faith in me and it was now time for me to repay that faith. It was time for me to make some sacrifices and become the best cricketer I could. It was up to me, I had a vision and I was focused. Over the next few months I spoke to as many people as I could who I thought might be able to help me as a cricketer. I was like a sponge soaking up information. The likes of Ian Chappell, Rod Marsh and Richie Benaud were all pleased to pass on advice and I was over the moon that they spared the time to talk. But it was a chat with Terry Jenner that really made me question my own commitment.

I had met Terry at the Academy and soon grown to enjoy his company. One night I rocked up at his place with a crate of beer expecting his first reaction to be to reach for the bottle opener and the second to say, 'G'day.' Instead, he really tore into me.

'You can put that lot down for a start,' he said. 'You've been picked to represent Australia and tour to Sri Lanka when you've done nothing to justify your selection. You've been playing for ten minutes, and what sacrifices have you made?'

'Not many,' I had to admit.

'Not many!' he snorted. 'Name me one.'

After much thought I had to admit that I had not changed my lifestyle one bit.

'You're drinking and partying and you're overweight,' he said. 'They've given you the opportunity to play for Australia which most cricketers can only dream about. What are you going to do about it?'

When I told him, he said: 'Good, I'm looking forward to seeing it.'

Even during my Test debut I had incurred the wrath of Errol

Alcott, our physio, by tucking in to a plate of party pies. My lifestyle simply had to change. For the next four months I would set off for a run before breakfast, have a swim in the morning and then hit the gym in the afternoon. Sundays I saw to be a day of rest. I didn't touch alcohol, even at functions when others were swigging beer. When one of my best friends, Merv Hughes, got married, I didn't touch a drop. As I said before, for the first time in my life I was focused. My diet consisted of fruit, pasta and cereals washed down with at least two litres of water each day. As soon as the weight began to come off I could feel a purpose about what I was doing. I even began to quite enjoy it and felt bad if I didn't push myself harder.

After all the work I had done to give myself the best chance at this level I thought that I might at least enjoy a change in fortunes when my international career resumed in Sri Lanka. Instead I went for 107 runs in 22 wicketless overs in the first innings of the First Test at Colombo and felt very low. We were 291 behind going in to our second dig and, even though we scored 471, my own confidence was still non-existent. I put down my turnaround to two people in that series, AB and Greg Matthews.

AB clearly sensed I was feeling down in the dumps as we sat together in the dressing room watching the innings unfold. 'Mate,' he said, 'I'm a big believer that hard work gets its reward in the long run. I know you've put in the effort and I know things will happen for you. Just keep believing and everything has a way of working out.'

Then, after the fourth day, I had dinner with Matthews at an Italian restaurant where he told me that if the selectors did not think I could do the job they would not have chosen me. Between them the pair gave me the reassurance I needed, and the following day AB handed me the responsibility.

Before lunch I had been trusted with only one over, which went for 11 runs. 'Here we go again,' I thought. Sri Lanka continued to make steady progress to the point where they needed around 36 to win with 4 wickets in hand. To my amazement AB tossed me the ball. My first thought was that the game might be over in the next six deliveries. I swear I was more nervous than I had been on my debut, but somehow I managed to put the first ball on a good length and go on to complete a maiden. That over gave me a massive lift. I remember Greg Matthews shouting, 'C'mon, Suicide,' (the nickname he gave me after the INXS song 'Suicide Blonde'). The encouragement from the fielders, AB especially, helped to calm me down and in the next two overs Mark Waugh held catches off Wickremasinghe and Anurasiri before Madurasinghe holed out to Matthews – all this without me conceding a run, so I finished with 3 for 11. For the first time I left the field thinking that I had contributed at long, long last. What a day! Another thing I remember is Dean Jones running in when I got a wicket and saying, 'Well done, mate, your average is 230 now.' Next time, he said, 'Mate, it's come down to 150 now.' He was trying to relax me with some humour, but I can assure you I didn't see the funny side at the time.

AB had clearly seen something in my character which I didn't even realise was there myself. He said in the press conference afterwards that I had held my hand up when it mattered. In reality the captain yanked it out of my pocket. He has often been credited with leading by example but I don't think people realise he was also a superb man manager, and there was another example of that ability during the home series against West Indies a few months later.

After our return from Sri Lanka I wasn't chosen for the First Test, which ended in a draw at Brisbane, even though we were on top for most of the game. AB said publicly that if Shane

Warne had been playing Australia might have been able to knock them over. To a youngster who had taken 4 wickets in as many Tests at an average only just below 100 those words were a real confidence-booster. In the next two Shield games I got two five-fers and two half centuries. I returned to the side for the Melbourne Test on 26 December 1992 and took 7 for 52 in the second innings as we won by 139 runs, the wickets coming in a spell of 14.4 overs that transformed my career and my life. It was the start of a great journey. Without the faith AB showed in me I couldn't have made that impression. From then on I felt I was good enough, if I bowled well, to be a Test cricketer. I went on to take 17 wickets in the subsequent series in New Zealand and could hardly wait to return to England for my first Ashes series. This time, I knew exactly where I wanted my career to go.

4

THE ASHES

I'M NOT SURE that a single delivery can change anybody's life. But that first ball I sent down in the Old Trafford Test in England to Mike Gatting on 3 June 1993 had a massive impact on mine. In the second or so it took to leave my hand, swerve to pitch outside leg stump, fizz past the batsman's lunge forward and clip off stump my life did change. Even now, eight years on from my Ashes debut, I am asked about it more than anything else. It remains one of the greatest deliveries of my career. As for being the 'ball of the century', as it has been described, I don't think that can be for anybody to say. So much of cricket's rich history has gone unfilmed. Beating Dennis Lillee's record as the leading wicket-taker of all time for Australia was one of my proudest, but my favourite moment in my career is my first appearance for Australia when the scoreboard read: 'Congrats Shane Warne on being the 350th Test Cricketer for Australia'.

What added to the drama that day in June 1993 was the fact that it was my first ball of the game and, as a leg-spinner, it takes time to find your rhythm. Despite performing pretty well against West Indies and New Zealand I had started the tour modestly. Worse, I was absolutely hammered by Graeme Hick at Worcester a month before the First Test and had been told I was not going to play in the one-day internationals so that

England wouldn't get a look at me. Although under instructions from Allan Border not to show Hick anything except my leg-break, because we knew he would play against us in the Tests, it was still a chastening experience when he twice hit me for 19 runs in an over.

At least I took some encouragement going into the game from the fact that the Manchester pitch had been prepared to assist turn. The England selectors thought the match could be won by their own spinners, Peter Such and Phil Tufnell. Such had actually taken 6 wickets as we were dismissed for 289 in the first innings. I had a reasonable stay at the crease and thought that if I put the ball in the right place I might be able to do something with it. Little did I ever imagine quite what!

I tried to give the first one a big tweak, but the priority was to make sure the ball hit the right spot and to generate a rhythm in the opening overs, gradually imparting a bit more spin and trying a few variations. Youth has a certain confidence, and when the ball left my hand on this occasion I could tell immediately that it felt right. The best leg-breaks should curve in to the right-hander through the air if they are spun hard enough. That is also, by definition, a good indication that it will bite hard off the surface. This time the ball followed the perfect course, although I didn't realise quite how far it had deviated until I saw a replay. Really, it was a complete fluke.

Ian Botham said afterwards that he hadn't seen the same look of wide-eyed horror on Gatting's face since somebody had stolen his lunch a few years before. In truth, I'm not sure there was much else that Gatting could do and we both laughed about it afterwards. You can plan a ball like that but for everything to work out requires a lot of luck. It happened to be my day. Other days Gatting has beaten me, but it has always been fun bowling against him. The way he stood at the crease as though he was dazzled by lights, however, could not have sent encouraging signals back to his colleagues in the dressing room. He even needed to turn to Kenny Palmer, the umpire at square leg, to confirm that he was out. Psychologically, I think, we had struck a massive blow for the rest of the series and none of the batsmen really tried to get after me. The funny thing is that people forget I had Robin Smith caught at slip in the next over with one that was probably just as good.

Despite getting a little bit over-excited at times, I still claimed 4 wickets as we managed to dismiss England for 210 before we piled up 432 in the second innings, thanks to a debut century from Ian Healy out of an unbroken sixth-wicket stand of 180 with Steve Waugh. With a lead of 511 we could not lose. Whether we could take 10 England wickets on what had become a comfortable batting pitch was another matter. The ball wasn't turning much and it was going to be hard work. England showed plenty of spirit and patience and were unfortunate when Graham Gooch was out handled the ball when instinctively trying to swipe it away from his stumps. After a magnificent century it was a shame to get out that way. Poor Merv Hughes went apoplectic with rage when he discovered he wouldn't be credited with the wicket, having worked tirelessly to make the breakthrough.

Batsmen were reluctant to go for their shots and it became a case of trying to out-think them during the course of the second innings. The dismissal of Alec Stewart gave me special pleasure. He had been playing forward with his bat behind his pad, allowing the regulation leg-break to pass the edge. I allowed him to settle into that habit before tossing in a zooter – the one that floats out of the front of the fingers and goes straight on off the pitch. It did not turn as Stewart expected and he gave a thin nick to Healy who once again took a good catch.

To complete a dream debut I was also named man of the match after returning the best figures by an Australian leg-spinner in

England, 8 for 137, since the great Bill O'Reilly fifty-five years earlier.

Another 8 wickets followed in the Second Test at Lord's, my first game at the hallowed ground. That gave me great pleasure because I remember walking into the changing rooms and soaking up the atmosphere from my spot and looking out over the ground. What a feeling. I was pumped for the game. Afterwards I was so fascinated with Lord's I took my fiancée Simone through and she loved it. We spent some time talking to the late Lord Cowdrey, a real gentleman.

We could already sense problems in the England camp. Gooch, initially appointed to lead them for the first three games, had his period of office extended to include the rest of the series, but then said he would step down if performances didn't improve. Mark Taylor, Michael Slater and David Boon all scored hundreds and Mark Waugh should have joined them, only to fall to Tufnell on 99. At the luncheon interval a gentleman knocked on the dressing room door and showed some of the guys a betting slip that revealed he had placed a wager on Australia's top four batsmen scoring hundreds. He had laid £100 at, I think, 1,000–1 – that's a lot of money to lose because of one single run. We were well on course for a third win at Trent Bridge, only to be denied by Graham Thorpe and Gooch, moved down the order to number five in a much-changed side, in the second innings.

Normal service was resumed with an innings victory at Headingley. We scored 4 for 653 and, if Border hadn't declared on reaching 200, I swear he would still be batting there with Steve Waugh now. With characteristic ruthlessness AB kept England in the field for two whole days and then Saturday morning as well, by which time their task had become hopeless. I remember Mark Lathwell was playing only in his second Test. He was in the field for a long time and then was dismissed very early, caught at the wicket. I'm sure he would want to forget that match. Gooch resigned as captain immediately afterwards but we extended the margin to four-nil at Edgbaston to make it a miserable introduction to captaincy for Mike Atherton.

I remember this particular game not for the chaos in England's camp but for the delivery that accounted for Gooch, restored to the opening berth, in the second innings. It probably turned as far as the 'Gatting ball' but was all the more satisfying because I was bowling to a specific plan. Over the series I think Gooch played me better than anybody and I enjoyed spending time with him, but I'd noticed when I bowled wide of leg stump he would thrust out his front leg a little casually. I thought that if I could pitch one a little fuller to beat his defence, and still get it to turn far enough, I might be able to bowl him around his legs. I discussed this with AB the night before and it is very satisfying when a plan comes together. This time it worked to perfection. Tim May and I took 5 wickets each to finish with combined figures of 10 for 171 from 97.2 overs which testify to the stranglehold the spinners now held over England.

Gooch was a player I really enjoyed competing against. I am still not sure whether he read me as well as some of the others but he had his own method, knew the strokes he could get away with and stayed in through sheer application, determination and pride in his country and his performance. He always put a high price on his wicket. I used to call him 'Mr Gooch' while he was batting, out of respect more than anything else.

Although we were beaten in the final Test at the Oval, I think the overall results reflected the difference between the sides. While I was delighted to take the man of the series award, having claimed 34 wickets – a record for a leg-spinner in a series in England – it had been a real team effort. My man of the series was Merv Hughes. He took some key wickets at crucial times, and nobody really knew the extent of his knee injury. It wasn't until he got home that everyone realised how bad it was. To get through was pure courage and a typical Merv big-hearted effort. Ian Healy was also sensational. I think this series was the best he kept to me and his batting was also very handy.

The 1993 tour is one of the highlights of my career. In many ways it is the best I have been on, and not simply because things worked so well for me personally. The squad just gelled from the first day. There was the right balance of youth and experience. There was no bickering, jealousy or backstabbing. We did everything together and genuinely enjoyed each other's success. But in a terrific bunch of guys I think Mervyn Gregory Hughes stood out for his influence on and off the field.

Much has been said and written about his character down the years. All I can say is that most of it is true. The bloke could be a downright nuisance but, like Healy, I don't think he has received the praise he warranted for his efforts in 1993. To see him after each day's play was an inspiration. He would sit with ice packs on his knees and maybe a groin or a shoulder, in what must have been terrific discomfort, and still manage to crack a joke.

He said that if he ever needed five packs instead of the usual four it was time to retire. That was his way – if there was a funny side to a situation then Merv would see it. All the time we wondered how long he could keep going. At the Oval he would hobble down to fine leg at the end of an over and still come back for another. Very often, too, it was Merv who made the breakthrough when we desperately needed a wicket. He was also a great help to me because his huge frame was always sure to leave nice footmarks to turn the ball from in the second innings.

What you have with Merv is basically a child in an adult's body, although he was smarter than many people thought.

Healy is on record as saying Merv was the quickest bowler he kept to for Australia. The bloke became a genuine cult figure and deservedly so. It was always amusing to see him going through his warm-up stretches on the boundary and see hundreds of people in the stand behind imitate his routine. We have become really good mates and these days he captains Footscray 2nd XI, batting at number eight or nine and fielding at first slip. His knees don't allow him to bowl very much, but it says so much for his love of cricket that he still wants to be involved and help the kids learn the game. Along with Bill Lawry he is one of the best after-dinner speakers I've heard.

My life changed during the Boxing Day Test against West Indies in 1992 when I took 7 for 52, but interest stepped up another few levels during those few months in England. That was when the whole world seemed to want to know everything about me on and off the field. People wanted to know how I spent my spare time and, more important it seemed, with whom. I remember one newspaper published a list entitled 'Ten things you never knew about Shane Warne' – and I swear I didn't know five of them myself. Having my life scrutinised to that degree came as a new experience, but fortunately people like Merv, David Boon and Allan Border were there to help guide me through.

One of the happiest memories is getting engaged in the Lake District midway through the tour. I had been given a few days off, so Simone and I decided to take in some of the beautiful scenery. We hired a rowing boat and it just seemed such a romantic place to pop the question. There was nothing premeditated about it, even though I knew from our first weeks together that she was the right girl for me. She was the one. The team were in Bristol at the time, so there were lots of celebrations when we returned, firstly with my parents and brother who were in Bristol and then with my team mates and the friends I had made from 1989. The people at Bristol Imperial CC have become a second family.

We had another great celebration when we eventually retained the Ashes at Headingley. By that time Craig McDermott had been forced to go home. He played through some of the early games, despite complaining of stomach problems, really through the healing hands and persuasion of Errol Alcott. A few of us wondered how badly he was struggling, but after a full-blooded operation on his bowel we knew. We thought he should be there with us to celebrate, so somebody, probably Merv, hit on the idea of finding a lifesize cardboard cut-out and bringing it along to the changing room. There was Billy, quiet as a church mouse for a change – with authentic cigarette drooping from his mouth and a can of XXXX stuck to his hand.

At the start of the tour I would have been happy to play in half of the Tests and just learn more about the art of bowling leg-spin for the rest of the time. Even after Old Trafford I did not expect to be so successful and I was genuinely embarrassed by some of the praise. All of a sudden people were comparing me with the likes of O'Reilly and Clarrie Grimmett. I did wonder if that was fair to be compared with two of the greats when I had only played for a couple of seasons. Needless to say, I thoroughly enjoyed that tour and I couldn't wait to bowl to England again on our own pitches in 1994–95.

After such a magnificent series it seemed too much to imagine that I would fare even better during our next encounter. I started with figures of 8–71, the best of my career, in the second innings of the First Test in Brisbane at the end of November 1994. The dismissal of Stewart gave me special pleasure because, as at Old Trafford, I set him up for the kill. This time I gave him a short leg-break so he could rock on to the backfoot and cut. I didn't mean for him to hit it for 4. Clearly tempted, he went back for what looked like a similar ball but was in fact a well-disguised flipper which hurried on and bowled him before he was through with the stroke.

I had felt comfortable in Shield cricket before the series began and was beginning to learn how to cope with the media interest that seemed to become more intense than ever in the weeks leading up to the Ashes. The only slight disappointment at Brisbane was that I missed a hat-trick by a couple of inches. Having bowled Phil DeFreitas and trapped Martin McCague leg before first ball with a flipper, I decided to try Tufnell with a googly. He misread it but, despite passing between bat and pad, the ball squeezed past off stump. Clearly I had used up all my good fortune earlier in the day when Graham Thorpe missed a full toss.

Chances like that crop up only rarely, so when I managed to send back DeFreitas and Darren Gough with successive balls in the Second Test at Melbourne and saw Devon Malcolm, looking like Robocop with all that padding on, striding to the crease I sensed the opportunity of a lifetime. A few months earlier Damien Fleming had taken a hat-trick in Pakistan on debut. As he went back towards mid off he told me that, after taking his first two wickets, he thought about all the options before deciding on his stock ball, the outswinger, because that was the one he knew best. It sounded like good advice, so I went for the top-spinning leg-break, knowing Devon would either slog, and possibly miss completely, or block, and perhaps bat-pad a catch to one of the close fielders. He chose the second option, but the ball bounced a little more than he expected and went via his gloves towards the direction of the keg at short leg where David Boon dived a long way to his right to hold on to an absolute screamer. We won the Test, I had a hat-trick and, as if that wasn't enough reason to party, this just so happened to be Boon's thirty-fourth birthday as well. What a night!

As in England eighteen months previously, the question now was not whether we would retain the Ashes, but by what margin. Although the retirement of Border had left a hole in our batting, there was still enough quality in the top order to post enough runs while McDermott, man of the match with eight wickets in Melbourne, proved a constant thorn in their side. But cricket has a way of producing the unexpected and the Third Test at Sydney was a thrilling match. It finished with Tim May and I having to bat for seventy-seven minutes to save the game after being bowled out for 116 in the first innings. This after Atherton had declared the England second innings with Hick 98 not out. Gough's down-to-earth, raw enthusiasm had made him a popular figure and he bowled superbly to take 6 for 49.

Maysie and I hung on but it wasn't without controversy. In the final hour of a Test match 15 overs have to be bowled, so the pair of us were watching the scoreboard tick along slowly and when it brought up the last over we thought, come on, only six balls to go. Halfway through the over I thought that we couldn't lose any more, so decided to have a slog. I hit a 4, then another 4 and the last ball drove to Devon Malcolm at mid off, where he dropped it. Irrelevant, I thought, and started to wander off, thinking, you beauty, only to see Mike Atherton talking to the umpires. He said there were still a few minutes left until the hour was up, and he was right. They had bowled their 15 inside the hour, so they were entitled to keep going until the hour was up. If Devon had held that catch . . . the mind boggles!

In Adelaide we slipped to 156 all out chasing 263 in 67 overs to clinch the series. Maybe we were over-confident, maybe a bit complacent, and a century on debut by Greg Blewett in his hometown was the only reason to cheer. The unexpected defeat brought us back down to earth and in the final game at Perth we produced our biggest win of the campaign, victory by a massive 329 runs with another hundred for Blewett. McDermott, the man of the series, completed the Test in thrilling fashion by knocking Malcolm's middle stump out of the ground. England had plenty of chances in this Test, but didn't hold their catches and suffered for it.

Since I had taken 20 wickets in the first two Tests, the media suggested I might be disappointed with the final aggregate of 27. The most important statistic was the three-one scoreline. The series was closer than that suggested, and I would be very happy with 27 wickets in every five Tests I play. A bowler can contribute without taking wickets by keeping an end tight. Stories about feeling burnt out and jaded were somewhat premature, even though I was starting to feel sore in the shoulder and needed massage on a daily basis. Midway through the series my workload in the nets was cut back by Errol Alcott, our team physiotherapist. I certainly didn't feel the Poms had suddenly seized the initiative. Indeed, it was a difficult tour for them which probably reached its lowest point when they failed even to reach the World Series Cup final ahead of an Australia A team.

I discovered a few years later that part of England's preparations for the series involved watching video tapes of Australian batsmen scoring runs and taking wickets. I guess the idea must have been to try to identify weaknesses, but what sort of effect would that footage have had on morale? If I was a batsman the last thing I would want to see before a Test match was a string of balls turning past my bat from a guy I was about to face. I didn't have a bad time in 1993, but I also sent down plenty of 4-balls which were dispatched in no uncertain terms. Those were the clips that should have been shown. The thing that we Aussies found funny was that whenever it rained in England during the 1993 and 1997 Ashes series the BBC always showed a lot of footage of the 1981 Headingley Test. It was either Ian Botham slogging us over the park or Bob Willis steaming in to take his 8 wickets.

The period between 1994–95 and the next Ashes series in 1997 was an interesting, sometimes worrying, time for me. In the darkest moments I wondered if my career was about to end. My shoulder and spinning finger were causing increasing problems and after much thought and listening to experts I decided to undergo surgery on the finger after the World Cup in 1996. It was causing so much pain and had threatened to blow up during the one-day event. It did just before the quarter-final against New Zealand. Errol Alcott gave me treatment and when he was working on my forearm my fingers were twitching and moving uncontrollably. Rest was no longer an option, and nor were further cortisone injections into the knuckle. Although I had made a gradual recovery through the series against the West Indies and South Africa, some critics were still not prepared to give me the chance to show them I could still bowl. They wrote me off. When we landed in England they also thought I was gone.

I was quietly confident, although I never expected to make an impact equal to the '93 tour. This time I was a known quantity, batsmen were better prepared and, although they did not say so explicitly, it became quickly apparent that England were going to be a very competitive side. But quite clearly, they underestimated the growing reputation of Glenn McGrath and Jason Gillespie.

England began the summer well, winning the one-day series in 1997 with Adam and Ben Hollioake, the brothers born in Melbourne, heralded as the latest saviours of the national game. The build-up to the First Test centred around Mark Taylor's bad run of scores and when we lost at Edgbaston by 9 wickets certain people and newspapers were quick to write off our chances. We had been caught cold on the first morning in seaming conditions after Taylor won the toss and batted. Nasser Hussain and Graham Thorpe put on 288 for the fourth wicket when England replied. I was robbed as I made 47 before Devon Malcolm took a screamer, diving forward to dismiss me at third man.

One huge positive we could take out of this match was Taylor's return to form in the second innings. He didn't bat particularly fluently to start with but played with determination in a great captain's innings. He gradually hit his straps. When he pushed Andy Caddick into the covers to reach his hundred we could almost sense his feeling of achievement and relief back in the dressing room. I was very happy for him because he had helped me a lot and was a great leader. One thing that was very strange, though, was that the manager, Alan Crompton, let some television cameras into our changing room to share our celebrations when the captain got his hundred, the first time that had happened in my career. When Taylor raised his bat for his hundred his expression was like steel. It was worth a million words. How much longer he would have continued in office had he failed again I don't think any of us really knows, probably not even Tubby himself.

The fact is that a dark cloud had been lifted from over his head. Although his innings was not enough to save the Test, I think it proved the turning point of the series. The next morning, after we had lost, we were having a training session. There was a new purpose about us as we worked out the following day and only rain prevented us from levelling the series at the first opportunity, after we dismissed England for 77 when we met again. McGrath's figures of 8 for 38 were the best in an Ashes fixture at Lord's and I could take quieter satisfaction at a ball that spun wickedly out of the rough to bowl Mark Butcher in the second innings. My other wicket was Hussain. I've had the wood on him and after the First Test wanted to get back on top.

Whatever the scoreline it was apparent by now to anyone

who knew anything about the game that we were starting to hit our straps. In a five-week period we gained emphatic wins at Old Trafford, Headingley and Trent Bridge to ensure we won the series as well as retained the Ashes. Manchester is one of my favourite grounds in England and, while nothing could match the impact of four years earlier, I still managed to take 9 wickets, 6 in the first innings, including Alec Stewart with a big-spinning leg-break, as we scored our first success. That was my best haul since the finger operation and along the way I passed Richie Benaud's record of 248 wickets for a leg-spin bowler. The ball was gripping out of the footmarks to such an extent that Healy decided to wear a helmet complete with grille in the second innings. The Test also gave me personal satisfaction because during the game our first child, Brooke, was born back home. When I received the first pictures of her I was so pumped up I went out and took 6 for 48.

The victory was set up by one of the best innings Steve Waugh has played for Australia on the first day. As at Edgbaston, Taylor gambled on batting first in almost ideal overhead conditions for pace bowling when the pitch was a bit moist, backing the batsmen to score enough runs to keep us in the game while the pitch deteriorated so that we could knock England over cheaply in the fourth innings. Whatever the batsmen might have thought as he signalled his intention after calling correctly, the decision was a huge vote of confidence in the bowlers and especially in me. Steve Waugh, playing with controlled aggression against the rising, moving ball, helped to vindicate a brave piece of captaincy. Then, in the second innings, he reached three figures again. His pain was evident as he kept taking a bruised right hand off the bat, but he continued to grit his teeth and stay out for more than six hours to help us towards an unassailable lead. Allan Border would have been proud of those two innings.

If the old guard had been behind the success at Old Trafford then three men on their first Ashes tours, Matthew Elliott, Ricky Ponting and Gillespie did us proud at Headingley – though not before we lodged an official complaint when David Graveney, the chairman of the England selectors, ordered the groundsman to change pitches a fortnight before the game. Apparently Graveney was furious when he turned up to find both ends shaved and demanded something more suited to his own bowling attack. It barely mattered as 'Dizzy' Gillespie scythed through the England batting. Our own first innings got off to a bad start before Elliott, badly missed by Thorpe early on off debutant Mike Smith, and Ponting added 268 for the fifth wicket on the way to an innings win. The only shame was that Elliott, who has been unlucky not to play many, many more times for Australia, could not keep out a fine inswinging yorker from Gough on 199.

As usual, panic seemed to engulf England officials. Speculation surrounded Atherton's captaincy, with some reports suggesting he had offered to resign on the eve of the Fifth Test at Trent Bridge, which we won by 264 runs. The selectors had said earlier in the series that they would stick by their players. Needless to say, wholesale changes then followed for Nottingham and they responded to newspaper pressure by giving debuts to the Hollioake brothers. Billed as the latest saviours of English cricket, they flattered to deceive and Ben, just nineteen, was dropped after only one game. Only in England could that happen. One thing that surprised us about Adam was that he had a bit to say before the game, that he would not be pushed around by the Aussies and that at school he let his fists do the talking. Those comments might have been taken out of context, but we certainly found them very interesting.

We retained the Ashes and – surprise, surprise – I received some bad press afterwards, this time for my celebrations on the players' balcony after we clinched the series. I had managed to claim a stump and I just did a little hip-swinging dance with it raised in two hands above my head. *Wisden*, rather flatteringly, called it 'the Warne wiggle'. Photographs confirm from the look in my eyes that I didn't mean anything nasty or provocative. The crowd were having what I assume was a friendly go at me and this was simply my way of acknowledging them. Surely we are allowed to show a little emotion after winning the Ashes. Also, what people didn't realise was that outside the dressing room about half of the crowd were Aussies and the other half English and we all had fun.

I think over-confidence set in at the Oval. We only needed 124 to win, but crashed inexplicably to 104 all out. The champagne was already on ice in the dressing room when Elliott and Taylor went out to open the innings. I remember Ian Botham coming into our dressing room for a chat and suggesting that it was a little bit premature. A couple of the players had already showered and a few of us were sitting around playing cards. All in all the atmosphere was completely wrong when we needed to concentrate on completing the task in hand. We wouldn't make that same mistake today.

It was the third time that year that we'd lost the last Test of a series already won. I suppose we were coming to the end of a long, draining and emotional tour. So many bowlers were suffering injuries that we had to call up Shaun Young, an all-rounder from Tasmania who was playing for Gloucestershire. To make matters worse, I hurt the aducter inside my leg near the groin and could not bowl off my normal approach. I came in off a couple of paces instead, and also had to bat with a runner. Did that make a great difference? I like to think so. The pitch was dry and crumbling and Tufnell helped himself to 11 wickets. A scoreline of four-one would have been nice, rather than three-two. We had shown a great deal of character and while my total of 24 wickets was down on the haul from 1993 I was happy with my tour. I also chipped in with some runs and enjoyed myself.

One of the frustrations with any injury is the way people keep asking if you are okay. It is nice that they care and take an interest but it can become annoying. If I thought the interest in my finger was a little over the top that was nothing compared to the attention that seemed to surround my shoulder in the months before the next Ashes series in 1998–99.

For all of the physiotherapy and the brilliant work of Errol Alcott and Lynn Watson it became increasingly clear through the 1997–98 winter that I could no longer afford to delay surgery. I was not at my best in India after my most successful summer ever, and the results of an arthroscopy when I returned home revealed more damage than we all expected. There were tears in the rotator cuff and they also had to shave down my bicep tendon, plus clean out a few other areas. One doctor even told me that if I had kept bowling for much longer the shoulder could have collapsed completely and ended my career. Simple rest was not an option.

After going under the knife I had to keep the arm in a sling for about six weeks before beginning a rehabilitation course that involved exercises four times a day. In many ways it was an enjoyable period. For a start, I managed to see more of my beloved St Kilda in the AFL than I can remember and I even turned up to watch the odd practice session. It is sometimes not a bad thing for a professional sportsman to sit in the crowd and watch from the other side. It is a reminder of how much you miss something when it is not there. When I watch St Kilda I feel as much a supporter as the next man. I cheer my side and, I must admit, have been known to get a bit hot under the collar at times.

Then, I was invited to a small celebration of Sir Donald

Bradman's ninetieth birthday on 27 August 1998 at his house in Adelaide, with Sachin Tendulkar. He still carried that aura, that force of personality and had lost none of his mental capacity. We had a good chat about spin bowling and in particular about Bill O'Reilly, the best bowler he said he had ever seen. It was interesting to listen to the master batsman talk about how much he loved the modern game; Sachin asked him about his stance and some other things but it was a privilege to be invited to his home and enjoy the day. Unfortunately The Don has left us, but his memory will live on.

Back at home, though, self-doubt crept in. This was a big operation and despite advances in surgical techniques there was a risk that I would never be the same bowler again. Richie Benaud, in that familiar, laconic way, told me that a similar problem hastened his own retirement. At times I was upbeat but at others I was down in the dumps. I didn't always find it easy to sleep, sometimes because the shoulder caused me some pain, but mostly through worrying whether I would be able to produce the big leg-break and the full range of tricks afterwards.

Initially I thought I might be able to recover in time for the First Test against England at the end of November. This was soon revealed as over-optimistic and, as I struggled initially for both St Kilda and Victoria, I wondered whether I might have to sit out the whole series. My shoulder seemed to be working pretty well – the medical people had assured me it ought to feel as good as new – but confidence only returned gradually.

Then, early in December, another bombshell dropped with the news that Mark Waugh and I had received money from a bookmaker in Sri Lanka four years earlier. I have discussed the issue itself in another chapter. Suffice to say here that it was an untimely distraction and set me back a bit mentally. I read out a prepared statement before the Third Test at Adelaide. The matter understandably dominated the build-up to the game, which Australia won by 205 runs to take an unassailable 2–0 in the series and make sure the Ashes were retained again.

Once again we took our foot off the pump slightly and to England's credit they beat us in Melbourne, meaning they would level if they could score a second win at Sydney. Meanwhile, I felt I bowled really well for Victoria against a full strength New South Wales side. Even though I didn't take a lot of wickets I felt I bowled well and was ready to make the next step. To my delight I was recalled for the final Test, in the first week of 1999 alongside MacGill. Some people suggested my re-introduction was premature and that I needed more wickets behind me in the domestic game. But I have always done better on the bigger stage.

As it happened, my return went superbly. Magnificent batting on the first day by the Waughs gave us a solid base and Glenn McGrath removed Alec Stewart to claim his 200th Test poll. When I joined the attack as the fourth bowler, butterflies were flying around my stomach just as they had on my Test debut seven years earlier on the same turf. I felt as though I was starting again, relieved to begin with a dot ball and annoyed when Mark Butcher whacked the next delivery through midwicket. I decided to send the fourth one through a bit quicker, hoping Butcher would be late on the stroke. The plan worked to perfection as the ball sped through to hit his pads plumb in front of the stumps. I didn't bother turning round, I knew it was out. Things couldn't have gone better.

From then on the match belonged to Slater with a magnificent 123 out of our second innings 184 and MacGill, who added 7 wickets to the 5 he took first time around. He bowled beautifully, fizzing his leg-breaks and wrong-uns. It was good for Australian cricket that we had another leg-spinner. The fact that I managed to beat the bat consistently at least showed I could still turn my stock delivery and my second-innings wicket was an important one – Butcher stranded down the pitch after misreading a top-spinner. I knew I had contributed against the oldest enemy. More important, I removed any nagging doubts in my own mind that my career was heading towards the end.

I have never played in a losing Ashes series and I would love to keep it that way. In fact, even when we went one-down in 1997, it has not crossed my mind that we would surrender the oldest prize in the game. At times in my experience the difference between the sides has been Australia's ability to recover when the chips were down. From my first appearance against England in 1993 to the last Test of the 98–99 series we have won thirteen of the twenty-two Tests while they have won five. Going back to 1989 the scoreline is twenty to five in thirty-two games.

In the past I have described England as being soft under pressure. They have had plenty of opportunities but not always managed to nail us down. In Brisbane in 1998–99, for example, they had us 5-down in the first innings but missed a couple of chances. One was to run out Steve Waugh. He went on to add 187 with Healy and there was another big moment they lost that contributed to the defeat. That has been the biggest difference between the sides during my career – when Australia see an opportunity we have generally grasped it. In the past, once England have fallen behind they have not shown the same fight as they are doing now. They tended to play to compete rather than to win. It is wrong to say they have gone into games expecting to lose. I just think that as soon as our noses are in front, as soon as Slater cracks 50 in the first hour, some of the players start to think, here we go again. They have never had somebody like Steve Waugh who has come in with 3 or 4 wickets down and consistently retrieved the situation.

Their body language in the field has not always exuded enthusiasm or expectancy. Some of them have needed to take a leaf out of Darren Gough's book. He was a guy who impressed us immediately because, as well as being a really good bowler, he wears his heart on his sleeve and gives his all. The public love to see a bloke expressing himself and enjoying the game like he does. With Gough they know they are watching somebody who will never give less than 100 per cent whatever the state of play. I don't know about his ancestry, but there seems to be a bit of the Aussie ticker about him.

Some of England's selection policy has been baffling. Hick is a classic example of a player who has really been messed around, coming in and out of the side instead of being a permanent fixture. He is purely and simply a quality player. As an outsider looking in, he seems to lack a little bit of confidence in his ability at that level, but how much of that can he put down to not knowing whether he has a regular spot? It is a shame the world has not had a proper chance to see his talent. He times the ball better than anybody else I can think of and his innings against us for Worcestershire in 1993 was magnificent.

We did not target Hick especially before the start of the series, except to make sure we tested him against the short-pitched stuff. Once he got out a few times, we started to detect a weakness and I think the problem then became mental rather than technical. I have seen Hick pull and hook with the best. He just seemed to get confused about his best approach, whether to duck, hook or swing inside the line, and Merv Hughes in particular started to get on top of him. That didn't make him a bad player. He just needed re-assurance and even Merv was pleased to help him out in that regard and to see the back of him.

Robin Smith is another player who seems to have been badly treated. He told me the reason he was dropped in 1993 was because the selectors didn't think he could play spin. But he was such a good batsman that if they felt he was vulnerable to slow bowling he should have been promoted to open. He has proved himself by batting in many different positions. In that series they dropped Smith, Hick and Gatting at various times. Amazing! If those three were not among the top six batsmen in the country then England should have been one of the best sides in the world instead of scraping around for the odd win here and there.

I like to think that Smith in particular would have been handled differently had he been an Australian. For England he was used in all sorts of spots and never really was allowed to settle in one position. Because he was their best batsman, along with Gooch, during that period he was always asked to fill the problem position and being the sort of guy who will go out of his way to help anybody, he always did what was best for the team, which is what you expect, but I think Robin was used as a scapegoat. In effect, the selectors compromised a strength to solve a weakness, and eventually it was the player who paid the price for their mistakes. It is amazing that he only played in fourteen victories out of sixty-two Tests. There must have been a few headaches.

Another difference might be the way we are prepared to utilise our talent from the past. In Australia now the system is in place where we can call upon the likes of Rod Marsh, Ian Chappell, Dennis Lillee and my own mentor, Terry Jenner. They always offer their time and service which is so valuable to us all. There is an equal amount of experience in England. The problem is that much of it sits in the television commentary box. Botham might have ruffled a few establishment feathers down the years, but he knows the game inside out and ought to be part of the set-up. He is an inspirational guy, especially to the youngsters. Then you have David Gower and Bob Willis – probably the best English batsman and bowler of their generation. It just strikes me as a great shame that they can't put something back in. People talk about our Academy, but there is no point having one unless there are quality coaches.

For any Australian or Englishman the Ashes remains the most important series in world cricket, simply because of the history and tradition, the personalities involved in all the memorable battles of the past. It is the oldest series in the game and the one that neutrals always look to. My opinion is that England is the favourite tour for most Australian players. It makes a big difference being able to travel from one town or city to the next in a coach instead of spending hours on end at airports. We are always well supported because people use the cricket as a reason to visit England on what represents the holiday of a lifetime. The same is true when England come to Australia. On recent tours their support has been fantastic, probably as vocal as at a home game if not more so. The Barmy Army have been great to their players.

The Lord's Test is always a highlight. While the MCG is my favourite ground – I have been lucky to have played and watched football there as well as cricket and I think of it as my home stadium and my own backyard – Lord's is up there close. As a player you can't help feel your skin tingle with the history that breathes around the place. To walk from the dressing room, down two flights of stairs and then through the Long Room, past the MCC members with their egg-and-bacon ties saying, 'See you in a minute' (and with me they generally do), is a wonderful feeling. All the walls are covered with pictures and paintings of great players from the past. It can be humbling as well as a very proud minute or so.

I remember standing at the window of the visitors' dressing room for the first time and being staggered by the incline of the famous slope. It measures something like eight feet from one side of the ground to the other. I never imagined it would be so pronounced and it did take a little bit of getting used to when I bowled in 1993. There are two honours boards in the dressing room for touring batsmen who score a hundred and bowlers who take 5 wickets in an innings in a Test. As soon as I saw the list of names I made it an ambition to join them. Unfortunately, I took four in each innings in 1993 and, with Glenn McGrath bowling superbly, I didn't get much of a chance four years later – maybe in 2001.

The recent one-sidedness has not diminished the contest. When we took the lead in 1998–99 I know some people suggested the series should be cut from five to three Tests, but I can't imagine that will ever be a serious consideration. These games are huge box office attractions. Australians will always turn out to see the Poms playing Australia, and in England the crowds are happy to see good cricket, which both teams provide. Maybe if England continue to spiral downwards people will start to get bored, but there is evidence of a recovery under Nasser Hussain and Duncan Fletcher.

5

CLOSE CALLS WITH SOUTH AFRICA

IN LESS THAN A YEAR my life had changed beyond recognition. From missing selection for the First Team against the West Indies twelve months earlier I had now become a regular member and one of the main bowlers in the side. My 7 wickets at Melbourne in the Boxing Day Test of 1992 had set me up for a fantastic tour of New Zealand, where I took 17 wickets, and an even better trip to England for my debut Ashes series. Where the previous year I wondered whether I was good enough to play against the best in the world, I was now full of confidence, enjoying the limelight and the opportunities that had started to come my way. I was also engaged to be married. As you get older you learn to pace your movements, but back in 1993 I could hardly wait to start bowling again.

One of the few blemishes of the previous season had been the failure to reclaim the Trans-Tasman Trophy in New Zealand when we lost the final Test in Eden Park. We felt we had been comfortably the better side, but could not recover from a terrible batting collapse in the first innings. When New Zealand visited the following summer we were determined to make amends.

The rivalry between the sides is of the friendly variety.

Although they won three series against us from the mid-80s we were the better side in the 90s.

New Zealand held their own for the first three days of the First Test in Perth in November 1993 but we gradually imposed our authority. Although they secured a first innings lead, thanks to a hundred by Andrew Jones, we scored runs far too easily second time around, declared, and New Zealand fought hard to play well and hang on for a draw. But we saw signs that we could beat them.

They have never had the biggest pool of players to chose from, and were seriously undermined when Martin Crowe returned home injured, having limped through the final stages in Perth with a brace on his knee. We heard rumours about strife in their camp and, whether or not these were true, we outplayed them for the rest of the series. At the time I had a deal with Puma and John Forbes, who worked for the sponsors, said before the next contest in Hobart that he thought I would soon take 6 for 36 in a Test match. I still haven't – but this time I went close by claiming 6 for 31 in the second innings for 9 wickets in the match. My favourite was bowling Ken Rutherford around his legs as he tried to sweep.

I was pleased to be back in tandem with Tim May. We had enjoyed a great partnership in England but the selectors decided on an extra seamer in Perth – rightly so – and the victory by an innings and 222 runs in Hobart more than justified his recall. The beauty of bowling with Tim was that he kept an end so tight. He was not a negative bowler. He had great loop and such good control that he rarely sent down a 4-ball. Batsmen have to score runs and when they feel bogged down they take risks. There was a good example in Hobart. Blair Pocock had blocked and blocked and blocked when, for no apparent reason, he decided to come down the track to me and give Ian

Healy a stumping. Clearly, frustration had got the better of him.

When everything is working I think an off-spin/leg-spin combination provides the best balance. I know that Clarrie Grimmett and Bill O'Reilly were successful as two wrist-spinners in tandem, but they were genuinely great bowlers and I can't think of another two leggies that have been successful over time. When the same type of bowler is operating from both ends batsmen can become settled. Grimmett and O'Reilly must have been very, very special.

By the end of the series New Zealand were clearly demoralised and we secured another innings win in Brisbane where the dry surface was well suited to spin. This time I took 4 wickets in each innings for 18 in the series, an Australian record against New Zealand and breaking my own from '93. But perhaps the most damning indictment of New Zealand was that seven of our batsmen scored hundreds. That also says something for the quality of our batting. In all it had been a one-sided, low-key series played in front of smallish crowds, no doubt waiting for the visit of South Africa in the second half of the season. But for us it had been important to avoid defeat and build some momentum. I thought we put in a thoroughly professional performance and I was still bowling well and felt like I was on a roll.

I think the South Africa series had been at the back of our minds all along. Deep down we expected to beat New Zealand, but our second opponents were to a large degree an unknown quantity. We knew what they were capable of through either playing or watching the 1992 World Cup in Australia, but had not faced them in Test cricket since their re-admission. In contrast to the New Zealanders, their presence had attracted a great deal of interest and the series managed to live up to the hype after a slow start when the First Test in Melbourne was badly affected by rain.

The game saw Hansie Cronje become my seventy-second and final wicket for the year. I had already set a record for spin bowler in a calendar year and at one stage it seemed I might even challenge Dennis Lillee's tally of eighty-five victims set in 1981. The following year I almost beat my own record when I took 70 wickets. Incidentally, my total was overtaken in 2000 when Muttiah Muralitharan reached 75 from only ten Tests – an incredible average of nearly 4 wickets every innings.

In Melbourne the sides spent a lot of time sizing up each other. Although the series was only eight years ago we did not have the resources to study opponents that are available today. Besides which, there is nothing to beat the evidence of our own eyes. This was our first look at Allan Donald – sharp, but not yet the force he would become – and also at a certain Daryll Cullinan. Of all their batsmen this was the guy who had intrigued us most. He arrived with a big reputation, having scored stacks of runs in South Africa, and the way he sledged continually from slip when we batted (even though he dropped a few catches) made us think he would be something special. Craig McDermott had him for a first ball duck, and I guess life against Australia didn't get much better for him. On that tour Hansie Cronje, with his slog-sweep, was very effective.

After the disappointing and unseasonal weather in my home city we were able to enjoy a proper game in Sydney. It evolved into a real thriller for the crowd and a bitter-sweet five days for me. As soon as I turned up and saw the pitch I thought I was in with a chance and Allan Border clearly agreed as he brought me into the attack inside the first hour. Nothing much happened before lunch, but afterwards it started to turn. Gary Kirsten, Jonty Rhodes and Cullinan all went to the flipper before Dave Richardson and Craig Matthews edged leg-breaks to slip. The wicket I most remember is that of the charismatic Pat Symcox. As I signalled to go around the wicket he made a big play for changing his guard from middle to leg stump, chuckled to himself and said: 'You won't get around there, China.' The next ball I did just that, bowling him around his legs to the dismay of Symcox and lots of clapping, jumping and laughing from Ian Healy.

A classic Michael Slater innings and typically gritty contribution from Border helped to establish a three-figure lead and when I sent back Kepler Wessels and Cullinan in quick succession they had lost 5 second innings wickets without retrieving the arrears. Then Rhodes and Richardson mounted a partnership with Rhodes finding spaces to score runs through an attacking field and sweeping against the spin, but the crucial stand saw Rhodes and Donald add 36 for the last wicket. Psychologically it meant they had a lead in three figures. There was also something inspiring about the way Rhodes had gone about the task, at one point hooking McDermott for 6. Even on a dusty pitch where the odd ball went through the top, a target of 117 should have been comfortable. From expecting defeat, however, South Africa must have realised they too had prospects and could really pump themselves up.

Our problems began just before close on the fourth day. From 1 for 51 we lost 3 wickets for 6 runs, including May, the nightwatchman. Next morning Border was bowled by a ball from Donald which he left, Mark Waugh and Healy followed and I was run out by a direct hit from Cronje. McDermott played some swashbuckling shots to get us close, only for Damien Martyn, who had batted well for more than an hour and a half for 6 runs, flaying to cover when we were only 7 runs short. I felt for Marto because he was my buddy and also the last recognised batsman. McGrath quickly followed to give them victory by 5 runs. Our dressing room was like a morgue afterwards, while McGrath could hardly move from the crease in shock and disappointment. I could boast match figures of

12 for 128 - still the best of my career – yet I couldn't manage a word or a smile.

A year earlier in January 1993 I had been in the side that lost by one run to the West Indies at Adelaide, when McDermott was last out, caught behind off Courtney Walsh when the ball just brushed his glove as he tried to evade a short ball. In that game I had only bowled 8 overs, but I stayed in for more than an hour in the second innings and helped us to inch towards the target. It was probably the most disappointing game of my life, and losing by one wicket to Pakistan in Karachi in 1994 was not much better. But this was slightly different. We had been in charge for nearly the whole game but thrown away the opportunity in the fourth innings.

Martyn received a lot of flak for his part in the defeat, but I think much of the criticism was unfair and to blame him personally for the result was outrageous. He had stayed there longer than most and if the shot had gone a foot either side of the fielder it was a certain 4. His strength is as a stroke-maker and he can be one of the most attractive players in the world. The fact is that if eleven international cricketers couldn't get 117 between us it was a pretty poor effort all round. Martyn and I were the first youngsters to come through the Academy and we joined a side with a number of very senior figures. We came through a lot together and remain good friends to this day, but unfortunately he lost his place after that innings and struggled to get back in because of the overall quality of our batting. He worked hard and is now doing very well.

While the South Africans were ecstatic, we still thought we could level the series. I cannot take anything away from them, because they saw a chance and grasped it. That is one of the attributes of a good team. But we arrived in Adelaide, after winning the World Series in the third and deciding final, determined not to give them another sniff.

It helped to have Steve Waugh back from a hamstring problem and, once he struck 164 to help us to declare at 7 for 469, we were well on the way to drawing the series and, although they narrowly avoided the follow on, we were able to set a target of 321 on a well worn pitch where even survival had become hard work. Having tied up an end in the first innings, I was now employed in a more attacking fashion and relished the challenge against batsmen who had struggled to cope with the big spinning leg-breaks and showed few signs of being able to read the variations. I had begun to develop a touch of tendonitis in the shoulder, but pain can be a state of mind, and when McMillan became my hundredth Test wicket, going back to a flipper, I felt as fit as a fiddle. A return catch off Richard Snell set me on the way towards 200 and ended a collapse which saw the last 7 wickets fall for 29 runs. I had taken 4 for 31 from 30.5 overs, figures which underline just how South Africa struggled against leg spin.

That haul meant I finished the Australian season with 36 wickets in six Tests – a couple more victims then in the Ashes series. I felt I was still improving as a bowler because I was learning with every game. It wasn't just a case of getting kicks by beating batsmen with huge leg-breaks any more. I sensed an edginess among the South African batsmen and really worked on confusing them. The number of wickets I took in that series with the flipper gave me great satisfaction. I also took a lot of pride and satisfaction from being named International Cricketer of the Year, earning me a pair of Toyota cars which the team helped to drive around the outfield at Adelaide as a way of saying thanks to the Australian public for their support. They have been great for a long time.

Although we should have won the series, the one all scoreline indicated that the teams were pretty evenly matched. Having said that, when we left for South Africa later in February we thought we might have a psychological edge as winners of the most recent meeting. We reckoned without the incredible pressure we would face in and outside the grounds. The country was facing a potentially explosive situation anyway with the elections that would bring in Nelson Mandela as president just a few weeks away. At times we played games while helicopters hovered overhead because the African National Congress happened to be staging a rally nearby.

When we landed in Johannesburg there seemed to be more people waiting to get a look at us than on Boxing Day at the MCG. The South Africans were fascinated by us and with me in particular as the new kid on the block who was somewhat mysterious. Ian Healy nicknamed me Elvis on that tour because of the crowds who wanted to see me everywhere we went. In the papers they called me the Wizard of Oz or the Sultan of Spin. All very flattering, but there were times when I wanted to run away from it all. I enjoyed the limelight and the novelty of signing autographs, as many as I could, but for a couple of weeks in South Africa I was a time bomb waiting to explode.

The funny thing is that I don't believe my bowling was affected, certainly not statistically. South Africa got away from us second time around at Johannesburg when the difference was only 3 runs from the first innings. They showed the very qualities we have grown to embody ourselves – courage, patience, discipline and a steely will to win. We thought we had chances to save the game on the final day with 8 wickets in hand, but none of the batsmen could go on and play the really long innings we needed.

A brief stay at Sun City came at a timely moment. We needed to chill out, forget the cricket, play some golf, get ourselves in the right frame of mind for the remainder of the tour. There was an amusing incident at Stellenbosch (which Merv nicknamed 'Still on the booze') where the groundsman explained an uneven pitch for our three-day game by saying that a snake had wrapped itself around the roller the previous day and refused to budge – not that he spent too long trying to persuade it to move. I must say that once we were out of Johannesburg, where a small group of people seemed intent on hollering abuse rather than watching cricket, the tour became thoroughly enjoyable. It could be that I had simply learnt my lesson from previous experience. I always try to look for a positive.

Cape Town lived up to all expectations – a beautiful setting to play and watch cricket in front of the picturesque Table Mountain. The Second Test in the third week of March proved to be a great match for Steve Waugh, who had suffered with a few niggles in the early weeks, including a back problem that arose on the waterslide at Sun City. On the eve of the game a newspaper reported that he was doubtful after being bitten by a poisonous spider. That was news to all of us, but it didn't prevent one admirer from sending eighteen red roses as a 'get well' tonic. They seemed to do the trick as he hit 86 and put on 108 for the sixth wicket with Healy in a partnership that had an important bearing on the match. It gave us a first innings lead but, just as importantly, kept them in the field for longer than they expected.

Because of injuries Stephen rarely bowls these days, and when he does turn his arm it is only for a few overs to try and buy a wicket. But at one point he was possibly the best all-rounder in the world, and in a crucial final hour on the fourth day we bowled in tandem to remove five of the South Africa batsmen, despite the pitch being devoid of any pace or bounce. That suited Stephen's skiddy type of delivery and he soon held a sensational return catch to dismiss Cronje and precipitate the collapse. I finished the session by removing Peter Kirsten and Fanie de Villiers, the nightwatchman, in the final minutes. Again, the timing made those wickets so important.

On the final morning we gave ourselves a target of 91 to win – simple, in theory, as long as we didn't think too hard about the way we had lost in Sydney less than three months earlier. After a quick pep-talk in the dressing room we decided there was no point hanging around. That might have been the mistake we had made before. This time, if the ball was there to be hit, then we would hit it, and 25 overs later, with Michael Slater relishing the plan, we were home by 9 wickets. The celebrations in the dressing room were so enthusiastic that we didn't have the energy to party back at the hotel.

So the series was set up at one all, or two all including the initial series in Australia. Everything was set for a thrilling finale in Durban. Unfortunately, it seemed to us that South Africa were happy to settle for a draw instead of going all out for a win. We were desperate to succeed because, with a Pakistan tour coming up, there was speculation that this could be the great Allan Border's last Test before retiring. He had given so much to Australian cricket and deserved to go out with success.

South Africa put themselves in a good position when they bowled us out for 269 early on the second day. Yet they had showed no urgency in scoring runs. They batted for fourteen hours in all with under 200 coming on the whole of the third day. I bowled 55 overs, more than in any other innings in my career, but ended with 4 for 92. Their tactics were difficult to comprehend. The pitch was pretty good, so they could hardly have expected to blow us away in our second innings. They needed to give themselves time to take 10 wickets and then chase a total. In the end, Mark Waugh and Border were left at the crease playing out for time. Short of winning, at least Border was there for the final moments, having removed any possibility of defeat. A month later he confirmed the speculation and hung up his bat to tributes from us all. An era in Australian cricket had ended and we felt sad, because he was Australian cricket and had helped us all so much.

One of the key moments in Durban came when Rhodes, on 2, seemed to be held by David Boon at silly mid off against my bowling. The umpires could not be sure the ball had carried and rightly gave the batsman the benefit of the doubt. Rhodes went on to score 78 before I trapped him with a flipper. Even then we couldn't cut through the tail quickly enough to be able to win. I think we would have put our foot on the accelerator in the second innings and tried to set a target, knowing how uncertain they had been against spin over the previous months.

The one-day series after the Tests proved just as tight, finishing level four all when David Richardson was run out off the last ball of the final game in Bloemfontein attempting the run that would have given South Africa victory overall. The sides were as closely matched as that. But we left the country for a short one-day competition in Sharjah thinking that we could and should have done better. I wonder if South Africa could honestly say the same about themselves. But I love touring the country, the nice people, the lovely scenery and the hospitality. I look forward to going there again.

6

MATCH-FIXING

I HAVE NEVER ATTEMPTED to fix a game or any part of a game in my life. I never would and never will. Nor have I knowingly received money from a bookmaker. As far as the business with the man I knew only as 'John' is concerned, I was stupid and naive to accept money. It didn't dawn on me that he might be involved with trying to fix cricket matches. I thought he was a wealthy man who liked a bet, who had won money on Australia in the past and wanted to express his thanks. I took it at face value and thought he was telling the truth. This is how I was introduced to 'John'.

The story is well known. We had travelled to Sri Lanka at the start of our 1994–95 international programme for a one-day tournament preceding the Test series in Pakistan. We were based in Colombo and on several occasions we went to a casino near the team hotel. On this particular night I suffered a losing run on the roulette wheel which left me down by $5,000 (US). I went over to join Mark Waugh, who introduced me to a gentleman called 'John', as somebody 'who bets on the cricket'. That is quite different from being a bookmaker.

Mark is one of my best mates in the game. Any friend of his is a friend of mine. 'John' said that I was his favourite player and that he had always wanted to meet me. He seemed a nice enough bloke and we spoke for around thirty minutes at the most before shaking hands and going our separate ways.

It turned out that we were staying at the same hotel and I was surprised next day after training to take a call from 'John' inviting me to his room. He continued to flatter me, as he had done to a lesser degree the previous night, in the way that most cricketers become used to on the sub-continent. So it was something of a shock when he pulled out an envelope full of money. I asked what it was for and he said it was a token of his appreciation and compensation for the money I had lost the evening before. He said that he was a very wealthy man and wanted to give me something as his way of saying thanks for the number of times he had won on Australia in the past. I said that I had money of my own, thanked him for his kindness but said that I didn't want his gift. He was quite persistent and said that he would be offended if I didn't take it. He stressed that he expected nothing in return. In the end I took it, thinking there were no strings attached (and promptly lost it again at the casino that night).

If something similar happened to a player today the bells would ring immediately. But in 1994 none of us imagined how aspects of the game might be corrupt. There were no whispers of anything untoward occurring in the world of cricket. The idea that bookmakers might be trying to buy up cricketers could have come from a work of fiction. We also knew there were some generous people in the sub-continent who were fanatical about the game. There were stories about players being given cars and gold nuggets simply as a mark of appreciation. Apparently, Bobby Simpson, our coach at the time, has said somewhere that he told us at a team meeting to be on guard against people offering gifts. I have no reason whatsoever to doubt his word, but it certainly didn't register with me. Team meetings, from my experience, can sometimes drag on – everybody will have his say about an opponent, discuss a few theories and then decide to play in the way that has worked pretty well for the last 120 years.

Looking back now, with everything that has emerged during all the investigations in various parts of the world, people might wonder how I could think that a near-stranger was prepared to show such generosity without an ulterior motive. At the time, as I've said, I took it at face value and it didn't register that I could be making a rod for my own back, even when 'John' rang on a couple of occasions to have a friendly chat. In one case he wished me a Happy Christmas and in another he said Happy New Year. They were the sort of conversations I might have had with my dad and brother. He didn't ask about the likely make-up of our side or team morale; he just inquired about the weather and whether the wicket would suit me. I was never under the impression that I was giving information to a bookmaker. I just assumed he was a mate of Mark's who was having a bet on the cricket. As captain of Victoria and occasionally Australia I gave the media more information than I gave to 'John'. Technically, I did give information for money, but it was not in the way that has been portrayed. I only met the man twice, for no longer than thirty minutes and twenty minutes, and that was seven years ago.

The next development came during the short tour of New Zealand for the Centenary Cup one-day competition in February 1995. Ian McDonald, our team manager, called me into his room to ask whether I knew anything about players taking money for providing weather and pitch reports. My response was no. I was not trying to deceive McDonald by being clever, because when 'John' gave me five thousand dollars he wanted nothing in return. Besides which, what we talked about was just general chat. I told McDonald that the only money I had received was from the occasional sportsmen's dinner and a gift from a guy who was a friend of Mark Waugh.

McDonald then said in a knowing way that 'John' would be the same guy with whom Mark had a business deal to provide information on pitches and weather. I remember getting that sinking feeling and wondering if I had let myself in for something after all. McDonald listened to the whole story sympathetically. Technically, I had accepted money from a man who was a bookmaker. And, yes, I did speak to him about pitches and weather. I remain adamant that I did nothing wrong. But I could see that McDonald was now in a tricky position.

How he got wind that there might be a problem in the first place, I don't know. He said that he needed to inform the ACB back home before taking the next step. When Mark and I boarded a plane in Sydney bound for the West Indies, the next leg of our schedule, we didn't know whether we would be sent back to Australia at the other end. Mark Taylor, the captain, had only been informed of the situation by McDonald the night before. It was an extremely nerve-racking flight, but in the end the Board decided to fine me $8,000 and Mark $10,000. We received the news during a stopover in London.

The ACB also decided that it was in the best interests of the game and of the Australian players to keep the matter in house rather than issue a press release. I had nothing to do with that decision. I didn't make any representation one way or the other and was never asked to. In hindsight I think it would have been better for all of us if the Board had made it public straight away. They were trying to protect us but I felt I'd done nothing wrong. We all make mistakes. When the news finally broke four years later people were naturally suspicious that they had kept the matter under wraps and that there was more to it. Innocently, the Board made a mistake trying to look after us.

By February 1995 the ACB were aware that Salim Malik had approached Tim May, Mark Waugh and myself to perform badly in games in Pakistan. Alan Crompton, the ACB chairman at the time, said subsequently he was concerned that if the 'John' affair had been made public it might have been confused with our allegations against Malik. Some people have speculated that the ACB would then have been under pressure to impose harsher penalties against Mark and myself.

It was only some time later I began to consider the theory that 'John's' $5,000 (US) might have formed part of a sting operation and that Malik was working with 'John' when he tried to bribe me to underperform during the First Test in Karachi at the end of September 1994.

Again, the basics of Malik's approach are well documented. The First Test was four days old with Pakistan on 3 for 155, chasing 314 to win. That evening Malik rang and asked me to come to his room at the hotel. I was a bit surprised because, although we would speak to each other on the field and at the cricket ground, and I think shared a mutual respect as cricketers, he had always seemed rather aloof and wasn't a guy I knew well. We chatted briefly about the first four days and then he said: 'You know, we cannot lose.'

My immediate reaction was that he just wanted to sound confident. I laughed and suggested that we felt we were in with a good chance. He repeated it once, before saying again: 'You don't understand. We cannot lose.'

When I asked what he meant he finally came out with his offer – $200,000 cash to be made available in half an hour for Tim May and myself to bowl badly the following day. 'Both of you bowl outside off stump and it will be a draw,' he said.

The offer left me utterly shell-shocked. I had never heard anything like it and never imagined that this went on. I said that we were going to beat them and returned to the room I was sharing with May. When I outlined the conversation to my spin partner his initial reaction was tongue in cheek. Then, as I expected, he told me to ring the Rat (our nickname for Malik, because of his resemblance to one – how appropriate!) and tell him we were going to nail them. We also told Taylor, who was captaining the side for the first time, about the approach because we knew the matter could not just be brushed aside. He in turn passed the information to Bobby Simpson, our coach and Col Egar, our manager, who reported it to John Reid, the match referee.

For much of the Test we were in charge. We made steady inroads to the point where they needed 56 to win with the last pair, Inzamam-ul-Haq and Mushtaq Ahmed, at the crease. What happened next amounts to one of the most frustrating periods for me on a cricket field as three very good appeals for lbw and a catch behind were rejected. With Pakistan needing three runs to win with one wicket in hand, Taylor and I had a chat and decided to leave the whole of the on side in front of square vacant to tempt Inzamam to hit through that area. This is what you dream about. The plan worked in that he tried and failed – but unfortunately Ian Healy missed the stumping chance and the ball raced to the boundary instead. Game over, we had lost. I felt so bad for my mate Heals who was devastated. The fact that I won the man of the match award came as little consolation and for Taylor it meant a losing start to what would prove a golden reign as captain. It was still a fair effort because we were down to a pair of fit bowlers, Jo Angel and myself, with injuries to Glenn McGrath and May. When I went up to the podium to collect my man of the match award Malik brushed past me and said that I should have taken the money. I wanted to nail him there and then with the old knuckle sandwich.

I feel that the most upsetting part of the whole business came during the original inquiry into the allegation in Pakistan where the original judge effectively exonerated Malik and accused Mark, Tim and myself of being liars. Malik, attempting to find a reason why I would have manufactured the story, said that it was part of a plot to unsettle his batting because I couldn't get him out. Now Malik was a fine player who has had the better of me on occasions, but I would always back myself against any batsman in the world by fair means. The odd spontaneous word at the crease is one thing, but making up a story as serious as this is quite another.

Nearly six years after his approach Malik was finally given a life ban by the Pakistan Cricket Board on the recommendation of Justice Mohammad Malik Qayyum, following a lengthy inquiry. The scale of his involvement has emerged. He was also alleged to have tried to fix games against New Zealand and South Africa, but Qayyum said it was due in a large part to my own deposition that the punishment should be imposed. At long last I had been vindicated in public and justice was seen to be done. I don't claim to be any sort of Clark Kent figure, but I was proved right and wasn't making it all up. Malik was also captured on film in England in 2000 telling a reporter what it costs for what in terms of fixing matches.

News that Mark and I had taken money from 'John' broke in December 1998. Once the original decision had been taken by the ACB and the fine imposed and paid I thought the matter was over. I certainly didn't spend the next four years worrying what would happen if it ever became public, because in my heart I knew I had done nothing wrong. I cannot speak for Mark but I believe what he has said about his involvement. No journalist ever approached me during the intervening period saying that he had been leaked information about Australian players taking money from a bookmaker. I don't know if the information was passed on by a member of the ACB, the ICC or a former player.

It was a difficult period because I was trying to concentrate on making a recovery after the shoulder operation and had only recently decided to give up smoking. I felt nervous as I faced the press in Adelaide to read a prepared statement. A week or so later, during a Shield game at Sydney, I decided I ought to try to clear the air and pointed out the differences between my own case and the situation regarding Malik. I am pleased that my story soon came out in the open. Initially, I think the Australian public were confused about exactly what happened. People had been ribbing me and some of my friends were asking whether I was involved. My integrity was being questioned and I was very unhappy.

Basically, with betting being illegal in Pakistan – another thing I didn't realise until everything came out – it was not unreasonable to be worried for our safety if May, Mark Waugh and I went over to Pakistan to give evidence at the original inquiry. In any case, we had given full statements to the ACB and had nothing to hide. Then, I did not go to Lahore to face Qayyum personally in 1998 because, unlike Mark Waugh and Mark Taylor, I was not with the team in Pakistan at the time. I was out with a shoulder injury. The Pakistani hearing in Melbourne was to be public so that everybody could hear our answers. That way the matter could be put to rest. Being cross-examined by trained lawyers who seemed less concerned with absorbing my evidence than trying to trip me up was a new, unsettling experience but I just had to tell the truth, like I've done from day one. I wondered if the aim of the Pakistanis was simply to throw in as many accusations as they could as a smokescreen. They tried to make a big deal of my gambling habits, which were hardly a secret. I confirmed that I played blackjack and roulette and bet on Aussie Rules, but never on cricket when I was involved.

Michael Shatin, the QC for Mark Waugh, asked what I thought was a pertinent question about whether Malik had ever challenged me over the allegations. After all, we had played Pakistan in 1995–96 and then during the 1996 World Cup. The fact is that he never mentioned the business at all. Gradually, people recognised that I had not been involved in anything like match-fixing. Thanks to the bravery and sense of Judge Qayyum, there is acceptance that I have told the truth all along.

I would love 'John' to come forward to confirm my version of the story. I have been upfront with the ACB, given evidence to the Pakistan inquiry and then to the O'Regan inquiry which was set up by the Board soon after the decision to fine Mark Waugh and myself became public. There is nothing more I can do, but if the cricket authorities think in the future I can still help them to get to the bottom of anything relating to corruption then I will be happy to assist. It was interesting that O'Regan, after interviewing more than sixty players, officials and journalists, recognised a possible link between the approaches of 'John' and Malik. O'Regan pulled no punches in his summing up and I'm sure that everybody involved has learnt from the experience.

Most people now realise what happened. A couple of newspapers, the *Age* in Australia and *Mirror* in England, decided not to continue using me as a columnist. The reason was that they wanted me to comment, obviously, but for legal reasons I was not allowed to do that. Most of my sponsors were prepared to take me at my word and support me. I thank them very much.

Given the revelations that have come to light in recent years I am sure all of us have thought back over our careers and wondered whether every player in every game was giving 100 per cent. In any case, it would be very difficult to interpret a match, to decide whether one side played well only because the other were playing poorly on purpose.

I do recall a Singer World Series one-day game against Pakistan in Sri Lanka in September 1994 as an occasion where cricket seemed unusually easy. Pakistan needed 180 to win, but finished their 50 overs on 9 for 151. I remember Salim Malik driving a lot of balls from Steve Waugh inside out straight to fielders. I also remember another player being stumped by a long, long way when he came down the pitch to me. Good players can make mistakes under pressure and Pakistan are known as a hot and cold team.

Like most people in the game I was really surprised when Hansie Cronje admitted his dealings with bookmakers. I found the whole scale of his situation mind-boggling. I knew Hansie very well – the international circuit is close – and always thought of him as a player guaranteed to give 100 per cent. He tended to take defeat badly. The fact that it was Hansie, with his reputation as a religious man and a tough competitor, made us open our eyes and wonder about the depth of the problem. He was the last person I ever thought would be involved.

Looking on as an outsider, and not having studied the evidence given to the King Commission in Cape Town, the affair seems very sad. We had to go to South Africa for a one-day tournament of three matches in April 2000 within a few days of his confession. I wasn't sure how the crowd would react, or even how many people would turn up to watch. In fact the grounds were full and the spectators rallied behind South Africa. They obviously realised that the eleven players representing their country were fully committed and as upset about being let down by Hansie as they were. In the circumstances it was a magnificent effort by the new captain Shaun Pollock and his team to win the series two-one. They recognised the huge responsibility on their shoulders and were determined to win and show they were giving it everything.

Like Hansie, Mohammad Azharuddin was another guy I never held under any suspicion, but who now is said to have been involved. I thought of him as a very polite, sensitive, quiet person who dressed extremely smartly away from the game. He was also a particularly high-class batsman, capable of taking batting to another level on his day. Again, like Hansie, he appeared to have a steely side to him. As a Muslim in the India team he must have possessed great inner strength and determination. He continues to protest his innocence of the allegations and to fight to clear his name.

Were the clues there that we all missed? I don't think so. I have played in Sharjah, where investigations have centred, and not, to my knowledge, set eyes upon a bookmaker. All I can remember is being smashed around on a perfect batting pitch as Sachin Tendulkar scored successive hundreds in 1998. If that place was a hotbed of corruption then I'm afraid, like Sachin's straight drives, it all went over my head.

I think it is the responsibility of each Board to make sure their players are above suspicion and to impose stiff penalties against anybody found guilty of match-fixing. In my opinion match-fixing warrants a life ban. It strikes at the very spirit of the game. I also think there is a duty on every one of us to pass on any information, however small and insignificant it might seem, to the authorities. In Australia, we now have a special investigator to look into allegations. The ICC, through the Anti-Corruption Unit, also seem to be making an effort to get to the bottom of the matter. Spectators, players, officials and everyone else want to leave the ground knowing that you outplayed the opposition. Here's to the great game of cricket!

7

TAKING THE WINDIES' CROWN

B Y THE END of 1994–95 we thought we were the best side in the world. Others were not so sure, and we needed to win in the Caribbean to convince those doubters. To be fair, we hadn't won in West Indies, Pakistan or India for a long time. The West Indies, indisputably the dominant force throughout the 1980s and early 90s, had begun to lose the veneer of invincibility, while we continued to take strides forward under Mark Taylor. Even though the West Indies were unbeaten in fifteen years and twenty-nine series, and had not lost at home since going down to Ian Chappell's Australians in 1972–73, we believed we could repeat what Chappell's side had achieved.

At their height there was not a single weak link in the West Indies side except, I suppose, the absence of a quality spinner, but with the pace attack they had they probably didn't need one. By the mid-90s, although still relying heavily on pace, they did not possess a complete quartet to strike fear into the opposition. In the absence of Gordon Greenidge and Desmond Haynes they had yet to settle on an opening partnership remotely comparable, while their batting overall did not have the depth of old. They seemed to be on a slow downward curve, while ours was continuing to slope upwards. It was purely a question of whether the two lines had yet crossed.

Touring teams had tended to go to the Caribbean preoccupied with the thought of facing four quick bowlers. The fear factor crept in, and the West Indies had become adept at being able to smell that fear. Once they thought they had that edge they were merciless. But our game plan was to fight fire with fire, to give them a taste of the medicine they had been dishing out to the rest of the world for so long. We had specific ideas about each of their batsmen and a collective strategy to intimidate numbers eight to eleven. If their bowlers were going to pepper our lower order, then they would get it back. If they didn't, then they would get it anyway. We were determined to be the side calling the shots, and in the weeks before the series began our practice sessions became more and more intense as the bowlers worked on short-pitched bowling and the batsmen grew used to ducking or swaying out of the way.

Those preparations soon realised rich dividends. After losing the one-day series heavily, we hit our straps from the opening overs of the First Test in Barbados. Brendon Julian bowled like an absolute dream before lunch as West Indies lost three quick wickets before Brian Lara and Carl Hooper started to counter-attack. By the first break the score was 3 for 116, which says everything for the frenetic pace. But once Julian struck again to remove Lara the West Indies never recovered. Some people tried to make an issue of that wicket. Steve Waugh juggled with the ball at backward point before taking the catch low down. The facts are that Lara asked Stephen whether it had carried and Stephen, who is an honest bloke and well aware of the traditions and the spirit of the game, confirmed that it was a good clean catch. Lara didn't seem to have a problem with that. Television replays were inconclusive, but it didn't matter, everyone was happy that Tugga caught it.

The fact that we managed to secure a lead of 151 – worth

almost double on a difficult pitch – owed a lot to a characteristically tough innings from Ian Healy, well supported by Julian, playing the best cricket of his life. It's a real shame BJ hasn't played a lot more international cricket because he could be a great player. We made early inroads into their top order again and managed to take wickets steadily through the rest of the innings before Taylor and Michael Slater hit the winning runs. For the first time in thirty years the West Indies had lost inside three days and it was a wonderful 'get well soon' present to our coach, Bobby Simpson, who had gone to hospital with thrombosis midway through the match. After suffering some early punishment I recovered to take 5 wickets on a bouncy pitch, while Glenn McGrath set the tone for the rest of the series with 8, including a brilliant off-cutter which beat Lara all ends up. Just as important was the way he declared our intentions by roughing up their tail.

The Second Test at Antigua in the second week of April could have been a real thriller but for some lousy weather. We were 229 ahead with 3 second-innings wickets remaining going into the final day and, despite evidence that Lara was back to his best, we would have backed ourselves to bowl them out in four and a half or five hours. Unfortunately, we couldn't get on until lunch and the game ended in a timid draw.

Timid is the last adjective anybody could use to describe events in Trinidad little more than a week later. Ominously, the pitch was green, wet and bouncy with an inch-high covering of grass – all in all the worst I have seen for a Test match. It made batting a hazardous business. This was the infamous game when Richie Richardson had to physically restrain Ambrose as he went eyeball to eyeball with Steve Waugh. I still don't know what upset Ambrose – pure frustration, perhaps. When he had a point to prove he really was lethal. For Stephen to withstand what followed was courageous in the extreme, but he was determined not to give any quarter. I was very surprised that there were no ramifications from such an ugly incident and that Curtly escaped any sort of punishment from the ICC. But I think it showed, more than anything else in the series, that we were really getting to the West Indies.

I soon realised he meant business as he chipped my right thumb with a particularly vicious delivery. The game lasted only 164 overs in total and finished well inside three days. No batsman except for Stephen passed 50. It became a lottery and I was surprised to be called upon to bowl as many as 16 overs because of the way conditions suited the pace men.

With my thumb swollen to almost twice its usual size, I managed to play in the decider at Jamaica. I wouldn't have made it but for Errol Alcott, our physio. He has a wonderful and sometimes magical pair of hands. There was no way I intended to miss out with such a wonderful series level at one all unless I couldn't physically bowl. I felt the occasional twinge of pain, and I can't say I particularly enjoyed batting, but the most important thing was that I could rest the ball on my thumb well enough to be able to bowl. More than that, I managed to have Lara caught by Healy diving forward in front of the wicket when an edge ballooned up via pad in the first innings. Then, in the second, I bagged four more including last man Kenny Benjamin with a big leg-break that he edged to Taylor at slip to clinch the series. By then the ball was kicking off a horribly cracked pitch. Healy had sent for a helmet after a leg-break somehow reared so sharply that it bounced over his head – immediately after one had gone through his legs. It meant a lot that I had managed to come through (with the help of pain-killers) to play a part in an outstanding and comprehensive success by an innings and 53 runs.

Steve Waugh's innings in Jamaica was one of his best for Australia, if not the best in his Test career. There are plenty to choose from. Watching from the dressing room as he and his brother Mark withstood everything the West Indies could hurl at them, we could see how they were draining all of the energy from the bowlers. It was fantastic to see the Waugh brothers batting like that. That game was the turning point in recent Australian cricket history. From those last three days at Sabina Park, Australia rather than the West Indies have been the team everybody else has most wanted to beat.

We were 3 for 73, chasing 265 on first-innings, when Stephen joined his brother and they proceeded to add 231 for the fourth wicket. What made Stephen's innings all the more remarkable was that he had been disturbed in his sleep by a thief during this game. His concentration never wavered and he batted for almost ten hours in all. Somebody estimated that he faced around 150 short-pitched balls in total. When Paul Reiffel sent back three batsmen, including Lara, for a duck before close on the third day we knew we were on our way, as long as we maintained our concentration for one final push in the field. Having come so far there was no way we would squander the opportunity to win the Frank Worrell Trophy.

People in the Caribbean love their cricket and have a keen understanding of the game. They had grown used to their own side winning all the time, so to find themselves not only in the process of being beaten, but in a way more typical of the manner they had flattened sides in the past, almost became too much. As Mark, playing commandingly at times, and Stephen pushed them closer and closer to defeat the place fell silent. What a contrast to the atmosphere in Antigua three weeks earlier when Chickie's disco blared out around the ground. It was nice afterwards that Allan Border and Dean Jones, two guys who had suffered at the hands of the West Indies quicks down the years, were able to join us for the celebrations that followed. We had set up chances to beat them in 1992–93, only to lose two-one after a magnificent spell of 7 wickets for one run from Ambrose in Perth.

When the series was over Richie Richardson described us as the worst Australian side he had ever faced. That didn't say very much for his own team. I thought his words showed a complete lack of sportsmanship when, in reality, we had won fair and square. I was brought up to play competitively but to be gracious in defeat and on the occasions when we lose I make a point of shaking hands and saying, 'Well done' to the opposition, however disappointed and even angry I feel inside. If Richardson genuinely thought we were such a bad side then he was entitled to that opinion. But people will be able to make up their own minds. I should point out that we suffered the disadvantage of losing all four tosses and saw possibly our two best fast bowlers at the time, Craig McDermott and Damien Fleming, forced to return home before the start of the series because of injury.

Looking back, this was the series when Glenn McGrath really began to establish himself as a top-class bowler. Seizing the opportunity presented by the absence of McDermott and Fleming, his accuracy and aggression strangled the West Indies and he began a personal battle with Lara that has continued since. As for Steve Waugh, the man of the series, he was probably already recognised as a great rather than just a very good batsman during the 1993 Ashes tour, but his performances in the Caribbean left no doubt. This trip was the making of him as an all-round competitor. At our post-match party in the hotel in Jamaica he was still wearing his whites and spikes and his baggy green cap that means so much to him until late in the night.

At the turn of the decade officials in Australia sensed that leg-spin would be the way to eventually topple the West Indies. As events transpired, we beat them in a pace-dominated series.

What a way to start! The look on Mike Gatting's face says it all as I introduce myself to England at Old Trafford in 1993.

My first injury.

At my worktable.

Together with Jason.

Mum and Dad's wedding.

Mum and Dad in the sixties.

Above The budding Aussie Rules player at Mentone Grammar School.

Left My childhood hero Dermott Brereton – any physical resemblance is purely coincidental.

East Sandringham Boys Club – I'm furthest right, second row from the back. My dad, the manager, is on the far left at the back and my brother far left at the front.

ESBC
U-11
1980

The late, great Trevor Barker of St Kilda, an inspirational player and man.

Professional for Accrington CC in Lancashire in 1991.

The successful Mentone team – I'm third from left on the front row.

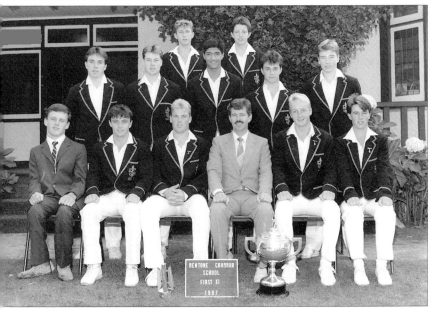

Above Bang goes that maiden hundred again – losing my way against India.

Left A champagne moment – with broadcaster Brian Johnston at Lord's in 1993.

Below Bowling on my Test debut against India in 1992 – fortunately my career went uphill from there

Above Robin Smith caught Taylor bowled Warne the First Test at Old Trafford, 1993.

Right Graham Gooch played my bowling better an any of his English colleagues.

Below Merv Hughes in the thick of proceedings after was named man of the match at Old Trafford, 1993.

Our three century-makers against England at Lord's in 1993 – Mark Taylor, David Boon and Michael Slater.

Allan Border (200 not out) and Steve Waugh (157 not out) after their unbroken 332 partnership at Headingley, Fourth Test 1993.

That could never have happened five years earlier. My role was to chip in with important wickets now and then rather than be the main strike bowler. When I was called upon for long spells I was happy with my consistency, particularly in the second innings.

I think the fundamental assessment of the West Indies was accurate, because they do have a weakness against leg-spin. Basically, apart from Lara, they only know how to block it or smash it. There is no in between, and their attacking shots in this series were not always very well controlled. Lara played me as well as anybody in that side, but then he was comfortably their best batsman. Our plan to restrict his scoring shots by maintaining a tight line and length applied to all of their batsmen. Grounds in the Caribbean are small and the outfields are fast. Anything that beats the infield usually races to the boundary so we needed to keep down the 4-balls. Like most plans that come to fruition, it was hardly rocket science. In fact I wouldn't put our success down to anything more complicated than having a simple strategy and executing it. That is the trick. You can have the best plans in the world but if you can't execute them, there's no point. We were also extremely well led by Mark Taylor, who kept the side together and focused when we struggled during the one-day series. It was just a thoroughly pleasant trip to be involved with, quite apart from the ground-breaking result.

After a West Indies tour we generally go to Bermuda for a few days, when the wives and girlfriends fly over from Australia to join us. We play exhibition matches and do some coaching with the local people, but basically it is a time to relax and unwind. Then, right at the end, the ACB were happy to pay for a party in appreciation of our victory. It turned out to be the night of all nights. We ate caviar and drank champagne until two or three in the morning, even though the taxis had been booked for approximately 10.30 and sat there outside with the meters running. Jack Edwards, the tour manager, who also happened to be the president of my club side, St Kilda, had clearly underestimated our ability to celebrate. The bill ran to almost $13,000 (US) and poor Jack was left with his ears ringing when he conveyed that news to the ACB back home. I think he's still in trouble now.

Brendon Julian was in a worse state than any of us. The next morning we were due to fly to New York for a holiday with our girlfriends, but when he couldn't get out of bed apparently Jackie had left him in the hotel and said she would meet him on the plane. The other three of us grabbed a taxi for the airport – with Brendon spending the journey hanging his head out of the window and throwing up. He probably didn't think so for a few unpleasant hours, but a king-size hangover was a small price to pay after such a memorable success. The West Indies tours are good fun. Acra beach in Barbados is really beautiful so, hopefully, I'll see it again. We had a great bunch of guys who gelled together. What a tour!

8

THE SRI LANKAN BOGY

MOTIVATION is something I never lack at any time, but especially not against a team such as Pakistan and when they came to Australia in 1995–96 I was fully pumped up. Only a year had passed since Salim Malik attempted to bribe Tim May and myself to bowl wide of off stump in a Test match. Worse still, just a couple of weeks or so before the series was due to begin the judge in Pakistan leading the first investigation had decided that Malik was not guilty, effectively branding us liars. So I desperately wanted to beat Pakistan to set the record straight and show there was some justice in the game.

To begin with I felt a little surprised that Malik was actually named in the party. He had lost the captaincy - though not, it was said, because of the match-fixing business – and been dropped recently for a series in Sri Lanka. I wondered if he would look for a reason to opt out of Australia, knowing the reception he would get from the crowds. He must have known he would be under pressure from the moment he arrived a week after the rest of the squad. While I held no animosity towards the other players, we wanted to nail Pakistan. With all of the interest surrounding our imminent confrontation and the verdict of Judge Ebrahim, I felt under the microscope and, despite being advised to say nothing about the matter for legal reasons, I felt I had to defend myself in public. I repeated what I told officials at the time, which just happened to be the truth. I just wanted the cricket to start.

We had decided at a team meeting before the First Test in Brisbane in the second week of November to give Malik the silent treatment while he was batting, although I was determined to give him the biggest send off imaginable if I took his wicket. I had to wait until the second innings for that opportunity to arise. When we batted he split the webbing in his hand taking a catch at midwicket to dismiss Mark Taylor. Our total of 463 still looked very strong and I was really pumped up to bowl, even though I couldn't be sure whether Malik would appear.

Unlike the Indians, I don't think the Pakistanis play leg spin particularly well. I can't imagine why that is the case because they have the advantage of playing against slow bowling a lot at home. For that reason I hadn't been bothered when a few of them suggested before the game that my variations wouldn't cause problems and that I didn't spin the ball as heavily as before. In fact, I had worked with Terry Jenner and Bobby Simpson earlier in the season because my action was getting a little high leading up to the Tests and I felt I was bowling really well for Victoria.

In spite of their confident words the Pakistanis showed little clue once I started to hit my straps. They either scratched around, using their pads nervously or, like Inzamam-ul-Haq, went for the big hit that didn't come off. When I had Mohammad Akram caught by Greg Blewett I had taken 6 for 10 from 56 balls, with figures of 7 for 23 overall. Not bad for a bloke supposedly in decline, and the only disappointment as we gathered in the middle was that Malik showed no sign of walking out to become what I hoped would be victim number eight.

I had to wait until Pakistan were six down in their second innings before he finally declared himself fit to bat. The crowd gave him a frosty reception – I was really happy with the way the Australian public supported me during a difficult time – and I told Taylor that I was going to give him three or four bouncers in a row. Even at my pace I thought I might be able to cause him some damage if I took him by surprise and managed to hit him. The captain, with his level head, asked what that would prove. He told me to concentrate just on getting him out. That is never bad advice, and after the batsman poked at three balls I sent one down a little slower, a leg-break pitching on leg stump, and as he tried to hit it through midwicket, he found a leading edge to give Craig McDermott a catch at mid off. The crowd went beserk, Malik could not get away quickly enough and we soon rattled through the tail. The pitch had good bounce and I finished with match figures of 11 for 77, the second best of my Test career and the best by an Australian bowler against Pakistan. I was especially pleased that I managed to keep my discipline. It took a lot of will-power but the satisfaction came from my figures and, most importantly, victory by an innings and 126 runs.

Cricket, however, can be as unpredictable as life itself and I soon came back down to earth when we moved to Hobart. Waqar Younis hit me on the big toe of my left foot with one of his familiar inswinging yorkers during what proved to be the penultimate over of our innings. I was really enjoying myself with the bat and had hit Mushtaq Ahmed for three sixes. A few balls later came the departure of Glenn McGrath and as soon as I removed my boot the toe started to swell. It was like watching somebody pump up a balloon and x-rays confirmed the worst fears of Errol Alcott, our physio. Yes, it was broken. I could only watch from the dressing room as we went two love up to seal the series.

How I managed to play in the Third Test in Sydney I'm not sure. It was certainly a case of mind over matter. The left foot is the one that I plant at the crease in my delivery and I had to cut a huge hole at the top of the boot to minimise the pain. The game was interesting and, not for the first time, I think our standards probably slipped because we had already won overall. Malik had not played in Hobart and when he got off the mark here he raised his bat, presumably in an attempt to win some sympathy from the crowd. It would take more than that to redeem his character and the Sydney folk responded with a series of boos.

Although I didn't manage to claim his wicket in either innings, I still took 8 in the game for a record of 19 at 10.42 in the series. Mushtaq bowled well in Sydney and if anybody was going to take Australian wickets I was pleased that he happened to be a leg-spinner. He, too, had a really good series, bouncing in like Abdul Qadir and playing with a smile on his face. He took 18 wickets and genuinely turned the ball, as well as finding enough bounce to trouble some of our batsmen.

The wicket I remember most in Sydney was that of Basit Ali, who arrived in Australia with a big reputation but had become a pain in the neck through the series. He always seemed to be holding us up, waiting until we were at the end of our mark before playing with his equipment or pulling away to check the field. We like to get through our overs in the right time because we don't enjoy overtime any more than the crowd. The odd sarcastic comment like, 'When you're ready, mate' didn't seem to have much effect. One ball remained at the end of the third day so I decided to call up Ian Healy for a chat in mid-pitch with the idea that we should give Basit a taste of his own medicine. That single ball took at least three minutes to bowl. Basit must have thought we had suddenly spotted something in his batting and were hatching a master plan. In fact, the conversation was all about where we should go to eat in the evening – Mexican or Italian. Finally, I asked Heals what I should bowl – a top-spinner, leg-break, flipper or wrong-un from over or around the wicket.

'Oh, just do something special, mate,' he said. 'Bowl him around his legs or something.'

So I sent down a big leg-break which Basit tried to pad away, only for it to turn sharply and bowl him through his legs. I'm convinced he had worked himself into a state and lost his concentration. Heals and I could barely stop ourselves laughing.

Even though the series ended with defeat, I felt happy with proceedings overall. I had started the season in a really good form and taken revenge over Malik where it mattered. We didn't speak to each other once throughout Pakistan's stay. There was no way I intended to shake his hand or try to make his life any easier. I'm not even sure I could have held my temper if he had tried to approach me. He brought the game into major disrepute. Apparently, he spent most of his time away form the ground moping around in his hotel room. Which brings me on to another bloke . . .

Because of some of the things I have said down the years people assume I just don't like Sri Lanka. That could not be further from the truth. I love the place itself. Every time I have been there the people have gone out of their way to be friendly and hospitable. Australian teams couldn't have asked for more. The 1992 tour was my first for Australia. I will always remember it fondly for the Test at the Sinhalese Sports Club ground in Colombo. It ranks as probably my favourite Test for Australia. There are no problems with Sri Lanka, or with the vast majority of Sri Lankan people. My differences are with Arjuna Ranatunga.

Without any question he is the most difficult opponent I

have come across. I don't mean that he was the best batsman. What I disliked was that he seemed to act in ways which were contrary to the spirit of the game, at times pushing the rules to the limits and making life difficult for the umpires. It often appeared that if there was a ruse Ranatunga could play to try and get under our skin he would do so.

I think their visit to Australia in 1995–96, following the Pakistan series, was the most discordant I have known. They were rubbed up the wrong way at one of the airports even before the First Test in Perth by the enthusiasm of some of the sniffer dogs, which they took as an insult. On the eve of the game there were problems with the size of the logos on their shirts. Then, when play began, there were soon questions about what had happened to the ball. It seems that Khizar Hayat and Peter Parker, the umpires, felt that something was wrong but decided not to replace it. Graham Dowling, the match referee, still reprimanded the side. From the dressing room it is often impossible to say what is happening in a situation like that. All I remember is Michael Slater hitting a magnificent double-century and the likes of Mark Waugh, Mark Taylor and Ricky Ponting (on his debut) piling up the runs – and Stuart Law scoring 54 not out in what proved to be his one and only Test innings. From that solid foundation we proceeded to win by an innings and I managed to claim my two hundredth Test wicket when Chaminda Vaas became a victim of the Warne/Healy combination.

If matters were starting to become fractious, then the series exploded at the traditional Boxing Day Test in Melbourne when Darrell Hair called Muttiah Muralitharan for throwing. Initially, he stood several yards behind the crease to take a close look before shouting 'no ball' on seven occasions. Ranatunga switched his bowler to the other end where Steve Dunne did not seem to have a problem, but once Hair said he was also prepared to call Muralitharan from square leg the bowler was effectively out of the contest. Again, I watched from the dressing room and, once I worked out what was going on, I felt sorry for the bowler. To have your action questioned in front of so many people like that amounts to a public humiliation. There are ways and means of doing something and I am not sure this was the best solution to a difficult problem. But Hair was right. If an umpire thinks that a bowler has a suspect action then it is his duty to call him.

Muralitharan's action is unique. It is different and unorthodox. When Allan Border faced him for the first time in Sri Lanka he played and missed at five out of six balls because he thought he was facing a leg-spinner rather than an off-break bowler. He had done his homework, of course, but out in the middle instinct tends to take over and Murali's action is not that of your average finger-spinner. The cricket grapevine was soon buzzing and there were rumours that both Hair and Dunne had expressed their suspicions to the ICC during a tournament in Sharjah shortly before the tour. Because Dunne did not have the same view as Hair in the middle of the MCG, it could have looked as though the bowler was being picked on by an Australian. Hair, as people in cricket know, is his own man and unlikely to have his opinion swayed by other people. Ranatunga's theory that Muralitharan was being no-balled as a conspiracy to halt Sri Lanka in their tracks as they were becoming a world-class side is too ridiculous to entertain. It seemed an insult to the umpires and, with defeats by an innings and 10 wickets in the first two Tests, he clearly had an exaggerated opinion of his side. He was always very quick to try and gain sympathy by portraying Sri Lanka as the new kids on the block when it appeared that they had become as adept as any side at gamesmanship.

Now that the ICC has officially cleared Muralitharan's action we all know where we stand. There are bound to be whisperings, simply because he looks so unusual, but there is a massive difference between looking odd and actually throwing. My concern is for young bowlers coming through in Sri Lanka and the rest of the world who might try to imitate his delivery. I expect that is happening already, because kids always try to copy their heroes, and those heroes are usually the successful players of the day. The ICC approved Muralitharan after much discussion because they were convinced that a deformity in his elbow meant that, although his arm is bent, it does not straighten. I ought to stress that I'm not saying Muralitharan throws – simply that coaches in Sri Lanka have a big responsibility to ensure their international players of tomorrow are completely above suspicion. What happens if a young Sri Lankan bowler copies Muralitharan and then when he is eighteen or nineteen tours with the Sri Lanka under-19 team and is called for throwing? His cricket career is over. We just have to be careful. I admire Muralitharan for showing as much strength as he has and for keeping smiling. I think he has handled the situation really well.

I do feel strongly that the decision of the umpires should be final, however wrong a player might believe it to be at the time. Muralitharan was called again in a one-day game in Adelaide against England by Ross Emerson in 1998–99. As the third team in the triangular competition, we had a big interest in the events. It also happened that I was captaining Australia while Steve Waugh was injured and I felt glad the episode had not arisen when we were the opponents. Ranatunga did not only complain to Emerson, he told him where he should stand when Muralitharan was bowling. He marked the ground and said, 'Stand there.' I thought that was disgraceful, but obviously the ICC didn't think so. It came as a major shock when he was not even fined for bringing the game into disrepute after his lawyers threatened the ICC with legal action. To think that just a few months later I was fined a percentage of my match fee purely for saying that Sri Lanka would be better off without him is unbelievable.

The anxieties from the Test series carried over into the World Series, coming to a head in the second final in Sydney. We batted first and scored 5 for 273 before thunderstorms hit the city. A reduced target left Sri Lanka needing 168 from 25 overs, a big ask and one that called for quick running between the wickets, as well as big hits. Ranatunga, needless to say, was keener on the hits than the running. He seemed to be calling for a drink or a new bat or glove at the end of every over to give himself breathing space. We were waiting for him to ask for a runner. Lo and behold, the inevitable request finally came, but to his great credit Steve Randell had the guts to turn it down. We objected, as we always did. When Ranatunga reinforced his point by suddenly beginning to limp, Randell could hardly refuse again. The runner just happened to be Sanath Jayasuriya, possibly the quickest man in the team. I remember on this particular occasion Ian Healy had a go at Ranatunga by making a critical reference to his fitness.

Tempers started to become frayed. Jayasuriya collided with Glenn McGrath and when I managed to get rid of Ranatunga for 41 I allowed myself a little extra celebration. Unfortunately that was not the end of his poor sportsmanship. Victory ensured we won the competition overall, but at the presentation ceremony afterwards he refused to shake hands with Mark Taylor, our captain. Taylor turned round to Healy and me who were right behind and said, 'Don't bother.' I think the rest of his side were more embarrassed than we were and I particularly felt for Dav Whatmore, their coach, who had played Test cricket for Australia and is a genuinely good, fair man. He was probably ordered not to as well. When some of the others tried to walk over to shake hands Ranatunga stepped in front of them and held out his arm. It was an ugly situation and none of us were really sure how to react.

Sri Lanka clearly realised that they needed to repair some bridges and the final Test was played in a far more civilised manner. It helped that Ranatunga pulled out because of injury and Aravinda de Silva took over the captaincy. Nevertheless, Ranatunga was his usual provocative self at a final press conference when he suggested his side had been hard done by in Australia. I guess the main reason the Sri Lankans stuck with Ranatunga was because he always backed his players. He comes from a powerful family in cricket circles on the island and it was only after the 1999 World Cup, when the side failed to reach the second stage, that his position as captain was seriously threatened.

Unfortunately, as the summer progressed, there had already been far more sinister warnings from others and a number of players, myself included, received death threats. In my case it took the form of a hand-written, personally delivered note in the letterbox of my parents' home. The thrust was quite clear – if I stepped on Sri Lankan soil I was a dead man. If it was a hoax then somebody out there has a pretty sick sense of humour. My family were not laughing.

Craig McDermott had a tip-off that a bomb had been placed in his house and Bobby Simpson, the coach, had also been threatened. You don't want to be scared off every time something like this happens, but you have to look at all the evidence, weigh it up and keep in touch with the Australian embassy. Obviously none of us was fully aware of the state of the civil war in Sri Lanka, but we knew vaguely about on-going activity involving the Tamils. We also knew that passions run high there. Then, just a few days before we were due to arrive in Colombo and a fortnight before the start of the competition, a bomb went off near the hotel we had booked, causing mass fatalities.

During the Australian season, when a few of us started to receive threats, we sat down with ACB members to clear the air. We just weren't sure what might happen. In a nutshell, would we be safe or not? We wanted to know and then weigh up the options. There was no way we wanted to pull out of any game in the World Cup but there was a feeling of apprehension. Denis Rogers and Graham Halbish, the chairman and chief executive of the ACB, said they had been told by authorities in Sri Lanka that we would be upgraded to the equivalent status of a head of state. We would have our own floor at the hotel which would be constantly patrolled by armed guards. So would those immediately above and below. Our phone calls would be screened and we would be supervised outside our rooms at all times. This told us that the Sri Lankans themselves were taking the threats seriously. By not going we knew we would concede two points. We did not think of this as a cricket matter to be discussed in isolation from the rest of the world. Interestingly, the Foreign Office were advising Australian people to stay away from Sri Lanka at the time.

Reports that a few of us were prepared independently to boycott this leg of the competition were wide of the mark. It had to be a situation where we all stuck together – we either went as a group or not at all. I thought it was a no-win situation for us and in the end the ACB, quite rightly, themselves decided that to go to Colombo simply presented too much of a risk. I was relieved at the time and am still convinced that it was the right decision. Had we been asked to play in Sri Lanka I don't see how we could have given the game our full attention. The West Indies also decided to forfeit the points and, inevitably, we took a fair amount of criticism in India and Pakistan as well as Sri Lanka. As usual, those who turned up simply wanted to see good cricket. I wonder how many of those who lambasted us for opting out of Colombo have ever had their lives threatened.

Australia had won the World Cup in 1987 and that team has a special place in our cricket history. Despite beginning two points behind one of the hosts, I really thought we were good enough in 1996, having come off a great summer in terms of results, to emulate Allan Border's team. We were among the favourites, and rightly so, but in the end I don't think anybody legislated for the thrilling way in which Sri Lanka themselves would pinch-hit their way towards the record books.

In Calcutta before the competition started we were confined to the hotel, except for practice sessions, because of security. Fortunately we had brought a stack of videos from Australia to help pass the time. When we moved to Bombay I soon went down with a stomach bug and missed a practice match ahead of our first game against Kenya. I remember vomiting in the toilet with Jim Wilson the Channel 7 reporter doing the same in the next cubicle. We were all pleased when we finally arrived at the ground on 23rd February to take on Kenya, who were to enjoy a great win later in the competition against West Indies.

Despite losing Taylor and Ponting early, a classy 130 by Mark Waugh helped us past 300 and towards a comfortable win. The only disappointment arrived when we heard confirmation that Craig McDermott had torn a calf muscle and would miss the rest of the event. We needed to show all our character to beat India in our next tie, in Bombay, which just happens to be the home city of Sachin Tendulkar. Much had been made of my personal contest with Tendulkar before the game. This always seems to be the case when we play India, but here he batted magnificently in the opening overs after we had scored

258, even overshadowing another hundred from Mark Waugh. I came into the attack inside the first 15 overs to try to tempt him into an error and the ploy almost worked when he skied a ball high to mid off, just wide and high of Stuart Law. But at least that gave him a sense of his own mortality and he wasn't quite so fluent afterwards. Frustrated, he eventually danced down the wicket to Mark Waugh who had cleverly slipped one wide for Healy to complete a stumping. My figures were 1 for 27.

From Bombay we travelled to Nagpur where we met some of the Zimbabweans, our next opponents, in the hotel for a chat a couple of days before the game. They had recently played Sri Lanka and told us they had not been allowed into Colombo until sixteen hours before the game. The travel arrangements seemed over-complicated throughout the competition with the organisers determined that as many towns and cities as possible would get a taste of the action, no matter how inefficient the airline service. I lost count of the number of hours we spent in various departure lounges twiddling our thumbs as one delay followed another.

We beat Zimbabwe comfortably on a wicket I would love to have packed and carried around for the rest of my cricket career. It was dry, crumbling and the pre-match assessment that it would turn square proved pretty close the mark. Even though Zimbabwe batted first there was sufficient assistance and I managed to take 4 wickets, including that of Andy Flower. Mark Waugh maintained his immaculate form to see us home with 14 overs to spare. Having begun with points to retrieve after conceding the Sri Lanka match we were now well on course for a place in the quarter-finals.

Maybe our defeat against West Indies in Jaipur was a lesson that we had started to drift along instead of making things happen. Quite clearly our opponents wanted to make a point after losing to Kenya, a result which would have brought unimaginable criticism back in the Caribbean. Curtly Ambrose and Courtney Walsh were certainly firing with the new ball and, in spite of an excellent 102 by Ricky Ponting, our total of 6 for 229 always appeared to be a few runs short. By this stage we realised it would be a high-scoring tournament because the openers could effectively take free hits in the first 15 overs. The hard ball came straight on to the bat and the quick outfields hastened the ball on its way to the boundary. At least the abrasive wickets and stubbly outfields had begun to roughen the ball by the time spin usually joined the attack.

Unfortunately, I was encountering problems with my spinning finger. Despite some cortisone injections before the tournament, the veins were starting to stick out through the knuckle and by the quarter-final against New Zealand in Madras I had a lot of pain. At our team meeting before the game we did not really speak much about Chris Harris, except to note that his recent highest score against us was around 15, before moving on to the next player. We did not see him as a player who could cause any trouble. How wrong we were.

Harris proceeded to play the innings of his life and added 168 for the fourth wicket with Lee Germon, the captain, who was another to feature little in our preparations. Germon, a wicket-keeper-batsman, had been brought in as captain without, strangely, an international appearance to his name in an attempt to restore discipline to the ranks and, like his partner, he must have realised early on that this was to be his day. Fortunately I tempted Harris to miscue attempting another big hit and Reiffel held a fantastic catch on the boundary. Given the carnage that had gone before, to contain them to less than 6 an over from the last 10 represented a comeback.

Nevertheless, the target of 287 bore a formidable look and at the fall of the second wicket I was promoted as a pinch-hitter to try to get the run rate back on track. There was nothing to lose because if I stayed in runs would come and if I failed we would not have fallen much further behind. When you are chasing a big score it is important to have recognised batsmen at the crease in the closing stages and the idea of me having a heave also meant the likes of Steve Waugh and Michael Bevan would stage an onslaught later. The plan worked pretty well – I struck 24 from 15 balls and put on 43 in just over 4 overs with Mark Waugh who, yet again, was batting like a dream. He proceeded to reach his third century of the competition, despite suffering cramp in both calves almost from the start of his innings, before his older brother and Stuart Law saw us home in clinical fashion with 2 overs to spare. We couldn't have gone about the run chase more professionally, our momentum was gathering nicely.

The following day I was on Channel Nine duty and they asked me about the batting. Obviously I was happy but sitting next to the pool was the captain of New Zealand, Germon, who was not so pleased and walked off. The ground at Mohali (Chandigarh),where we were playing the West Indies in the semi-final, was extremely picturesque. Unlike some of the media – who had to commute on a six-hour trip from Delhi on the day of the game – at least we were allocated a hotel. My abiding memory is of Taylor rushing round complaining that a rat had scurried across the floor of his room. I think it was quite an unnerving time for Tubby because on the morning of the game our coach driver seemed to hit 100 miles per hour as our ashen-faced captain begged him to slow down. On the sub-continent a clear road is a luxury and drivers tend to make good progress while they can. It is a case of buckling up, closing your eyes and listening to the headphones.

It was interesting to note that none of the four semi-finalists – India, Sri Lanka, West Indies and ourselves – had reached the last four in the previous competition four years earlier. What that says, I'm not sure, but we were extremely confident of pulling off two more wins to lift the Cup. In the other semi-final India lost to Sri Lanka by default in Calcutta when the home crowd rioted with their side well in arrears. If the reception that greeted Pakistan's defeat to India in the quarter-finals had been a little on the harsh side then the pounding subsequently taken in the press by Mohammad Azharuddin was many times worse. The fires in the stand were a bit much, but that is how fanatical they are. For our part we were delighted at the possibility of meeting Sri Lanka again. We had beaten them comfortably back home only a couple of months earlier. Besides which, Ranatunga was always guaranteed to pump us up.

For 90 per cent of the semi-final we didn't seem to have a chance of securing that date in Lahore. Mark Waugh's incredible run ended when Curtly Ambrose struck with the second ball of the match and Taylor soon followed. At 4 for 15 in the tenth over we wondered whether the floodlights would need to come into play. When we are in trouble, though, somebody always puts his hand up and steps to the plate. This time Michael Bevan, playing with typical concentration and good sense, paired up with Stuart Law in a stand of 138 and with a useful 31 from Ian Healy we grafted our way to 8 for 207. At least it gave us a chance.

We needed to take wickets to put them under pressure, knowing that the total was not large enough to be able to contain the likes of Brian Lara and Richie Richardson. The early breakthrough did not materialise until I joined the attack and held a return chance from Courtney Browne with my first ball. However, Shivnarine Chanderpaul and Brian Lara took the score to 93 before Steve Waugh bowled Lara with a jaffa. Then Chanderpaul and Richardson added a further 72 to leave

West Indies on 2 for 165, just 43 short, with 45 balls remaining and 8 wickets in hand. The game was getting away from us, but in a situation like that one wicket can make a tremendous difference. New batsmen do not have time to adjust to the light or play themselves in and by keeping the established part-ner away from the strike panic can quickly set in. That is what must have happened once Chanderpaul fell trying to hit Glenn McGrath over the top.

Roger Harper, promoted to try to clout his side away from danger, became another victim of McGrath 8 runs later and when I joined the attack I had Otis Gibson caught behind almost immediately. Jimmy Adams showed no sense of timing and, suddenly, West Indies had only 4 wickets in hand. Nothing epitomised the transformation more than the ugly swing that brought Keith Arthurton his downfall to complete a dreadful run of scores in the competition – 1, 0, 0, 1 and 0. It had become a question of who would hold their nerve – Damien Fleming, bowling superbly at the other end, and myself, or the West Indies lower order, who desperately needed to give Richardson the strike. I added the wicket of Ian Bishop in my last over and with six balls left they needed 10 more with 2 wickets in hand and, crucially it seemed, Richardson facing. The other issue was the lights. They were low and it was hard for the new batsman to adjust. Bobby Simpson had always told us that when the lights are low to pull our hats down so the glare stays out of our eyes. This was a situation when we definitely needed to heed his advice.

When their captain swung the first ball to the boundary the odds moved in their favour. Yet even such an experienced guy as Richardson had made what proved to be a crucial mis-judgment. An edge against Fleming went through to the keeper and Healy's direct hit was enough to run out Curtly Ambrose on a television replay. Instead of going for a single to

give Richardson the strike, Courtney Walsh chose to try and
finish the match with one stroke, only for Fleming to beat his
wild slog and hit the stumps. We had won – improbably – by
5 runs and reacted by just screaming and shouting in delight.
The players who were in the squad but didn't play were on
the ground as quickly as we turned around. It was a great
feeling.

I still can't pinpoint one dominating reason why we lost the
final at Lahore. Sri Lanka had the advantage of an extra day
to prepare, but there was a certain flatness about us from the
start. Because we had played them so often in recent months
we had very little to say at our team meeting the night before
the match and an official dinner in the gardens next to the
hotel turned out to be a hopelessly-organised and long-winded
affair. Word reached us the following morning that the game
would be delayed because of a saturated outfield and when the
call came that we should go to the ground as planned after all,
because of a remarkable change in the weather, it took us
by surprise. Then the lights weren't working properly. It was
chaos.

Having said that, we were still in a superb position to post
a match-winning score as Taylor and Ponting took us to 1 for
137 by the twenty-seventh over. We should have been looking
to double that. With wickets in hand we generally look to
double our score from the 30-over stage and generally we get
very close. Instead, wickets started to fall and we never recovered that momentum. To their own dismay our second-wicket
pair both fell to the occasional spin of Aravinda de Silva in
quick succession to leave new batsmen coming in against desperately slow bowling to try to work the soft ball around. The
one consolation was that our total of 7 for 241 was comfortably
better than the one we managed to defend against the West
Indies and our hopes rose when Sanath Jayasuriya, sub-

sequently named player of the tournament, and Romesh Kaluwitharana fell in the opening 6 overs.

The problem facing the bowlers by this stage was the heavy dew that made gripping the ball a nightmare, particularly for a spin bowler like myself who likes to give it a good rip. What made this especially disappointing was the way the pitch had started to break up. The old cliché about the ball becoming harder to handle than a bar of soap rang true. De Silva went for his strokes right away and, to add insult to injury, Ranatunga was there to see his side home by 7 wickets at the end. We dropped catches in the field and didn't play as well as we could, but Sri Lanka outplayed us fair and square. It was probably our worst one-day performance of the season and I cannot remember a dressing room being so quiet afterwards. Looking back, the only consolation is that defeat in Lahore made victory at Lord's in the next competition so much the sweeter.

But we did do well to make the final. The presentation was tough after events in Australia, but we shook hands and said, 'Well played.' When Ian Chappell got up on the podium with the whole of Sri Lanka it looked funny, then it collapsed. Only in that part of the world would that happen. We made up for it in the 1999 World Cup.

9

VICTORIES HOME
AND AWAY

I HAD SUFFERED the odd twinge here and there, had my toe broken by Waqar Younis and needed to monitor my shoulder almost constantly, but until the operation on my spinning finger after the World Cup (1996) on the sub-continent I never wondered whether my international career was drawing to an end. While I had every faith in the surgeons there is always an element of risk in any surgery and, for me, the ring finger on the right hand, along with the shoulder, is probably the most important tool of my trade.

The months after the World Cup disappointment spent in recuperation and then gradually starting to bowl again were a difficult time, and not just for me. I felt sorry for Greg Hoy, the surgeon, as the whole of Australia wanted to have its say on how I should be treated and whether I would be the same bowler again.

As far as I was concerned the question was not so much whether the finger could be rebuilt, but whether I would have the same confidence in it as before.

Originally, I hoped I might recover in time for a one-day series in Sri Lanka – where the security problems were beginning to ease – and a one-off Test against India in Delhi. I soon realised these targets were highly optimistic. Despite working hard in rehabilitation the finger remained stiff and, worryingly, bowling just didn't feel the same. I struggled in my first game back for St Kilda and then again on my debut as captain for Victoria.

Despite improving week by week and declaring myself ready for the First Test against West Indies in Brisbane on 22 November 1996 I felt apprehensive at the start of the international season. Nerves were the major reason why I was not at my best in that match, but we still won on the back of a determined first-innings total of 479 compiled in around eleven hours, which included an unbeaten 161 by Ian Healy, the highest Test score by an Australian wicket-keeper. Healy followed that with another good performance in the second innings as we set up a declaration. However, even in 2000–01, when the West Indian decline had reached what I hope will be its lowest point, people would be reluctant to write them off while Brian Lara remained at the crease.

Once he slashed at Reiffel early on the final morning, they switched to defence, and with little assistance from the slow pitch we needed to keep our patience and snaffle any chances that came our way. Despite feeling my way back gently, however, I still claimed a couple of wickets in each innings, including Jimmy Adams, who can be an obdurate customer when he gets set. As long as Glenn McGrath and Michael Bevan, with his chinamen, were taking wickets at the other end, I was happy to support. I didn't spin the ball as far but I felt my control was good.

In the posters advertising the series Courtney Walsh and Mark Taylor had gone eyeball to eyeball proclaiming the series as the world championship decider, as though it was a heavyweight title fight. Because we held the Frank Worrell Trophy, after winning in the Caribbean in 1995, we were effectively defending that title and the events in Brisbane confirmed that, if anything, the gap between the two sides had widened. That was underlined in the next contest at Sydney when again we were able to declare, set them a fourth-innings target and dictate terms. All sides have an advantage in their own back yard and, along with India, I think we are the hardest to beat on home soil.

I made far more of an impression in Sydney than Brisbane. Terry Jenner had helped me and I felt confident going into the match. In fact I turned the ball consistently as far as I ever had and from then on I didn't have any doubts about my finger. In that respect it became an important – and memorable – game. The ball to remove Shivnarine Chanderpaul ranks as one of the best of my career. It spun more than the Gatting ball three years earlier, pitching outside the line of the left-hander's off stump and nipping back wickedly to bowl him off his pads. It could not have been more timely, coming on the stroke of lunch, as Chanderpaul and Carl Hooper had been showing signs of resistance. Once that stand was broken we managed to bowl them out before tea, but personally I was gaining self-belief and momentum even before that wicket. I had taken a good return catch from Chanderpaul in the first innings and also confused Hooper into becoming an lbw victim not playing a shot – always a satisfactory dismissal for a bowler. In all I took 7 wickets and conceded less than 3 runs an over against batsmen who do not need an invitation to attack. I knew from then I was back and ready to go.

Four years earlier I had taken 7 for 52 at Melbourne, but this time the MCG gave more assistance to the pace bowlers and Curtly Ambrose in particular took advantage. I don't think we took our foot off the pump. Maybe we didn't bat as well as we can, as an all out total of 122 in the second innings suggests, but quite simply, when a player of the quality of Ambrose gets it all together he can be devastating. He is the best bowler I've played with or against. The West Indies chased 87 to win, but they eventually made it in comfort to claw their way back to two-one overall. They bounced back, as all good sides do.

Spin, in contrast, proved the dominant factor when the series resumed in Adelaide after the World Series one-day event at the end of January. Bevan, recalled for his left-arm wrist-spin and his batting, bowled beautifully to take 10 wickets. It was nice to bowl a long spell with a spinner at the other end, something that had not really happened since I worked with Tim May, and I was delighted to get Lara twice in this match. West Indies desperately missed the injured Ambrose and I think some of their batsmen thought that Bevan represented easy pickings because in their eyes he was not an established frontline bowler. They did not show him the respect he deserved and paid the price.

Bevan went on to enjoy a golden summer. I hope it will happen again for him. He always wanted to be considered primarily as a batsman – still does – and he gave us tremendous depth coming in at number seven. Until this period he had seen himself as a part-time bowler, but when he was called upon he really stepped up to the plate. He has had his troubles in Test cricket against the short ball at times, but one thing about Bevan is his dedication to work on fitness and technique. If he can land the ball consistently well as he did against the West Indies and South Africa, then I think he still has a huge future at Test level. With so few bowlers of that type in the world, he can be a surprise package, especially as he also has a great wrong-un. Having a genuine all-rounder in the side makes a massive difference to the balance – just look at the current South Africa team. Bevan could give us the option of playing three pace bowlers and two spinners, without affecting the quality of the batting. Both he and Adam Gilchrist are definitely capable of filling the number six position.

The three–one scoreline after Adelaide ensured we retained the Frank Worrell Trophy and re-inforced our position at the top of the tree. Unfortunately, and not for the first time, the pitch prepared for the final Test at Perth was not very good. Ambrose and Walsh in particular exploited the cracks in an ill-tempered affair that we lost by 10 wickets inside three days.

In many ways I felt relieved when the contest finished. Difficulties arose on the second day when Lara became angry and agitated at some of the verbals we were directing towards Robert Samuels, their young opening batsman. I didn't think we had stepped over the line. Some people might think that sledging should not be part of the game, but it is the way of the world and, contrary to popular myth, we are not the only team that tries to get under certain opponents' skin occasionally. If a player complained every time he copped a word or two the game would move very slowly. As Samuels batted for more than five hours on this occasion he seemed to be acquitting himself pretty well.

For a reason best known to himself Lara decided to go public with his opinions at a press conference that evening. I would not want to strangle free speech, but I firmly believe that what happens in the middle should stay in the middle unless the line is crossed and the words become offensive. I can give an example. During the 1998–99 series in the Caribbean Nehemiah Perry, their off-spinner, turned to Lara when I came out to bat and made a comment. I objected about that to both Lara and Clive Lloyd, the West Indies manager, because Perry had stepped over the mark. Back in Perth, we were not impressed with Lara squealing to the press, and when he came out to bat as a runner for Walsh the next morning he clearly calculated to antagonise us further. Words were exchanged again before Walsh and Taylor came together to call a truce after the umpires stepped in.

That was not the end of the controversy. Towards the end of the game, when we were clearly heading towards defeat, Andrew Bichel and I suffered the full wrath of Ambrose as he suddenly developed a no-balling problem. One over lasted fifteen balls. He did not overstep by an inch or so, but by a couple of feet or more. He had fractured my right thumb with a short ball in the previous series and to have him releasing bouncers from an even shorter distance coming around the wicket would not have been pleasant on the flattest pitch in the world, let alone this cracked surface.

The crowd, beginning to boo Ambrose, clearly thought something was amiss. One ball hit Bichel on the back as he tried to take evasive action, but even so late in the series neither of us could afford to give an inch. A few years on I can take satisfaction from that innings and the way we stood our corner. At the time my heart was racing. After the game Ambrose said he would be retired before the chance to tour Australia arose again. It was a sad way for such a great player to leave our shores. We were not close friends but we respected each other immensely – he tended to cut a remote figure sometimes where the opposition was concerned, even though he was supposed to be the dressing room prankster in his own camp.

As for Lara, he had just not been himself during the series. I don't know what his problem was, whether he had personal difficulties, but there were situations he didn't handle well at all and I think they affected his batting. They might even have had an adverse effect on the rest of the side. After being dismissed in the Second Test he came into our dressing room while we were on the field to say that Healy was no longer welcome in their dressing room because he thought Heals had claimed a catch that didn't carry. Television replays showed clearly that Lara was out legitimately, and his actions were hardly those of a man who wanted to make friends. The feeling was becoming mutual because we didn't really want him in our dressing room either. He has set himself high standards with the bat, but scored only one hundred and that in the final Test when the series was over. When he is at his best, fully focused, he is as close as anyone can get to Sachin Tendulkar. The difference is that Sachin has that consistency and never loses concentration. I don't want this to sound like a personal attack, because I enjoy Lara's company away from the game and count him as a mate, but on this tour his mood could swing from one day to the next. To his credit he seems to have lightened up over the last couple of years.

Overall I was happy with my performance, especially as I started so apprehensively in Brisbane. I bowled more overs than anybody else in the series and only McGrath took more wickets.

One way or another it had been a compelling, sometimes difficult, series. We could have done with a good break afterwards to recharge our batteries but, as is the way with international cricket these days, we could start accumulating air miles again within a fortnight. South Africa was to be the next destination. In the three years since our last visit to Johannesburg I thought the place had changed. The sheer novelty of the sport had worn off among the people and we were not met with the same curiosity at every turn. The grounds were usually far from being full and we were allowed more space away from the game.

I rank the Wanderers ground among the most intimidating places in the world to play cricket, but this time I was prepared for the reception. To try to help some of the others Geoff Marsh, our coach, asked me to speak at the team meeting before the First Test about playing here and my experiences on the 1994 trip, about how the atmosphere had made us aggressive when we ran out, and about what to expect from the crowd. I suggested that we all take those few extra seconds to make sure we were quite calm before bowling or facing a delivery. Really, as always, it was a case of each individual finding a way to cope.

I don't know whether my words made a difference but the result – in my fiftieth Test – was our second biggest ever win against South Africa, by an innings and 196 runs. And this after they passed 300 in the first innings. Greg Blewett and Steve Waugh batted throughout the third day – only the tenth pair ever to do so in Test cricket. This was fantastic viewing for all of us, especially the bowlers who enjoyed a good rest. By coincidence the last pair who achieved the feat, our own Taylor and Marsh, watched along with the rest of us in admiration from the dressing room. For one batsman to do that is amazing, but for both to keep going without making an error is incredible. Putting myself in the shoes of the South Africans, the experience must have been demoralising as well as draining, as we found out in India in 2001. Their subsequent collapse in the second innings didn't come as a surprise.

Once again, the Bevan/Warne partnership caused some problems. We had taken 4 wickets between us in the first innings and shared 8 more second time around, with Bevan claiming the last 4 in 12 balls. We had decided to go in with two spinners and two pace bowlers, following the success against the West Indies, and the selection paid rich dividends. As far as I was concerned South Africa seemed to play spin so cautiously they rarely looked like scoring runs, even in the first innings on a fresh pitch. They dug themselves a big hole. Maybe that was a legacy from our previous series. In this case I thought I bowled better in the second innings when I re-imposed my authority over Daryll Cullinan as he edged his tenth ball to Healy.

Victory in our next Test at Port Elizabeth in mid-March was as narrow as the success in Johannesburg had been convincing. On a thickly-grassed strip we squandered the advantage of winning the toss. By the end of day two South Africa had a lead of 184 with all second-innings wickets intact. That night we had a big team meeting back at the hotel, led by Taylor. He stressed that things would not happen for us unless we believed in ourselves. It was one of those really good, open, honest chats where no fingers were pointed but everybody left feeling on top of the world and knowing exactly what was expected. The main thing was that we still thought we could win.

The next morning Jason Gillespie was just sensational. He not only bowled with genuine pace and hostility but also put the ball in the right place and generated good out-swing to send back Gary Kirsten, Adam Bacher and Daryll Cullinan inside the first hour, with Jacques Kallis run out in between. It was inspirational stuff. The rest of us took up the baton as South Africa's batting went to pieces. Bevan and I shared the last 5 wickets for 31 runs and I had to laugh when Paul Adams nicked an attempted reverse sweep to Taylor at slip. For a lad who was trying to make his way at international level his strut had surprised us at Johannesburg and, despite that defeat, his self-opinion had not diminished.

I don't mind players having confidence in their ability, but no one should be arrogant. Adams had tried and failed with a few reverse sweeps earlier – this at a time when South Africa had been pegged back and needed to graft out every run they could – and I couldn't help offering a friendly word of advice.

'How about trying to play a normal stroke first, buddy?' I suggested, not-so-secretly hoping he would continue to make himself look ridiculous and present his wicket on a plate. There is never a place for humiliation on the cricket field because we all try our best and can make a mistake, but in this case his whole innings had been a huge misjudgement.

As a result of our fightback and the tomfoolery of Adams

we needed 270 to become the first touring side to win a series in South Africa since their re-admission in 1991. That was still a tall order, given that the highest total of the match up to that point was 209, but at least it gave us a chance as long as we batted well and one of the top order made a big score. Mark Waugh duly put his hand up and scored a brilliant hundred in more than five hours, mixing watchfulness in defence with some of the most elegant strokes imaginable. His innings spanned over two days and just reminded everybody how good a batsman he is. He deserved to be there at the end, but instead fell to Kallis, and when Cronje accounted for Bevan I had to walk out with 12 still wanted to win.

I thought the best idea was to play my natural game and quickly brought down the target by driving Hansie Cronje back over his head for 3. However, that proved to be my one and only scoring shot because I was soon adjudged lbw to Kallis. We were still 5 short with 2 wickets in hand. Gillespie blocked out the remaining five balls of the Kallis over, but Healy must have sensed that it was down to him as he swung the devastated Cronje over long leg for what must have been one of only a handful of sixes in his career.

Such a fantastic comeback showed just what can be achieved with self-belief allied to talent and imaginative leadership. We went wild in the dressing room afterwards. I remember Gillespie and Matthew Hayden, their faces smeared with Vegemite to look like warriors, acting out how animals hunt and kill. The renditions of our favourite team songs, 'Khe Sanh' by Cold Chisel and John Williamson's 'True Blue' – a favourite of Steve Waugh but not all of us – were louder than ever. Brian McMillan and Jonty Rhodes joined us for a drink, only to get into trouble with Bob Woolmer, their coach, for socialising with the opposition.

Jonty has become one of my best mates in the game. This

always surprises outsiders because on the surface we have very little in common except our occupation. He doesn't gamble or drink beer, while I'm not exactly on first name terms with our local vicar. But we hit it off immediately on the 1993–94 tour and did some coaching together in the townships which I found an immensely rewarding experience. More than anything, though, I admire the way he plays the game and is such a team man. Those who point to his batting average in the early to mid-30s and say he is lucky to have played so many Tests can't know much about the game. He saves so many runs in the field and provides the heart that beats through the team. Both of us play cricket for the friendships as much as the performances. When we retire we will not talk over the barbies about hundreds and five-fers, or victories and defeats, but of the fun we enjoyed on and off the field.

With the series in the bag, we lost yet another dead game, in Centurion. I think South Africa had been chastened by their two defeats, while our cause was not helped when we heard the news that three of our side, Hayden, Matthew Elliott and Justin Langer, would be returning home before the one-day series. This was the first stage of the new term 'separate team'. I went without a wicket and all in all it was an anonymous match. Defeat certainly didn't detract from our earlier successes.

After a difficult start on the previous tour, I had grown to like South Africa as a place. Sure, there are enormous problems with poverty and crime in certain areas. We were advised never to go out alone and preferably not even in twos, which sometimes made it hard to act spontaneously. But there is also so much going for the country. Most of the people are extremely pleasant and helpful and Sun City, the holiday complex a couple of hours from Johannesburg, is sensational. From an Australian viewpoint the climate is very similar, so we encounter no problems in adjusting. The beaches are beautiful and there is a lot to do there. I have no doubt in saying it is one of my favourite tours and the series in 2001–02 promises to be perhaps the most important in determining the real world champions since we visited the West Indies in 1994–95. I only hope I am around to be part of it. Fingers crossed!

10

INDIA

THERE ARE TIMES in my life when I've felt on top of the world and others when I've wondered if my luck will ever turn. In 1997–98 I fluctuated between both extremes. I will remember the summer in Australia fondly for taking my three hundredth Test wicket, and then in India setting a new world record for a spin bowler by passing Lance Gibbs' total of 309. I also filled in as captain of my country for the first time. Those were the high points. But I also endured a difficult time in my first Test series in India, trying desperately to contain Sachin Tendulkar and his colleagues, and finally arrived back in Australia knowing I had to undergo surgery on my shoulder to even stand a chance of being able to continue in the game.

New Zealand arrived in October 1997 as our first opponents, at a time when the dispute between the Cricketers' Association and the ACB over pay and conditions, described at length later in the book, was nearing a potential crisis point.

Nobody would describe the situation as being an ideal lead-up to the series, particularly as many of the moves were played out in public. In the circumstances, we did extremely well to win in Brisbane and Perth against a team who always raised their game against Australia, and who were clearly going places under the adventurous leadership of Stephen Fleming.

I began the season with 264 wickets in 58 Tests and set

myself the challenge of reaching number 300 in Australia. That meant I needed to take an average of 6 wickets in each Test. It was the first time in my career that I set myself a personal goal in terms of statistics.

The First Test at the Gabba was to set the tone for the first part of our summer – long spells and a good haul of wickets. New Zealand almost held us on first innings before collapsing to 132 all out on the final day. My match figures of 7 for 160 from 67 overs included the wicket of Adam Parore to one of the best catches ever taken off my bowling by Mark Taylor, who had to dive backwards to his left after being unsighted initially as the ball turned across the batsman. In the words of the great Richie Benaud: 'What a catch!'

Six more wickets followed at the WACA as we clinched the series with an innings win and we were only one wicket away from a clean sweep in Hobart after Fleming declared New Zealand's first innings 149 behind in a bold move designed to make up for play lost to rain. Having gone two–love behind he had nothing to lose, and his side proved equally adventurous in going for a target of 288 in two sessions. That in turn raised our chances of claiming the 10 wickets. The first of my 2 wickets were both stumpings – Chris Cairns, promoted up the order to help the run rate, and then Fleming himself. Having collapsed from 1 for 93 to 4 for 95 they decided to dig in, but the ball was now turning sharply from around leg stump and I felt confident of forcing an edge or glove to one of the close fielders. Once again, I needed a really good catch to account for Parore. This time Matthew Elliott flung out a hand as he slipped at deep square leg. We gradually winkled through the lower order until Simon Doull and Shayne O'Connor, the last-wicket pair, managed to hold out for more than 10 overs to earn a draw.

From my experience New Zealand have always lifted

themselves against us. If Richard Hadlee was still around they would be a genuine force. Guys like Nathan Astle, Craig McMillan and Fleming himself are capable players in the middle, while Chris Cairns and Parore are extremely handy at seven and eight, but they haven't really found the openers to give them the starts they need.

Although the possibility of a strike had been averted, another off-field issue overshadowed the climax of the series. This time the headlines were made by an announcement on the final day of the Third Test that Taylor and Healy had been dropped from the one-day squad for the subsequent Carlton & United series against New Zealand and South Africa. Significantly, with Taylor certain to lead the side in the Tests against South Africa, this now meant that Australia had separate captains for the limited overs and five-day games for the first time in our history. The ACB had talked to the selectors and wanted to start to build a specialist one-day team with the 1999 World Cup in mind and only five of the team that played in the final Test against New Zealand featured in the initial Carlton & United game against South Africa.

Having two captains made for an uneasy period in the dressing room initially. It was a new concept for all of us, especially with Taylor saying publicly that he thought it was not the ideal situation, and he was right. To my mind, the selectors faced a difficult decision. They had either to install separate captains, or pick a guy for the one-day side they did not think was in the best eleven. It may happen again in future, but I think the selectors would much prefer to have one man in charge for both formats. There are always crossover periods in the year where the one-day series becomes a topic for discussion during a Test match, and vice-versa. It is awkward at the best of times because not everybody playing in one format has been chosen for the other and those guys can feel left out. When that player happened to be the captain, Taylor, it left us all slightly on edge.

As a consequence of that decision the selectors appointed me as vice-captain to Stephen in the one-days. That was an honour in itself, and when he went down with a hip problem during the C&U tournament I stood in to take charge of Australia for the first time, against New Zealand at Sydney. Leading Australia is a greater privilege, and I relished the extra responsibility. After the game some of the guys said they ran out feeling as pumped up as if they were playing Aussie Rules. I ended my team talk with the words, 'Let's put on a show' – and they did exactly that.

The game couldn't have gone much better. I won the toss – which is always a good start - and had the luxury of joining the attack with 4 New Zealand wickets already in the bag and a formidable total of 250 to defend. The highlight was Ricky Ponting running out Craig Spearman and Craig McMillan from backward point sensationally on the way to victory by 131 runs. All in all, though, it was a strange tournament as the selectors experimented with players deemed to be one-day specialists. We lost our first five games to South Africa, only to win overall when we took the deciding final in Sydney by 14 runs.

That was another example of the way that we seem to have the edge over them in tight situations. This also held true when the Test series began. They arrived confident of beating us for the first time since being admitted back to the Test fold after two drawn series home and away in 1994, but lost heavily by an innings in the Second Test at Sydney and squandered the opportunity to level the series in the final match in Adelaide. Having taken 19 wickets in the three matches against the Kiwis, I proceeded to claim 20 at an average of 20.85 against South Africa to pass my target for the summer.

I had felt confident in all three of our previous meetings since 1993–94 and saw nothing to concern me this time. Certainly not hype about a supposed personal battle with Daryll Cullinan. For such a good batsman against other countries, and a bloke with a triple-hundred in first-class cricket to his name, I have never figured out his problem against us. He is an intense, prickly guy, and I can only imagine he developed a bit of a phobia. This time he was run out for 5 in the first innings before I bowled him for a duck in the second, having twice beaten him as he pushed forward nervously. There is such a thing as playing the ball rather than the man and poor Daryll's mind seemed to be in knots. The selectors put him out of his misery by dropping him for the rest of the series.

Despite having the better of Cullinan once again, that contest in Melbourne became an increasingly frustrating affair as South Africa showed a lot of fight. I bowled 35 overs on the final day with South Africa batting merely to survive, but despite turning the ball past the bat on countless occasions I just couldn't get the edge. Jacques Kallis came of age as an international cricketer that day. He showed a good tight technique in defence and an assured temperament as he completed a maiden Test hundred. His composure under pressure was really impressive for a young guy and I'm not surprised by his progress since. In my opinion he and Chris Cairns are the best all-rounders in the game.

After such a tiring effort I hoped we would bat first at Sydney three days later, but sadly it wasn't to be. After Hansie Cronje won the toss South Africa showed little inclination to score at more than 2 runs per over. They missed a prime chance to grasp the initiative. On the second morning I felt far perkier, turned the ball more sharply and claimed all 5 of the remaining wickets, including David Richardson with one that turned almost as wickedly as the Gatting ball to stretch my overall tally to 294.

Adam Bacher and Gary Kirsten failed to survive the new ball and further wickets tumbled almost as soon as I joined the attack – one, two, three, four and then Richardson for the second time in the match to reach 299. Given the difficulties I had in eventually passing Dennis Lillee's Australian record two years later, it seems funny to think how quickly I went from 290 to 300. For much of the game the weather had been thoroughly miserable. The sky was grey and a good percentage of the crowd had clearly decided yet another shower would end play for the day. Miraculously, though, the weather relented, the floodlights were switched on and, not knowing whether a storm might break during the night, we pushed hard to tie up the contest with a day to spare. When Kallis misread a top-spinner from around the wicket it gave me my three hundredth Test wicket and a very, very special moment. Paul Reiffel soon claimed the last 2 wickets in the rain and the umpires had decided to call it a day at the end of the over. So the celebrations began.

To reach 300 wickets requires consistency and stamina as well as sheer ability and, despite the ever-increasing amount of cricket played these days, it says everything that only seventeen bowlers have reached that landmark. I felt very privileged to join such elite company and to be the fourth quickest to get there in my sixty-third Test, behind greats in Dennis Lillee, Richard Hadlee and Malcolm Marshall, and the second youngest after Kapil Dev. It is something I never thought would happen. I don't think I could have bowled any better than I did at Sydney. It was one of those games where everything seemed to click, every leg-break seemed to bite and find the edge and every variation worked like a treat.

Maybe my success in Sydney encouraged the selectors to bring in a second leg-spinner, Stuart MacGill, for his debut ahead of Michael Bevan when the Test series resumed after a break for the C&U series. The game is best remembered for a magnificent innings by Mark Waugh at his best under pressure in the second innings and South Africa's failure to square the series. They had enough chances after scoring 517 in their first innings but dropped a total of ten catches – incredible for a team that prides itself on its fielding.

There was also a moment of controversy when Mark Waugh, in the process of saving the game, brushed the stumps with his bat and dislodged the bails after being hit on the arm by Shaun Pollock. I was batting at the other end at the time and it was obvious from the non-striker's end that he had swung the bat in disappointment. The third umpire decided he should be adjudged not out because he was in control of what he was doing. If he had not been in control he would have been out. None of us in the middle knew the exact rule, but once we checked after the game it was clear that Mark could not have been given out. However, Hansie Cronje queried the decision and his composure was not helped when Bacher soon dropped the same batsman. Mark proceeded to reach three figures as we secured a draw and there were some claims that Cronje speared a stump through the door of the umpires' changing room afterwards. If that was the case then I'm sure it was in frustration more than malice because the result denied South Africa the chance to go home on level terms. They knew they had squandered an opportunity. For us, it was an important success that justified our unofficial standing as the best in the world.

I had the added honour of being named man of the series, but an intensive year of almost full-time cricket had left me feeling drained. In the six Tests against New Zealand and South Africa alone I had bowled nearly 360 overs. The immediate priority was clearly the Test series in India four weeks later so, in conjunction with the selectors, I decided to pull out of a one-day series in New Zealand to give my shoulder the rest that it needed. I was having problems with it all through the summer, but for some reason the ball kept coming out of my hand so well that I was reluctant to change anything. I thought that if I continued to work on strengthening the muscles around it I would get by. After all, on the evidence of the Australian part of the summer such a policy was proving successful.

However, the actual soreness refused to go away and there seemed to be a knock-on effect of dreadful migraine headaches when I tried to sleep. I could have pulled out of the tour to India with every justification. I had only played two Test matches against India even in Australia – and those right at the start of my career when I felt completely out of my depth and bowled garbage. With help from Errol Alcott and Lynn Watson, a shoulder specialist who gave me a series of exercises, I had managed to get through the New Zealand and South Africa series and I saw no reason why I should come unstuck in India.

There is an old saying in sport – if you fail to prepare you should prepare to fail. I did not know it at the time, but as I was recuperating in Australia, Sachin Tendulkar was practising intensively for the series ahead by deliberately scuffing up an area outside leg stump in the nets to face the local wrist-spinners.

I suppose I should take it as a compliment that he felt he needed to do that before he took Australia and me on. I have nothing but admiration for the guy and as the series progressed he showed why he is the number one.

Although the series was billed as Tendulkar v Warne both of us tried to play down that individual element. Every series is country versus country, even though there are interesting battles within that. We had not won in India since 1969–70, while their unbeaten record at home stretched back eleven years. So I was looking forward to our warm-up game against a Bombay side including Tendulkar, who had asked to play to try and pick up clues for the serious business ahead. From the second ball, which he smacked over midwicket for six, I wondered if I might be in for a long, hard slog. A couple of times he sweep-slogged me against the spin, which is very unusual for him, while being in complete control. I had forgotten just how good a batsman he was.

When I bowl to somebody I know will feature subsequently in the Tests I don't usually reveal much of my repertoire. The consequences can be quite dramatic, as Graeme Hick showed before the Ashes series in 1993 and Tendulkar underlined here, but I still think it is wise to keep my powder dry for the big event. I resisted the temptation to try and confuse him with a sequence of flippers and wrong-uns, even as he raced to a hundred and finally finished 204 not out at a run a ball. My 16 overs cost 111 runs – although I was unlucky not to win an lbw appeal when Tendulkar was on 14 – and while I was prepared to save myself for the bigger dates ahead, it seemed that he wanted to strike a psychological blow.

The First Test was played in the heat and humidity of Madras on the east coast. It was here that Dean Jones was rushed to hospital for a saline drip to recover after his double-century in 1986–87. Apart from the pitches in India, such harsh conditions explain why so few sides come out on top. We played a one-day international at Cochin where the temperature soared into the fifties in the middle with a humidity of 90 per cent. No wonder that particular game was scheduled for April Fools' Day. There were a number of times during the tour when we went back to the hotel with diarrhoea or started vomiting or felt dehydrated. And the next day we had to go back and play cricket again. Even the Indian players struggled in some of the extreme temperatures, though they were used to the climate.

I must say, though, that food did not present quite the problem for me that people might have imagined from some of the newspaper headlines and pictures of tinned spaghetti and baked beans being shipped out with the words 'to Shane Warne in India' plastered all over the crates back home. That episode began after I went to see Geoff Marsh, our coach, in his room one morning and saw him tucking into some spaghetti. He said that he'd packed a few tins in his suitcase and would have one for breakfast occasionally. I then sought out Errol Alcott, our physio, to ask whether there was any chance of the ACB sending over a few tins so that we could have them on toast occasionally in the mornings.

Somehow a few journalists sniffed something out and wrote it as Shane Warne sending an SOS back home before we wasted away. Wasting away? To what, a block of flats? From quietly asking for a few tins I now had tonnes of the stuff – thanks to SPC. At least the story had a happy ending. We took a few tins each (baked beans every day is not a very sociable idea) and the rest were distributed to charity and under-privileged children. I have struck up a great relationship with SPC who are an Australian company.

As far as the cricket itself was concerned we held our own for most of the first three days in Madras but eventually lost by 179 runs thanks to a great knock by Sachin. On a personal note the game began promisingly with 4 wickets. After the carnage in Bombay the highlight had to be removing Tendulkar. He drove his first ball to the boundary, but I beat him twice before he edged a leg-break to Mark Taylor at slip.

We felt quietly confident with a lead of 71 on first-innings. Tendulkar, though, soon changed the course of the game with an unbeaten 155 second time around – again after surviving what I thought was a realistic shout for leg before before he had scored. In fact, although my figures did not make happy reading I did beat him several times again. The difference between missing the bat and taking the edge can be a fraction of an inch, beyond the judgement of any batsman no matter how good. Tendulkar played some brilliant strokes, but I certainly didn't feel disheartened by the experience. It was simply a great innings.

One batsman I never felt received the credit he deserved during the series was Navjot Sidhu. His onslaught at the end of the third day began to swing the balance, set up the situation for Tendulkar and set the tone for the rest of the series. He had a fantastic eye for the ball. Three or four times I thought I had beaten him through the air, only to see him swing the bat and hit the ball ten rows back into the stand.

The Second Test, in the huge concrete bowl of Calcutta, ranks as my worst for Australia. India's total of 5 for 633 was their highest ever against Australia and my figures of 0 for 147 are the second most expensive of my career. But at least when the Indians hammered me for 150 on my debut six years earlier I had the consolation of taking a wicket. Some consolation, you might think, as Ravi Shastri had 206 to his name, but it was still a wicket. Calcutta was the same in 2001 thanks to V.V.S. Laxman and Rahul Dravid. They won and became the fifth side ever to win after following on.

To put India's innings in perspective this time, Tendulkar was only fifth highest scorer even though he had 79 to his credit. All of their top order played magnificently. We were exactly 400 behind on first-innings and although our batsmen came in for some criticism it is very hard to be mentally in tune to retrieve such a massive deficit after spending so long chasing the ball in stifling heat. Unfortunately that left us two-nil down. We felt we had established ourselves as the best in the world after beating West Indies and South Africa, but after winning our previous nine series in all we found ourselves outplayed by India. They and Sri Lanka on their home soil would have to remain the final two nuts to crack.

Although there was no way back from being two-nil down we showed character to win the final game at Bangalore in the last week of March, especially as we had a string of players injured, including Steve Waugh, and conceded 424 in India's first innings – 177 to Tendulkar in another blistering knock. The climate in Bangalore, well inland, was far more to our liking. I was having problems myself in the groin and shoulder areas but felt pleased with my bowling overall on another dead surface to take 5 wickets in the match, including that of Rahul Dravid with a leg-break that pitched well outside leg stump but clipped off, to overtake Gibbs' record of Test wickets for a spin bowler. I cannot think of a reason for it, but I have always done better against Dravid than the other Indian batsmen. I feel I have the wood on him. All in all, I didn't feel that the batsmen were able to dominate as they had at times in Madras and Calcutta. Tendulkar was named man of the series and his run of scores, which brought an aggregate of 446 at 111.50, drew comparisons with Sir Donald Bradman. Obviously I never bowled to The Don. But if he was consistently superior to Tendulkar then I'm only glad he was an Australian. One guy who was fantastic all tour was Michael Kasprowicz. He led the attack and busted a gut, fully deserving his 5 wickets in the last Test.

I am not using the shoulder as an excuse but I felt I had not done myself full justice and desperately wanted the chance to atone when we returned there in 2000–01. Unfortunately that didn't happen; they beat us again 2–1. At the end of the series Mark Taylor and I sat down for a chat and he suggested that I consider going home instead of staying on for the one-day games and a tournament in Sharjah. But I thought that for the sake of a few more games at the end of the season I might as well keep going and see a specialist afterwards. We duly won the Pepsi Cup in India and lost in the Coca-Cola Cup final in Sharjah where we were once again Tendul-corized. A week later, in the nick of time according to the experts, I went under the knife.

11

WORLD CUP

LEAVING the West Indies for the World Cup in 1999 I really wasn't sure which direction my career would take. It hurt me greatly to be dropped from the side for the Fourth Test. Except for injury, I had not been left out of the team for eight years and the passage of time, reputed to be a great healer, was not making me feel much better. Although I was the leading wicket taker and bowled well in the one-day matches following the Test series, I was determined to play both forms of the game, not just one-day cricket. As anyone who has gone through the same situation will vouch, to be dropped is hard to take and, looking back on the whole situation, I think it made me more determined and hungry to play.

It was Steve Waugh's first series as captain and I think he felt he needed to be seen to be doing something in what had become a difficult position. Australia had won the First Test convincingly but lost the next two, largely through the individual brilliance of Brian Lara and calming influence of Jimmy Adams. I felt that my overall record in tough situations and big matches should have counted in my favour. To be fair, though, I was not bowling as well as I could, but then neither was Stuart MacGill who was trying to take my place. All the way through my career I had produced when it mattered and I thought the selectors should have backed me, but it was not to be.

I did not beg or plead for my position at the selection meeting – contrary to what some people have written and said – which I attended as vice-captain. I simply stated the case as I saw it. Although everything was conducted in a calm business-like atmosphere, it was not a run-of-the-mill meeting. Usually on tour the captain, vice-captain and coach pick the teams and the chairman of selectors is on a phone link-up and between everyone the team is selected. Trevor Hohns, the chairman, had his say through the link-up and Allan Border, a selector who was on one of his tours to the Caribbean, also joined in discussions. At the subsequent team gathering, the captain said that leaving me out was the hardest decision he had ever had to make. Those words meant a lot because Stephen and I have become good friends over a long period of time.

Because I felt removed from the action, watching events unfold in Antigua was a funny situation. I was delighted that we won to level the series. And looking back objectively, the whole business probably helped me as well. It is said that you only truly recognise how much you enjoy something when it is taken away, and this episode reminded me of my love for the game. It also told me that if I wanted to play at the highest level I needed to work harder than I ever had, to prove to myself that I was still capable of performing at that level. I decided to concentrate entirely on the World Cup, to put everything I could into the competition and save a decision about my future for afterwards. In other words, the tournament would be either the beginning of my rebuilding process or a swansong.

The 1999 competition began very inauspiciously. Before we had bowled a ball in anger I found myself in trouble for an article I wrote in *The Times* on the morning of the opening match between England, the hosts, and Sri Lanka. My thoughts about Sri Lanka and their then captain Arjuna Ranatunga in

Merv Hughes shares his thoughts with Alec Stewart at Headingley, 1993.

Merv Hughes bowls through the pain barrier at The Oval, 1993.

Peter Such becomes another victim in the Second Test, 1993.

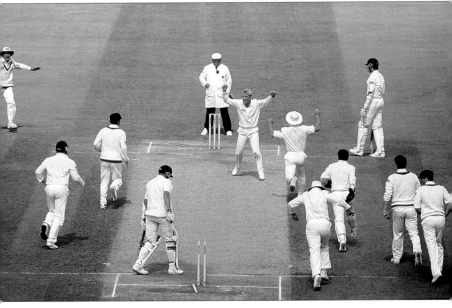

Above My three Australia captains – Steve Waugh, Mark Taylor and Allan Border.

Left One of my worst days on the field – going too far with the verbals after dismissing Andrew Hudson in Johannesburg, 1994.

Below The Newlands ground in Cape Town is one of the most picturesque in the world.

Sitting it out with a broken toe courtesy of Waqar Younis at the Bellerive Oval in 1995.

International Cricketer of the Year, January 1994.

Tired but delighted, with Damien Fleming after another success in the World Series.

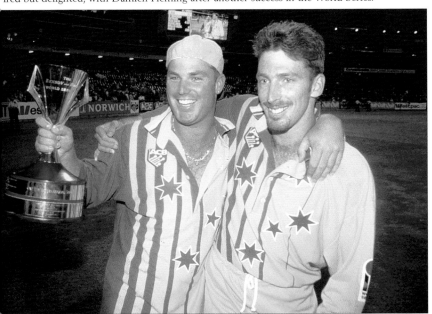

Hat-trick – David Boon takes a great catch as Devon Malcolm becomes my third wicket in as many balls in Melbourne, 1994.

With Steve Waugh and Brian Lara before a one-day international in Trinidad.

Richie Richardson had to pull Curtly Ambrose away from Steve Waugh in the Third Test at Trinidad in 1995.

Mike Atherton never enjoyed dealing with the press.

Muttiah Muralitharan is a great bowler, but I wouldn't want kids to copy his action.

Mushtaq Ahmed and I have passed on many tips to each other down the years.

Abdul Qadir flew the flag for leg-spin during the '70s and '80s.

The look says it all as Arjuna Ranatunga turns for another run and the World Cup slips away from Australia.

Aravinda de Silva helps Sri Lanka towards victory in the 1996 World Cup final.

Above Greg Blewett and Steve Waugh pass another landmark against South Africa at Johannesburg, March 1997.

Above right Curtly Ambrose was never more fearsome than in the Perth Test in 1997.

Below right Brian Lara falls victim to the Healy/Warne combination at Perth, 1997.

Below Michael Bevan, here celebrating the wicket of Jimmy Adams, could be a top-class all-rounder if he worked more on his bowling.

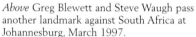

particular are no secret, and I have already elaborated on the way I think he acted in a manner which was contrary to the spirit of the game. I wrote that Sri Lanka and the game overall would be better off without Ranatunga, and that remains my view.

One of the match referees, Cammie Smith, had been ordered to listen to the case. David Richards, the chief executive of the ICC, swooped on our team hotel in Worcester with a dim view of the article. They pointed out that contracts for the competition stipulated we should not say anything derogatory either about players, teams or the World Cup itself. I was fined half of my match fee and given a suspended ban for bringing the tournament into disrepute. Ridiculous! I thought so.

In my opinion some people are so worried about appearing politically correct and saying all the right things that they never express what they really think. It seems a strange society when you cannot express an opinion – and that is all it was. In the press conference after that first match, which Sri Lanka lost easily, Ranatunga made a comment about the heritage of Australian people. I thought his comments were more offensive than anything I had written, but not for the first time in his career, he got away with it without even a fine. Everybody hates the person who says 'I told you' but, for the record, Sri Lanka failed to reach the second stage of the competition, as I predicted, and Ranatunga lost the captaincy soon after returning home. Much of my column proved to be accurate.

Nevertheless, I thought it would be wise to try to keep a lower profile for a while, to stay in the background and keep my nose clean. Typically, though, things did not go quite as I wanted. Our first game, against Scotland at Worcester, should have been a straightforward affair. Their team was comprised mainly of amateurs who had performed beyond all expectations to qualify at all. They were followed by an enthusiastic and vocal bunch of supporters, wearing the full national uniform, including kilts and sporrans, eager to make the most of what might be their only appearance in a World Cup. Inevitably, I was targeted for the loudest verbals and I decided to have a bit of fun back. So, after they had finished one particular chant, I turned towards them with a smile and gave them the good old-fashioned Aussie bird. It was not done in an angry way, it was banter and we were all laughing and it was taken in the spirit of the occasion, a friendly riposte to a bunch of supporters who were enjoying their day out.

The next morning I opened the newspapers to see photographs of myself giving the bird, out of context, and blown up to huge proportions. I should have thought of the consequences first. Cricketers are part of the entertainment industry and I am all for a bit of banter with the crowd. It wasn't that long ago that I was a spectator myself, having a beer and a pie and I dare say offering the odd piece of advice at a fair volume. I'm worse at the football when watching the Saints play. Sometimes I do the wrong thing at the wrong time and this latest bout of bad publicity was down to me. But it does seem to be a shame that interplay with a crowd has to be toned down for fear of being misinterpreted.

We ultimately came away from the game itself without too much trouble. I was impressed with the way the Scots approached the contest, from the moment Bruce Patterson struck the first ball of the match to the boundary. We did not bowl or field as well as we could and Gavin Hamilton, who was disappointed not to have been picked by England, batted as though he was Mel Gibson from *Braveheart* with a point to prove. I thought that I bowled pretty well to finish with 3 wickets, including Hamilton. Chasing 182 there was a brief scare for us when Ricky Ponting and Darren Lehmann fell with the score on 101, but the Waugh boys and Michael

Bevan managed to see us home with 5 of the 50 overs to spare.

Having been based in Cardiff for our preparations, let me take this opportunity to say thank you to everyone at Cardiff. They went out of their way to make us feel very welcome. We returned to Wales for the second game, against New Zealand. This was probably our lowest point of the competition but for me personally the highest. One of the few occasions in my career when, deep down, I was not really switched on. This time I think I could be excused. Just before midnight on the eve of the match, I received a telephone call from Melbourne to say that my wife Simone had given birth to our second child, a baby boy we decided to call Jackson. Being away during the pregnancy had added to the strain I felt under. We were coming up to nearly six months away from home and so much had happened. Obviously she was unable to fly out with some of the other players' wives and girlfriends at the end of the West Indies tour and no amount of calls could make up for her absence. I desperately wanted to be with her and the kids, but it was impossible in the circumstances. Any father can confirm the worries of the days before birth and the sheer distance between England and Australia compounded my concern. When the good news finally came through I felt a huge release of tension. Brendon Julian, Tom Moody, Damien Martyn and Darren Lehmann joined me for a beer and a cigar and I did not sleep much that night. I was so happy about things back home, but at the same time frustrated at not being there. I was thinking back to the 1997 Ashes series when our daughter, Brooke, was born. I wondered what the little boy looked like and whether he was okay. I lost focus on the task ahead.

New Zealand always find something extra against Australia because of the historical rivalry and on this occasion they out-played us all the way. They are a good one-day side because bowlers like Gavin Larsen are so difficult to get away. There

SHANE WARNE: MY AUTOBIOGRAPHY

is no pace on the ball to be able to work it around and Geoff Allott, a left-arm seamer who had enjoyed a moderate career so far, came of age during the competition. They definitely had the better of the conditions and, although we took their first 4 wickets for 49, we could do little as Roger Twose and Chris Cairns batted beautifully. Cairns struck me so far that I turned around and thought that's going to have some frequent flier points on it when it gets back.

That night was one of the strangest I have known. Anybody who saw us in the Italian restaurant would have thought we'd just won the World Cup and the Ashes rolled into one rather than lost by 5 wickets to a team we were expected to beat. We partied like never before, fortunately in a room upstairs away from most of the public. The two sides of the long table squared up for competitions in sculling pints of beer and shots of spirits. We even had a singing competition against a group of priests, who had doubtless arrived expecting a quiet, civilised meal. I had been a bit down in the dumps and it meant so much that the boys had put this on to celebrate Jackson's birth. These are the things that I will mostly miss when my time comes to retire, these are the most enjoyable times and the things you don't forget.

The fact remained, however, that our cricket needed to show a marked improvement if we were going to win the World Cup. When we lost the third game, against Pakistan at Headingley, the pundits effectively ruled us out of contention. While I understand why outsiders came to the conclusion we could not challenge Pakistan and South Africa, the form sides of the time, those of us on the inside look back to that defeat in Leeds as the turning point of the campaign.

On a good batting pitch we felt that 250 would be a par score. But Inzamam and Abdur Razzaq added 118 and Moin Khan smashed an unbelievable 31 from twelve balls, hitting

McGrath all over the place at the end. It was an amazing innings, to leave them with 275. That was a monumental target with Shoaib Akhtar and Wasim Akram always likely to find reverse-swing and ultimately we finished 11 runs short. Our attitude, though, had not been that of a side expecting to be beaten. In between innings we decided that if we were going to go down we would at least go down with a fight. I remember one particular shot by Ricky Ponting that said everything about the way we intended to stay in the competition, when he charged Wasim and hit him back over his head for 4. Our attitude has changed and that's what it is all about, having the right attitude and positive thoughts.

The Pakistanis managed to drag out our innings for more than twenty minutes past the scheduled close – had they bowled first they would have been deducted overs for their own innings under the rules of the tournament. Although we lost the game, our display with the bat set the tone for the positive cricket that followed and the team talk we had the next day was honest and upfront and we all made a pact with each other that we would stick to Steve Waugh's slogan of 'No Regrets', meaning extra hits in the nets, fitness, helping your mates out etc. From that point on, we behaved and played like men possessed.

Some of the players were beginning to feel jaded, not travelling well and perhaps even starting to succumb to a bit of homesickness, myself included. Steve Waugh, in an interview with ABC, was asked about rumours that he and I were not getting on as captain and vice-captain, and that the team were not happy. We couldn't believe it. I said to him that it was just another bit of poor journalism and not to worry about it, but we were both very disappointed because it wasn't true. Where that story came from, I have not got a clue to this day. The two of us have been mates for a long time and the idea that we could fall out was extremely disappointing. If it was an attempt by somebody to try to undermine morale in the side then it failed dismally. Between us, we managed to quash the rumour very quickly.

The morning after the Pakistan defeat Geoff Marsh, our coach, called the squad together at the meeting where we made the pact. It was one of the most open, frank, honest and purposeful team sessions. Nobody pointed an accusing finger or expressed negative thoughts, but we all had something to get off our chests. Everything was directed towards doing that little bit extra to reverse the opening results and create our own history, like the 1987 team.

By now, our task was clear. We had a maximum of seven more games and could not afford to lose any of them. Given the way that fortune plays such a part in one-day cricket, we knew that would be a tall order, but we were prepared to give it a go and back the undoubted ability within the group.

We agreed that in future we would do everything together. This was a once in a lifetime opportunity for those assembled in that room to succeed. We would never be together as a group again. For some, it would be the last chance to win the World Cup.

Every Australia trip is given a title these days and Steve Waugh's 'No Regrets' was a good one. I said a few words, as Stephen's deputy, about 1987, and how we should aim to create our own piece of history.

The team came up with the idea of banning alcohol once we had finished dinner. I think some people sat down to eat at 10.30. Dinner was getting later and later but we were all serious and no one had been drunk. (To be honest, I think we made up for it a little later.) By all means have a beer or a glass of wine over dinner, but when the plates were tidied away it was time to hit the fruit juice or go home. We also agreed on a midnight curfew. None of these issues was forced. By deciding to set our own rules as a squad we avoided picking on any specific players who might have been slacking or losing sight of the main objective. The bottom line was that we wanted to give ourselves the best possible chance of making a success of the trip. I am not suggesting these decisions eventually made the difference between winning the competition and falling short. But they definitely helped to instil the extra discipline that had been lacking. We were all grown-ups and big enough and ugly enough to know when enough is enough, but it was a group decision and I think it helped. It's amazing how a little 1 per cent thing can flow on to the cricket field.

The immediate result was that we left Leeds for Chester-le-Street in the north-east full of confidence and undaunted by the size of the challenge ahead. This new spirit manifested itself when we beat Bangladesh by 7 wickets, having taken less than 20 overs to pass their score of 178. We knew by now that net run rate might dictate whether or not we reached the second stage, so Brendon Julian and Tom Moody were promoted up the order. Moody, one of two survivors along with Steve Waugh from the 1987 squad, responded by scoring the fastest half-century ever in the World Cup from twenty-eight balls.

The selectors drafted in Moody for this match because of his experience with Warwickshire and Worcestershire in England, although there was very little to choose between the two. The selectors made the right choice. Moody releases the ball from around ten feet in the air and when conditions are in his favour he can be a handful. The other significant change was to introduce Paul Reiffel. We thought initially that Adam Dale would be a handful on seaming English pitches, but for some reason it just didn't happen for him in the first two games. He never quite managed to hit the deck as we anticipated and didn't bowl with his normal accuracy. We decided to ditch the plan of using Glenn McGrath first change and handed our leading pace bowler the new ball instead with the task of making that early breakthrough and immediately putting the opposition on the back foot.

The new plan worked to perfection when we faced the West Indies at Old Trafford. McGrath removed Sherwin Campbell, Jimmy Adams and Brian Lara within the space of thirteen balls to leave them 20 for 3 and finished with figures of 5 for 14 overall. The one that bowled Lara was up there with the best in the tournament and, with their biggest threat removed, we knew we were on course. By the time I came on they had lost more wickets and were back on the defensive trying to rebuild the innings. I bowled 4 maidens in my 10 overs and claimed the important wicket of Shivnarine Chanderpaul, as well as Curtly Ambrose and Reon King. Once again, Manchester had proved to be a happy hunting ground. It was my most economical bowling in one-day cricket: 10–4–11–3.

A target of 111 represented little more than a formality, despite slipping to 62 for 4, but the way Steve Waugh and Michael Bevan went about completing the task caused a lot of controversy with accusations that they went against the spirit of the competition by taking as long as possible to secure victory. Under the rules three countries qualified from each of the two groups for the next stage. Those level on points would be separated by a series of factors. The first consideration was results in head-to-head matches, then net run rate. By this stage three countries – New Zealand, West Indies and ourselves – were competing for two places to join Pakistan in what was known as the Super Sixes, effectively the quarter-finals. However, results from the first round against sides who went through were taken into the Super Sixes. It got confusing at times. Having lost to New Zealand and moved to within a few runs of beating West Indies, it was clearly better for us if Lara's side went through. That is why we took our time to reach the target, to try to lift West Indies above New Zealand on run rate.

The rules were there in black and white. We were playing smart cricket. What our critics failed to acknowledge is that we were able to control the game because we had put ourselves in such a strong position by bowling beautifully early on. I thought the rules were pretty good overall. Every match meant something because results in the first stage carried points in the second. I believe that the best two teams in the competition ultimately made the final. That means that the ICC and the ECB did a great job in deciding the format for this World Cup. As events transpired, New Zealand beat Scotland so comfortably in the last group game that they reached the Super Sixes anyway, along with ourselves and Pakistan.

We now had to play the top three sides from Group A – South Africa, India and Zimbabwe. Four of the six countries were to progress to the semi-finals but, when the points from the first stage were totted up, we were bottom of the six now left in the competition. The task was clear – we needed to win all three matches. If this sounded like a tall order then the way we demolished India at the Oval confirmed we had started to hit our straps. McGrath and Fleming knocked over the top order, this time the batsmen had already laid the foundations with a big score.

Mark Waugh and Adam Gilchrist put on almost a hundred for the first wicket and everybody chipped in with twenties or thirties down the order until we reached 282 for 6, a formidable total even on a good pitch.

The Indian batsmen had really captured the public imagination in the initial matches. Sourav Ganguly, Rahul Dravid and Sachin Tendulkar all scored hundreds brimming with rich, wristy strokeplay. This time they met their match. In some outstanding bowling from McGrath, Tendulkar and Dravid were caught at the wicket, then Mohammad Azharuddin, to leave India 4 for 17. Ajay Jadeja and Robin Singh managed to put some respect on the scoreboard but we won comfortably.

The second game followed a similar course. Zimbabwe, the form team, put us in to bat, watched us pile on the runs before losing wickets in a bunch when they replied. Again, too, Mark Waugh top-scored for us, with a brilliant hundred, supported by his brother, Stephen, who struck 62 from sixty-one balls. The one difference between this and the India contest is that Zimbabwe started aggressively before collapsing in mid-innings. I admired the way they went about their business. My prediction at the start of the tournament that they would reach at least the Super Sixes and possibly even the semi-finals raised a few eyebrows, but they had become an experienced one-day side and I expected them to be well-suited to English conditions. After McGrath removed Grant Flower, Neil Johnson and Murray Goodwin really went for their shots to the extent that I joined the attack at a very early stage.

They needed quick runs and the captain and I agreed that a change of pace was required and that I might be able to tempt them into making an error. Unfortunately, the plan backfired as Johnson hit lots of boundaries. For successive games, my figures did not make pleasant reading, but we won the game which was all that mattered and I had to find some inspiration. The demise of Goodwin heralded a collapse and, despite Johnson finishing unbeaten on 132, they were well short of our 303. People had begun to notice how our batting was firing and suggesting that, where Pakistan and South Africa had started the competition emphatically, we were building towards our peak at the right time, building our momentum. We knew that if we could beat South Africa we would go all the way.

We have always felt confident against the South Africans and were looking forward to the encounter. We've had the wood on them for some time now and, more important, they know it too, especially in the really big games. I would always back us to beat them in a tight situation simply because we have won from so many close positions in the past. They are a good one-day side and arguably the best fielding unit in the world. They are organised and well-drilled. But they do not have the variety of ourselves or Pakistan. While there is nothing wrong with their bowlers individually, they are pretty much the same pace which means that once a batsman gets in he is not forever having to size up another line of attack. They can be a bit predictable. Nicky Boje could be the answer, he looks good and with his batting this might be what they need.

The game at Headingley was a beauty and will go down as one of Steve Waugh's finest hours for Australia, if best remembered for Herschelle Gibbs' dropped catch when Stephen was on his way to a hundred. There was all sorts of talk going round about what Stephen remarked at this point. Steve said, 'You've just cost yourself the game.'

Whatever he does for the rest of his career − including defending himself against match-fixing allegations − Gibbs will be forever synonymous with that miss. As far as I am concerned, it was an accident waiting to happen. I said as much at our team meeting the night before the game!

We had gone through our usual business, run through the game plan and assessed the strengths and weaknesses of the opposition when Geoff Marsh asked for any final comments. I put my hand up and said that if Gibbs took a catch we should stand our ground and make the umpire give a decision because I did not think he held the ball long enough before beginning his celebrations. He had taken a catch quite recently which I considered to be debatable. The observation received short shrift from the squad. The meeting broke up amid laughter and a few shouts of 'Shut up, Warnie.' Okay, maybe it was a bit silly but I thought it was worth raising. It is uncanny how things happen. If the next day he had waited for just another second before attempting to throw the ball in the air instead of being cocky and smart-arsey about it, then we might have been on the next plane home. Hansie Cronje tried to take some of the pressure off Gibbs at the post-match press conference by saying that the ball hit a tender spot on his hands. But he knew – like we knew – that the mistake stemmed from downright cockiness.

Along with his 200 against West Indies in Jamaica in 1994–95 I think Stephen's 120 not out at Headingley was his best innings for Australia. He has certainly never played better in the limited overs game. Before the contest, it was rumoured later, he was possibly going to be dropped as captain and player for the one-dayers if we went out of the World Cup. True to character, he just picked up his bat and steered us into the semi-final. What an innings – and no one at the time realised that he was playing for his career.

Now that Gibbs had been able to reflect on the game he will realise how close he was to becoming a hero himself. He had top-scored in South Africa's innings with 101 and helped them to a defendable score of 271 for 7. Earlier in the tournament, I think that would probably have been too many for us. Having gone for a few myself in the previous matches, I was pleased to be able to stem the flow of runs midway through the innings as well as take a couple of wickets. I needed to get back on track with my bowling and to bowl to Daryll Cullinan gave me the confidence again. I got Cullinan and then Cronje first ball. Lance Klusener got away from us right at the end. It was a mystery that such a phenomenal hitter who was in the best batting form of his life did not come in higher than number six.

Steve Waugh arrived at the wicket at 3 for 48. He began carefully, but we knew that Jacques Kallis would be unable to bowl because of an abdominal strain and had decided in advance to target their fifth bowler. The tactic proved sound as Cronje and Nicky Boje cost 79 between them in 10 overs. Whereas we could have called on the likes of Damien Martyn or Mark Waugh for variety, South Africa did not have the same full hand of options and from the players' balcony it was interesting to see Cronje become increasingly animated as the runs began to flow. Stephen and Hansie always had little digs at each other and were always at each other's throats. Stephen had reached 56 when he was reprieved by Gibbs and proceeded to bat more and more aggressively. Ricky Ponting and Bevan offered good support to the point where we needed exactly a run per ball from the last 3 overs.

I can't think of many more dependable players in a situation like this than Steve Waugh. Even when only 3 runs came from Shaun Pollock's next over, we all felt confident - as well as somewhat anxious. Needing 8 to win from the last six balls, Moody hit 2 from the first and then squirted a 4 to the backward point boundary. You could see the energy drain from the South Africans, the disappointment apparent even though they were assured of being in the semi-finals. We eventually came through with two balls to spare amid scenes of pandemonium on the balcony and back in the dressing room. I remember our coach, Geoff Marsh, sounded like a commentator on the ball – 'Go on, get in there, go, go, go' – while riding his chair like a jockey and calling for the whip on his leg.

Although South Africa were many people's favourites, we were delighted to be able to play them again in the semi-final. We believed that the psychological hold established over a number of years would grip tighter than ever when we met again at Edgbaston. We also looked upon this game as our final.

We thought that Pakistan would beat New Zealand in the other game, but that our team was full steam ahead and there was no stopping us. We had great momentum. Having played in one memorable game against South Africa, however, we could not have imagined we were about to participate in arguably the greatest one-day match maybe of all time.

People can easily recall the final thrilling climax, when the last pair of Lance Klusener and Allan Donald were practically stranded at the same end needing only 1 run to win with three balls remaining. They forget the way that fortunes ebbed and flowed through the preceding 99.3 overs.

I have watched the game in its entirety twice since at home and it still has me captivated, even knowing the way the plot unfolds. There are so many great pieces of fielding or smart running between the wickets that went unrecognised at the time. The lesson for young players is to treat every ball as if it is the most important of the match.

Once again, we did not get off to the best of starts. Steve Waugh and Bevan consolidated the innings by adding 90 for the fifth wicket, but by the time I walked out we were 6 for 158 and looking as though we might fall short of our original target of around 230 as a potentially winning score. Bevan is the best at summing up the situation and is one of the best one-day batsman in the world, he paces his innings perfectly, so I tried to offer him support for as long as I could and knew that if the remaining batsmen could chip in with a few clean hits at the end, and we fielded well, we could retrieve the situation. I managed to score 18 in a stand of 49 and, although the last 4 wickets fell in quick succession, we were back in with a chance.

Herschelle Gibbs, batting like a man on a mission to redeem his soul, and Gary Kirsten caught us slow out of the blocks with a stand of 48. Our opening bowlers had done a great job all tournament and I was thinking before the game that this was the time to step up to the plate. The captain has written in his diary of the competition that he threw the ball to me in desperation. At this stage the possibility of containing South Africa seemed remote in the extreme and we needed wickets. It was strange to think that my argument about being the man to perform when it mattered had cut no ice in the West Indies two months earlier, but I had an opportunity now. I relished the challenge and decided to bowl the most lavish leg-break in my armoury to Gibbs. It seemed to follow a similar trajectory to the Gatting ball six years earlier, dipping in to his legs in the flight, biting off the pitch and fizzing past his bat to take off stump. This gave me great confidence. I knew I was back to my best, the extra time healing and strengthening my shoulder during the World Cup had worked and it enabled me to rip my leg-break again.

That single delivery restored all of the confidence that was slipping away in the previous weeks. Being dropped in the Caribbean, conceding runs against India and Zimbabwe and being away from the new baby boy had all affected my approach. Whenever I really tried to rip the leggie I was apprehensive, but after that ball the situation of the match changed and away we went. I was so pumped up I had to take deep breaths to concentrate. I had been turning the ball, true, but relying on the batsmen to think that the big one might be on its way, releasing it only every now and then. The chips seemed to be down and I thought to myself that this would be it, this could be the end of my career or the last game if we lost. 'Come on, give it your best shot,' I said to myself. Buoyed by taking the wicket of Gibbs with one of my best, I pumped myself up to the absolute limit.

In my next over I spun one past Kirsten's attempt to heave me through midwicket and then, in my third, Cronje gave a catch to Mark Waugh at slip. I had no doubt that he hit the ball, but replays suggested it went to Mark via his foot or bat. Cronje was a bit unlucky, maybe. Although these decisions tend to even themselves out down the years it was a bad moment for their captain to suffer. By this time the game had moved in our favour and Cullinan, never comfortable against us, contributed to his own downfall with a run out. Clearly, though, South Africa had learnt from Headingley. When Steve Waugh and Bevan had rescued our innings four days earlier, this time Kallis and the ever-reliable Jonty Rhodes repaired the damage for them. The atmosphere in the middle was so tense, I was bowling as well as I could and expecting to get a wicket with every ball. That spell of 8 overs for 12 runs with 3 wickets is one of my most important and best in any format of cricket for Australia.

Kallis was still there when I returned in the forty-third over. I settled straight back into the groove, but time was running out for South Africa and they needed to raise the tempo. They again held back Klusener on the demise of Rhodes to leave so much pressure on Shaun Pollock, the new number seven. Pollock began nervously before hitting me for a 6 and a 4 in my last over.

In a situation like this it is important to keep a clear mind and be in control of your emotions. Experience counts for so much at moments like this. With Kallis now on strike I stayed a little longer at the end of my mark just to make sure I was fully composed. Those extra seconds proved time well spent. Kallis could not score off the next ball and the next ball I slowed a little and he hit it to Steve Waugh at cover. My last ball was to Klusener and he blocked it and I was hoping that my 4 for 29 was going to be good enough to get us over the line.

Klusener's introduction could be delayed no longer. But was

it too late? They needed 39 when Klusener replaced Pollock, bowled by Damien Fleming.

If we could keep him away from the strike or, better still, send him back to the pavilion, we would surely be in the final. Easier said than done. Klusener's brute strength, a feature of the competition, soon re-asserted itself, the ball disappearing to the advertising boards like a tracer bullet. Then, in the penultimate over, Paul Reiffel misjudged a hard on drive off a full toss against Glenn McGrath which became a 6 instead. Worse still, Klusener took a single from the last ball to keep strike with 9 wanted to win.

I didn't envy Damien Fleming having to bowl the final over, especially to the undisputed player of the tournament. There was nothing at all wrong with the next two balls, but Klusener still somehow bludgeoned them to the boundary. The famous Australian self-belief was seeping away. Klusener took a huge swing at the next ball, only for it to dribble towards Boof Lehmann. Perhaps through nerves, or possibly because the call from Klusener was drowned out by the noise from the crowd from anxiety to beat us, Donald kept running. A direct hit by Darren Lehmann would have sealed their fate. Agonisingly, his shy at the stumps missed by millimetres. I thought that was our chance.

On any other day, Klusener would have treated each of the last three balls on merit, either clouted one of them over the infield or waited for a clear single. It's amazing what pressure can do. He could always have taken a risk with the final ball if need be, but sometimes in these situations clear thinking isn't high on the agenda, the thinking is on the outcome – win, win. But this was not just any situation. It is hard to convey the tension out in the middle. I think that Klusener's approach was dictated by the near miss the ball before. His head must have been spinning, so that when he miscued for a second time he decided to keep running anyway. Donald, heeding the recent lesson, saw no chance of a run and headed back to the non-striker's end. By the time Mark Waugh flipped the ball to Fleming both batsmen were at the same end. With Donald flapping desperately, Fleming rolled the ball to the other end for Adam Gilchrist to break the stumps. Luckily we had been tenpin bowling that week and learnt from it.

As we ran off, Steve Waugh turned to me, screaming, 'Are we in? Are we in?'

'We're in, mate, you beauty,' I shouted back.

Our captain was so overwhelmed and pumped with what had just happened it shows he's human. The changing rooms at Edgbaston are adjacent and I dare not imagine what it must have been like for the South Africans, silently playing over that last ball in their minds while they could hear our celebrations begin next door. It must have been even worse than the mood in the Australia shed after we lost the final in Lahore three years earlier. Stephen and I had to go and collect our prizes and we saw Hansie Cronje. We said, 'Bad luck,' but Cronje just couldn't reply. It was quite chilling to see a man so shell-shocked that he kept opening his mouth without words coming out. After seeing Hansie like that, and seeing how much it meant to him, I was shocked to learn what happened later.

The mood afterwards was ecstatic, but thoroughly pro-fessional. Our attitude was that, having come so far in the last fortnight, we would not do anything to jeopardise our prospects of going all the way. There was also a feeling now after what had happened that this time, unlike 1996, was to be our World Cup. From then until the final we stuck to light training and kept things relaxed. We were so confident I could not imagine losing. Personally, I felt more at ease than at any stage of the tour previously. I felt very confident in my bowling.

Then, another bombshell landed to knock me backwards again.

David Hookes had been on the radio back home to say that a story was about to break relating to Australia and the match-fixing issue. He claimed that there was more to come in relation to me. As has happened so many times, nothing more came out about me because there was nothing to come out. But this was the straw that broke the camel's back. I had told the ACB everything I knew. There was nothing more to come out as far as I was concerned and to suggest otherwise struck me as being ill-informed speculation. I was sick and tired of constant rumour and innuendo about everything in my life, of people alluding to something without offering evidence. To hear a former player, who knows how it feels to be the subject of false gossip, saying things like this made me feel even worse.

With our hotel in London located right next to Hyde Park, we went on a team walk. Steve Waugh and I were talking and I opened up to him. So much for a rift between us – here I was about to confide my deepest, inner thoughts. I told him I was finally sick and tired of the innuendo and rumours and then having to prove myself innocent. All I ever wanted to do was play the game, but other people were not prepared to let me get on with it. I felt that I was having to justify myself all the time. I acknowledged that I brought some of the problems on myself, but that did not ease my frustrations. I told Steve that enough was enough. Plain and simple. In a nutshell, I was ready to quit. My tone had clearly taken him by surprise. But he is a good listener. He let me say my piece, get it off my chest and then warned me not to make a decision rashly. His advice was to go home after the tournament and think about the future in calmer circumstances. I returned to the hotel no happier with Hookes, but pleased somebody else really knew how I felt. Steve's response was very sensible. He did not attempt to make a decision for me, he was there for me, which meant a lot, so was the coach, Geoff Marsh.

Some people have suggested the final was an anti-climax. And in truth, while we were supremely confident after the two games against South Africa, we did not imagine the ultimate victory would come so easily. We dominated from the start and never loosened our grip on a side who seemed overawed by the whole occasion. Wasim Akram, the Pakistan captain, said afterwards that he was proud of his side for getting to Lord's. I wonder if some of them genuinely believed they had the ability to end our winning streak.

There was some talk afterwards, perhaps because our 8-wicket win was so emphatic, that they must have thrown the game. I just do not believe that. Whatever they had been up to in the past, I cannot imagine any player would deliberately give less than his best in any game, let alone a World Cup final. Victory might have meant some of the previous misdemeanours could be swept under the carpet. That would have been entirely wrong, of course, but who knows what would have happened? Those who have never been to the sub-continent can hardly begin to imagine the sheer passion for the game out there and a World Cup success would have made heroes of the entire team overnight. The rewards, in the long run, would have been far greater than money. Then there is the simple matter of pride. What price can you put on a World Cup winner's medal? The plain fact is that the better side won on the day, and the best side in the tournament triumphed overall, but I think that the best two sides played in the final. So the ECB must take a lot of credit for running a great competition.

Unlike the semi-final, this game passed in a flash. There was nothing wrong with the pitch whatsoever, but once Mark Waugh held a brilliant catch in the slips to remove Wajahatullah Wasti, there was just no stopping us. I think that catch set the tone for the rest of the day. When I came on in the twenty-second over it was a case of building on the foundations laid by the pace attack. Fortunately, almost everything went right. And the one that bowled Ijaz Ahmed was up there with the best, pitching just outside leg stump and hitting off. Ijaz can be a gritty customer and I think because the delivery turned so much the rest of their batsmen thought they needed to score quickly before they copped a similar one. At 4 for 77 we could afford the odd boundary in exchange for wickets.

It didn't take long for Moin Khan and Shahid Afridi to follow. When Wasim Akram holed out it meant the end was not far away for Pakistan. Rather than plod towards the target of 133, Mark Waugh and Adam Gilchrist went berserk. I was especially pleased for Gilchrist, who had not shown the crowds just what a destructive player he can be in the World Cup. We won eventually with almost 30 full overs to spare; the game had spanned less than five hours.

After the presentations and the first wave of celebrations the captain and I went over to a marquee at the Nursery End of the ground for the formal press conference. The captain and man of the match do this after every game. It was only a matter of time before somebody asked if I was still thinking of retiring. The honest answer was, yes, I had still not decided whether I wanted to continue as an international cricketer. At this stage, to my knowledge, only the two of us knew about our conversation a couple of days earlier. I wasn't out to make a public threat, from a position of strength, saying to the selectors, 'Pick me or I'm off', contrary to what certain media people thought. Playing one-day international cricket is an honour and a privilege, but, as I have written previously, I was not sure whether I really wanted to continue my career if I was playing one form of the game. I had to decide whether deep down I'd had enough or whether I was going to fight for my spot. These were the questions I was asking myself, so when I was asked the questions by the press I answered honestly. With a tour to Sri Lanka coming up I had to decide quickly. There was also the question of county cricket in England, a big ambition of mine. Above all else, though, was the commitment to my wife and family, especially with the new addition to the household.

For this frankness I was nailed for apparently taking the gloss off the World Cup success. Would people have preferred me to hold something back, or even lied? At that time I genuinely didn't know where my future lay. Imagine the flak in my direction if I had said there were no plans to retire and then decided to pack it in a couple of months down the line. Once again, it was a situation where I just couldn't win. What I will say is that none of the reports did take anything away from winning the competition, not as far as the players and management were concerned. As usual, it was just a few print journalists trying to sell papers or dig the knife in.

As much as the final itself I will never forget the bonding afterwards. Three or four hours after the game, when everybody else had left the ground, we strode out to the middle for a special rendition of 'Underneath the Southern Cross I Stand' with Ricky Ponting leading the singing sitting on Tom Moody's shoulders. We were all pretty drunk by this stage and Adam Gilchrist and I tried to relive the dismissals by placing beer cans on the actual wicket where the balls had pitched. It was an unreal situation to be there, mates together on the most famous square in the world, a place breathing cricket history, with absolute quiet all around us. For those few minutes it felt like we really owned the place. I had been through some tough times, the hardest of my career, and to get through them the way I did to bowl the way I did in those two finals I felt proud. To contribute with man of the match awards in the two biggest games made me feel as tall as the combined height of Ponting and Moody.

Back in the privacy of our hotel we stayed up for most of the night singing, laughing and raising a few glasses. Some of the guys were still in their yellow tops because they just didn't want to change. Unfortunately, we had an early start next morning. I reckoned on about one or two hours sleep before the alarm went off. We all had to go down to the lobby to deliver our passports. I slapped on my favourite pair of silver Nike tracksuit pants which I usually wear around in my room and my white shirt, the only one I could find. Little did I realise the photographers would be out in force in the hotel foyer and the room where we had to deliver our passports. Of all the cures for a hangover I can reveal that the flashing lights of a hundred cameras rank among the least effective.

And there was still a serious matter to address. Where would my career go from here? And what was the Man Upstairs trying to tell me? I don't pretend to be a great follower of religion, but I realised there was a message there and couldn't for the life of me work it out. I needed time. Was he saying after what you've done for cricket and what you've achieved in the game, this is the right time to bow out, when I was at the top? Or was he showing that I could still cut it among the best and should go on playing? A long flight home with a throbbing head was not the time to be searching for the answer. Although I did think about it, I slept most of the way.

After the World Cup I told Allan Border I was going to retire and he told me that you are a long time retired and to think about it a bit more. We had the build-up of the parades, and he told me to see how I went. Well, the parades were unbelievable and I remember sitting there with my captain, Stephen, just thinking wow, this is amazing. They made me realise what I would be missing, the dressing room humour and sharing all the great times with my team mates. I was ready to fight if I had to. I knew in my heart that if I was 100 per cent fit I was the best spinner in Australia. If not 100 per cent fit, then I would come back to the field, so I was ready.

The rest is history. I got 5 for 52 in the First Test against Sri Lanka and all the fuss was squashed – at least until the next injury or bad game. At the time I thought, I'm back, let's go.

12

HAMPSHIRE

THE CHANCE TO PLAY county cricket in England held a great attraction long before I finally joined Hampshire in 2000. I would like to thank them for giving me the opportunity. As far back as 1989 I spent the summer in Bristol with Imperial and in 1991 I returned to play for Accrington in the Lancashire League. I love England and could easily live there. I have many good friends from those two years. In different circumstances and with better luck I might have joined a county club sooner.

During the 1993 Ashes tour I received some very good offers to play county cricket the following season, the best being from Northamptonshire. To put those deals in perspective, they were potentially more lucrative than the one I finally accepted with Hampshire. However, the ACB stressed that they did not want me to spend six months playing in England. They thought it would be too much and wanted me to be 100 per cent fit to play for Australia and with the international itinerary jam-packed for the next two seasons I also decided I wanted to stay fresh. I had only played for Australia for a few seasons so I was trying to do my best at that level and establish myself. Although there was no actual order from the ACB, I felt I had no option but to reject the counties.

Interest next arose in 1998, as is usually the case for any

player from any country after an England tour. This time Sussex were keen for me to join – I'd had a meeting with Tony Pigott, their chief executive, while we were there for the 1997 Ashes. Ironically, given my eventual destination, we met at Ocean Village, Southampton. Once again I was very tempted, but my shoulder was becoming a problem and in the end surgery was calling. The more I thought about it, the more 2000 seemed to be a feasible option, and a few feelers went out during the World Cup campaign. Once again there were some interested parties.

I spoke informally to Alec Stewart of Surrey who promised to pass on my interest to the club's committee. Tom Moody had recommended them to me, but by that stage they had already decided to stick with Saqlain Mushtaq. A similar situation occurred at Lancashire. They wanted a spin bowler and I was attracted by the prospect of the Old Trafford pitch. I had a very positive meeting with Jack Simmons, the chairman, and Jim Cumbes, the chief executive, when we played West Indies there during the World Cup. Indeed, as the coach pulled out of the ground, I felt sure I would be returning the following year. But they also decided to stick with who they had, Muttiah Muralitharan – and why not? As events transpired, Sri Lanka's commitments meant that Muralitharan became unavailable and they ended up signing Sourav Ganguly, a very different type of player and character. I don't think he was anywhere near as popular as Muralitharan.

Brian Ford, the Hampshire chairman, has said that negotiations began at Buckingham Palace when the World Cup squads and officials were invited to meet the Queen. I do recall an informal chat. It's amazing sometimes how things work out. Be that as it may, Hampshire soon made their interest clear through Robin Smith and the more I looked into the county, the more I thought that something could work. Smith, the captain, had always impressed me as a good bloke and a great player with considerable integrity.

He told me that Hampshire were a small county side with plenty of ambition who were getting into winning positions and making lots of runs but could not quite deliver that killer blow. They claimed the most batting points in 1999 so were looking for a bowler who would create some interest around the beautiful Southampton ground. Hampshire were due to move to a new ground on the outskirts of the city the following season, so 2000 was going to be a massive campaign. By now, I was becoming increasingly convinced. A chat with Ian Botham, a very good friend, effectively sealed the decision in my mind and it then simply became a question of my people thrashing out a deal with the club.

Rain lashed down when I arrived at the Northlands Road ground directly from Australia's short one-day series in South Africa in April. Little did anybody realise just how appropriate that was, given the terrible weather that stayed with us for much of the season. The first whiff of scandal over Hansie Cronje had broken a week or so before and, inevitably, I was asked for my opinions at the first press conference. By this stage the world and his mother were throwing in their two bob's worth about what should happen to Hansie. I wanted to wait to hear all the evidence first before forming an opinion.

Other than outlining my ambition to record a first-class hundred and win some silverware, my targets were not too high publicly, but inside they were huge. It soon became clear that the club itself was aiming high, and rightly so. After the batting success of the previous season in theory the recruitment of Alan Mullally and myself would convert a side on the fringes to potential champions in both four-day and one-day cricket. Such hopes, of course, were unfulfilled. With hindsight those expectations may have been a bit high. We were relegated from the first division of the PPP Championship and failed to earn promotion in the 45-over National League. The highlight of the season was reaching the semi-final of the NatWest Trophy and the Benson and Hedges Cup quarter-finals.

So what went wrong? Well, basically we just did not play well enough when it mattered. It really was as simple as that. There is nothing profound in this statement, but I believe that cricket is a game best kept simple. Long post-mortems after defeats usually go round in circles without any purpose, and I genuinely think we were a better side than our results suggested. I think that Jimmy Cook, the new coach, is very impressive and definitely on the right track. He would have learnt a lot about each player after his first year and be the better for the experience. We were in positions to win at least eight of the sixteen four-day games, but in fact we secured victory in only three. For example, we lost by 2 runs to Surrey, the eventual champions, when Dimitri Mascarenhas, our last man, was out to a pull shot that would have soared to the boundary if he'd connected as well as he had on more than one occasion previously. In another game, the Kent tenth-wicket pair of Paul Nixon and David Masters put on 125 and we lost by 15 runs. You cannot legislate for a tail wagging like that. The list goes on. No doubt other teams who didn't enjoy a good year would have similar stories.

The fixture list did us no favours. Such was the imbalance that, after playing Somerset at home in the first game, we had to play four of the next five away – against the sides who were to finish in the top four places. In between, it looked as though we might beat Lancashire before rain fell incessantly for two days. The end result of all this was that with the season near the halfway point we were at or near the bottom. We wanted to be about mid-table with a big run home against the bottom sides with the sun shining and wickets turning. But it wasn't to be. After a start like that it was hard to fight back, although our spirits were still quite high and lifted further when we managed to bowl out Durham for 83 and 93 to win by an innings and 164 runs at Basingstoke. Maybe if that match had taken place earlier in the season, who knows what might have happened.

Our exits from the two knockout competitions were particularly disappointing. The Benson and Hedges quarter-final against Glamorgan was played on one of the worst pitches I have seen. That is not an excuse because the opposition shared the same view. The previous winter Glamorgan had allowed a marquee to be erected on the square to accommodate corporate hospitality for the Rugby Union World Cup. Consequently, all of the grass had been killed off. I was not the only one to be bowled by a ball that actually shot underneath the bat from a normal length. Then, when we played Warwickshire in the NatWest semi-final, I was unfortunately back in Melbourne for the return one-day series against South Africa, while Allan Donald, Warwickshire's overseas player, was playing for his county, Warwickshire. To have reached a one-day final at Lord's would have been great for the members and for Robin Smith because they deserved it for sticking by us through a difficult campaign, but we were beaten by a better side on the day. I was proud that we had a good crack at chasing a difficult target.

Statistically, my own season was pretty successful with 70 wickets in the Championship, the most in Division One, at an average of 23.14. Only Glenn McGrath with Worcestershire took the honours overall and it was interesting to see that Phil Tufnell delivered the most overs. Because our batting proved to be so frail at times, in contrast to the previous season, I rarely enjoyed the luxury of being able to bowl to attacking fields with big targets on the board and the opposition chasing a total with plenty of fielders under their noses. Invariably we would be behind on first-innings, and often the opposition did not need to bat twice.

As an overseas player you want to be the leading run-scorer or wicket-taker as well as make a good impression by contributing off the field. I wonder whether I did let people down, because I am sure they expected me to win more games for the county. So did I, but having thought about this at some length, I am not sure what more I could have done. The weather was far worse than I experienced on my previous trips to England. The wickets did not really help spinners until the last third of the season. I felt that it was up to me to get us back on track in the games and at times I probably tried too hard. On other occasions I was unlucky and didn't always bowl as well as I would have liked, having set myself high standards.

The man I felt most sorry for was Robin Smith. He is one of the nicest guys I have ever met in cricket circles and doesn't have a single enemy on the circuit. He wears his heart on his sleeve for Hampshire and unfortunately he had a bad year with the bat. Being captain was a great honour for him and he desperately wanted Hampshire to have a successful season. Those who know him as a powerful batsman, capable of murdering the bowlers, will be surprised to discover that he takes everything to heart and it upset him deeply when results started to go against us. I don't think that anybody on the outside could appreciate how badly he took being relegated. I felt I let him down personally and I hope I have the opportunity to pay him back – just give me a chance, Judgie!

Robin could make a very good captain, because he has a lot of experience in the game at all levels and is very perceptive of other people. He has the respect of the team and his communication skills are outstanding. He said to me that he might be better off simply as a player. I don't agree. I guess as a player he would still worry about his own game – even if he was rattling off hundreds in succession – but not about everybody else's too. I have no doubt that in a good season his captaincy would flourish, but in 2000 everything weighed heavily on his shoulders and it must have been a relief in some ways when the season finished. The expectation on Hampshire from the public, media and members was enormous. Smith's own expectations were also very high and his concern at the form of the side was visible. I worried about him a lot. After play on some days we would sit in the team bath and have a drink and a cigarette. He just wanted to get things off his chest and I thought he could do with the company. I couldn't leave him by himself. That is how much Hampshire cricket means to the Judge.

As for the hundred I desperately wanted, it did not materialise, and I only have myself to blame. I had reached 69 against Kent at Portsmouth and felt this was going to be the great day. Min Patel, the left-arm spinner, had put a ring of fielders around the boundary, so I simply needed to push the ball around. Sounds easy. Instead, like a fool, I saw this as a challenge and was bowled recklessly trying to clear the rope. Then, in the last game of the season, against Yorkshire, I again reached 69 before giving a dolly of a catch to mid on when I was seeing the ball well. That was a particularly frustrating match because the surface really helped spin, but in the second innings I bowled the worst I had all season. Maybe I will never get there, but I'll have some fun trying.

Then, to make matters worse, Hampshire were docked eight points by an ECB Pitches Panel after they deemed the wicket to be poor – even though Yorkshire won in the last over and the decision carried no bearing on where we, or they, finished. Given some of those produced at Headingley which had gone unpunished, I found this an extremely harsh judgement. I appreciate the need for pitches to be better prepared in England to help young players to learn the game properly, but one of the flaws in the system of having pitch inspectors was that they did not attend every game. This brought about inconsistency. As for the pitch at Southampton for the Yorkshire game – the last first-class match at Northlands Road after 115 years – it produced a very entertaining game of cricket. Smith couldn't believe the decision. Cricket is a game people describe as being a great leveller but sometimes it just seems purely unfair. As players what we most want is consistency. Deep down I believe that everything happens for a reason and that reason isn't always obvious.

It was interesting to see the ways in which English batsmen tried to play me. In the first third of the season I must have taken 20 or so wickets when they decided to sweep. Word must have gone round the circuit pretty quickly because that soon stopped. Not many of the home players really used their feet. Matthew Maynard, a very talented batsman from Glamorgan, got on top of me in a one-day match, but there wasn't too much aggression. On a few occasions people such as Paul Nixon from Kent chanced their arm. That day at Canterbury he was rewarded with a great hundred. On other occasions I am sure I profited because of my reputation. Sometimes batsmen play the man rather than the ball. In other words, they might treat a shortish delivery as a flipper when really it is a rank long hop that deserves to be planted over midwicket.

Those I thought coped best of all were Rahul Dravid, in a contest at Portsmouth that some spectators told me afterwards was the most captivating they had seen in county cricket, and Darren Lehmann. Boof and Mark Waugh are the two best players of spin in Australia. Overall, though, I have never known a season where so many chances were created but didn't find the hands, where balls have narrowly missed the edge of the bat or missed the top of the stumps by inches.

The standard of domestic cricket in England generally was

higher than I expected. This was partly because my previous experience of playing against the counties was for Australia when sides tended to rest their overseas player and the main bowlers. Having said that, I believe that certain players fall into a comfort zone where they are able to earn a good living from simply playing county cricket and are not prepared to push themselves that extra mile to put their names up for selection for England. Some are not brave enough to risk failing at the highest level but, equally, I think that the structure of the system is largely to blame for fostering those negative attitudes.

Because of Hampshire's poor start to the season, we were not sufficiently upbeat and intense during the middle of the campaign and the schedule does not allow opportunities to take stock and work on weaknesses. There is not time for proper practice. Ideally, there would be three clear days before a Championship game to be able to work on technique and really think properly about a detailed game plan. It is very difficult to try to rediscover form against a bowling attack which includes Darren Gough, Craig White and Matthew Hoggard on a pitch at Headingley offering lavish assistance to the seamers, but that is the nature of the English game. The practice sessions are in the middle under pressure.

In recent years a number of Australians have come to England and done extremely well. It reflects creditably on us all that counties know when they sign an Aussie they are getting somebody who will give everything to the club. Just as the West Indian fast bowlers were in the 1970s and 80s, Australian players now, in particular the batsmen, are seen as a safe bet. At Yorkshire they cannot believe that Darren Lehmann is not playing regular Test or one-day international cricket. Neither can I. The same is true with Essex and Stuart Law, and Jamie Cox at Somerset. But who would our selectors omit? The fact is that Australian cricket is extremely strong at the moment and, to a large degree, I think that is down to our system.

In England there are sixteen four-day games, sixteen matches in the 45-overs league and two knockout competitions – that is before matches against the touring sides and the Universities and your pre-season. Generally, there is cricket on five days of the week as a minimum, as well as a travel day for away games. Much more goes into playing cricket than the public sees and players inevitably become products of their environment. An English season is draining, mentally as well as physically. Concentrating all the time is very difficult and those who are not used to such a crammed schedule find it tough going. The hardest part for me was being motivated and pumped up for every game.

The ones who do know the system realise when to go full throttle and when, maybe, to hold back – in nets, warm-ups and benefit games for example. It means that sometimes a bowler, on a given day, could bowl much faster than usual if he is feeling a little fresher, but it is the schedule which does this. With more rest, he would be able to charge in on a flat wicket, instead of settling for defensive fields and negative bowling to conserve energy. Then the selectors would be able to find out how good some players really are. I think that central contracts for the leading English players were long overdue. It is no coincidence that Darren Gough and Andy Caddick proved so effective against the West Indies last summer when they were not rushing back to perform for their counties between Tests. It is difficult, because these players started their careers in county cricket, but everyone has to think of their country first. Where batsmen are concerned it is a little different. I believe that the sheer volume of cricket means they can keep on a roll or come out of a trough. In England, you rarely go longer than three days without a hit. Failure back home might be the last opportunity for a month.

The answer, to me, is quite simple – reduce the amount of cricket. This will also mean that players will have time to get over the niggles that inevitably occur during any season. I think the two-division system is a huge success because every game counts. You don't lose interest midway because it can have made the difference between winning the Championship or staying up at the other end of the table. Each county should aim to contract eighteen professional players as a first-team squad, with the 2nd XI made up of youngsters and trialists who are going all out to gain a contract. Areas such as Yorkshire are particularly strong, so to ensure those on the fringe do not miss out they could go into a national pool, or have a drafting system, to be picked up by another county. This might not suit the stronger counties, but it means more good players will get their chance.

What is important is that the best players outside the Test team play against each other frequently, and that there is hunger, passion and desire for places. Unfortunately, I do not for one minute expect this to happen immediately. I hope that it might over time. One problem in England is that the counties make the decisions and sometimes think they are more important than the national side. Back home, the states know that if Brett Lee or Steve Waugh is taking a rest there is a good reason for it – he needs one. It is not a case of trying to get an insurance claim or pulling wool over somebody's eyes. Sometimes a player like Glenn McGrath might want to keep playing to maintain his bowling rhythm, or a batsman might want to keep hitting the ball to stay in form. It's all about communication and being professional.

In Australia we have only six state teams, against eighteen English county sides. Just look at the first-choice New South Wales side: Michael Slater, Corey Richards, Mark Waugh, Steve Waugh, Michael Bevan, Shane Lee, Brad Haddin, Brett

Lee, Stuart MacGill, Nathan Bracken and Glenn McGrath. Or Western Australia: Murray Goodwin (Zim), Mike Hussey, Justin Langer, Damien Martyn, Tom Moody, Simon Katich, Adam Gilchrist, Jo Angel, Brendon Julian, Matt Nicholson and Brad Williams.

When any of these guys goes away to play for Australia there is intense competition to fill the places and try to cement a regular place. We are in a very lucky phase of Australian cricket where our pool of talent explains why we have become the best team in the world. However, if a player like Giles White, who impressed me a lot at Hampshire as a good, consistent batsman with a determined attitude, was to join the Australian system for a period of time I am sure he would make the next steps. The same goes for Will Kendall and Dimitri Mascarenhas who have genuine quality.

There has been criticism of over-indulgence on the social side in England, but without unwinding over a beer or soft drink there would not be much chance to unwind. The English season is the equivalent of three Australian programmes back-to-back in a month less. Maybe there are occasions when sides, even Hampshire, could have had more discipline off the field, me included. I don't mean treat players like schoolkids with curfews and drinking restrictions because we all have to live by our actions, and every person is different. I strongly believe that discipline away from the game – on issues such as punctuality and having shiny shoes for example – is reflected in aspects of play such as shot selection, match awareness and summing up the state of the game. It just means thinking of your team mates and having pride in yourself. But I can understand why the odd night might go on later than is ideal. I will admit there were times when I stayed out a bit later than I probably should have, but you need sometimes to relax and unwind. There are too few opportunities for that in England because of the schedule of day-in, day-out cricket and the travel that goes with it, so when the chance arises you take it with both hands.

The fitness side became a talking point with all the counties. I know that the Australian Cricket Board were very unhappy that some county physiotherapists did not travel to all the away games. The home physio would look after the visiting team as well as his own, but, with no disrespect at all, it is better to be treated by somebody who knows your history of injury and things like your flexibility etc. If we are talking about being professional on the field then that should be backed up off it. Fortunately, I did not suffer any more than the usual niggles with my shoulder, knee and thigh, but there were a couple of away games where I felt uncomfortable asking the opposition physio for help. At Leicester, I needed something for my leg and they were very good about it, but I still felt uneasy. It is hard to ask for treatment to keep you on the park from a guy who is employed by the opposition. I do not think it puts the physio himself in an easy position either.

In weighing up county cricket I think it is easy for anybody to say that this and that are wrong. What must happen is for those who run the game to identify the problems and correct them, to think of the bigger picture rather than the interests of their own county. The England team must be the priority. The authorities must also think of the players first and not the bottom line, because if the players are performing to the best of their ability then that bottom line will look after itself, the cricket will be entertaining. The groundsmen, I believe, should prepare the best possible pitch they can, not one simply to suit their own overseas player and team. I think the answer is to do away with the toss and let the visiting captain choose whether to bat or bowl.

These are just my own opinions. I have tried to be constructive. Despite the results, I enjoyed the experience immensely.

I would love to come back in 2002 after the Ashes series if the circumstances are right. The players and officials could not have done more to make me welcome and the members let me enjoy my privacy.

It was hard work, but I am pleased to say that, looking back, I enjoyed the six months and made a lot of fabulous new friends, which is what my life is all about. Indeed, at this stage it would be hard to play for somebody else, having made so many good friends at Hampshire. If I could not return there then I might have played my last season of county cricket. Trying to weigh that loyalty against the need to make a living where and when I can would be a difficult balancing act if I had to make that decision.

In 2000 my wife Simone and the children came straight from South Africa in April and spent the whole summer in England. It was very hard for all of us and looking back, we made the wrong decision, which was compounded by the bad weather and some events off the field.

It was in this period that I became involved in an incident that attracted a lot of publicity – and which eventually cost me the vice-captaincy of Australia. It came about when some of the players were in a nightclub in the middle of Leicester following a county match. A girl approached a group of us making herself available, particularly to me. She bent over and asked me to autograph her back, which I refused. Then she tried to lift up my shirt and said that she would sign my body instead. I told her that was out of order, not going to happen and thought nothing more about it.

Situations like this happen from time to time and the thing I have learnt from experience is to deal with them, firmly but politely and without making a scene. This time, however, I made a mistake. Perhaps drink got the better of me, because with hindsight the sensible move would have been to up and leave straight away. Instead, the girl kept hanging around and, as we were on our way out, she said that she was a very good talker on the phone.

It was over a week later when I phoned for the first time. What developed next was explicit talk between two consenting adults. She rang back a few days later and the same thing happened. I am not claiming any moral high ground, merely stating facts. People can work out for themselves how private conversations and messages came to be repeated in a newspaper.

We were in the final day of our Championship game against Lancashire at Liverpool when the *Daily Mirror* reported the 'news' on its front page, with a further double-page spread inside. I should have spotted the signs long before – on that night in the club, to be honest – but it did not register that the newspapers would become involved until I was asked for a reaction – thinly disguised as an invitation to give my side of the story – the day before publication. Even at that stage I did not realise it would be displayed so conspicuously, detailing phone calls and portraying the girl as the poor innocent party in the whole business.

Once the story had come out it should have been left as a personal matter between my wife Simone and me. I telephoned Simone as soon as I saw the paper to let her know what had happened and we had a good chat when I returned. Needless to say, she was disappointed and upset. She was entitled to be. If it had been the other way round I would have asked the same questions, too. I apologised to Simone and she accepted my apologies. She has known me long enough to realise that what appears in the papers isn't the complete story.

For the family this was a major issue, something we needed to confront immediately and tackle head on. I came straight out and apologised. It was very unpleasant, but it was better to get everything out in the open rather than let it simmer and then bring up the issues six months down the line.

I told Simone that I could understand if she wanted a break from England and to go back to Melbourne. Her view was that we said we would stay for the whole summer in Southampton and that she would stick to that commitment. I admired her attitude and felt very proud of the dignified way she handled the situation, especially as she was thousands of miles away from her family and friends. It would have been easy for her to fly off the handle, but she listened to my side of the story before making any judgement. It took time for the marriage to get back to where it was before, but we eventually succeeded through talking and love. Indeed, when we put our family home on the market last year and I was tipped off that a newspaper was about to report that it was because we were getting a divorce she wanted to ring the journalist concerned straight away to correct him.

At the time she could easily have gone home and it would have been very hard for me to be without my family. As it was, we did not have a great deal of time with each other – and every relationship needs quality time together. It would have been great to see more of Hampshire and do a few special things with her and to get to know the other cricket families a bit better. Because it seemed to rain every other day she was often inside with the kids watching videos. It can be difficult abroad to find a baby-sitter with whom the kids are comfortable and whom you can trust. Naturally, they want the security of having mummy around when daddy is away all day from 6 am to 7 pm.

One way or another it proved to be a tough time for Simone. She was thinking of returning to Australia when I went back in August for the games against South Africa, but opted to stick it out. I feel very proud of her for that. She went to Spain a couple of times to at least remind herself of what the sun looked like, and then her mother and father came over for ten days or so. Alan Mullally's wife, Chelsea, was sensational the whole time and both have become really good friends, along with Rod Bransgrove, who succeeded Ford as the Hampshire chairman soon after I returned, and his wife, Mandy, to single out a few.

Simone understands that cricket is my livelihood. Sometimes it is very hard being a sportsman's wife because of all the time spent apart. As well as playing, I had commitments with Nike, the postal service in Australia launched a Shane Warne stamp, I did a few television programmes, a column and a commercial for *The Times*, as well as radio work for *Talk Sport*. I also tried to play in benefit matches or attend functions for Adie Aymes, our wicket-keeper, who was fantastic the whole season, whenever I could. The schedule was so tight that I was never able to meet Alan Brazil, an ex-footballer who presented our *Talk Sport* show. Generally, when there was the chance to have a day off I really tried to keep away from cricket and spend it with the kids. The only real time Simone and I had to ourselves was between 9.30 and 11.30 at night.

I hope this does not sound like a bitter man having a cheap whinge. I owe Hampshire an awful lot and can honestly say that when I left in the middle of September, the day after the end of the season, I took back with me some great memories and sat on the plane with a smile on my face. I would love another opportunity at Hampshire. I learnt a lot about the place and I thoroughly enjoyed it. The second time around we would all do a lot better.

13

REWRITING THE
RECORD BOOKS

THE FACT that I was watching from a TV commentary box instead of bowling or fielding at first slip didn't reduce my sense of pride when Australia completed the innings defeat of West Indies at Perth to set a new world record of twelve successive Test wins. I had played in the first ten of those as vice-captain and would have joined the Waugh boys, Glenn McGrath, Michael Slater and the rest of the boys but for the broken finger that ruled me out of the series. Having been involved in most of the team's greatest moments in the previous decade, I could imagine the feeling of sheer elation. Mark Taylor and I joined them for a couple of beers in the dressing room and then let them celebrate.

After all, I had become quite used to breaking open the champagne the previous summer. From the middle of October in 1999 through to early April the following year we played nine Test matches and won all of them. On a personal level, too, it was a memorable season because I overtook Dennis Lillee's Australian record of 355 Test wickets – not a bad follow up to the World Cup success. I had not thought of that landmark when I was young or started playing. It was beyond my wildest dreams. So when I achieved that milestone I felt very, very proud.

As the wins began to accumulate people started to ask for the secret of our success. There is no real secret about it. What we have is basically a group of talented, highly-motivated players with a strong team ethic and excellent back-up. We have always been confident and held each other in great respect, but that grew even stronger as victory followed victory. When Justin Langer and Adam Gilchrist, in only his second Test, led us from 5 for 126 to within sight of a massive target of 369 against Pakistan at Hobart in November 1999, we knew then that we were capable of winning from any situation. I think it was a real turning point in this Australian team.

Once the momentum starts to build it becomes easier for a new player to slot in. Damien Martyn, one of my best buddies at the Academy all those years ago and still now, would have played fifty Tests now for any other country and only Andy Flower from Zimbabwe had a better batting average in the year 2000, but the fact is we have incredible depth at the moment in all departments and we need to make the most of it.

Steve Waugh, as captain, has ensured we don't become complacent. It would be easy to take things for granted, but he remembers the taste of failure from his early days in the Australia team when it was hard to see where the next victory might come from. It left a bitter taste and I think the days when we perhaps took our foot off the pedal at the end of a series when it was already in the bag are in the dim and distant past.

The competitive spirit is visible even in the nets. Our sessions can become almost as competitive as some of the games themselves. Some first-class games in Australia are harder than most Test matches. The importance of practising hard and having a game plan and mentality was drilled into me very early by Allan Border. These days I don't bowl too much in the nets because I want to preserve my shoulder and fingers for where it matters most, in the middle, but when I do roll my arm over it isn't to give the batsmen an easy ride. Every fielding routine, too, has purpose, and we all want to improve.

So much of team spirit comes with success. A winning side tends to be happy, but there are some ideas we have adopted to improve bonding away from the game. The most interesting is probably the poetry-writing introduced by Dave Misson, our ex-fitness trainer. Some ex-players might think this is over the top, but times have changed and it was funny watching the boys. Michael Slater was as nervous as I've ever seen anyone – he was physically shaking. The idea is that we take it in turns to compose a few lines of verse and the author then reads out his effort after the warm-up, before we hit the field proper. Some of them are fair efforts and I have known guys stay in their rooms at night to give the exercise proper care and attention. There is also a task where we have to speak to the rest of the team on three different topics: the history of Australia, the history of Australian cricket and a subject of our choice (I chose blackjack and roulette with tips on how to win – a few of the guys either didn't listen or didn't read my paper closely enough).

The serious point behind this is to heighten our appreciation of what it means to play for Australia, to understand the sacrifices that have been made for us to enjoy the present. Steve Waugh is particularly interested in the history of Australian cricket, as I am, and even put in a bid for Victor Trumper's cap when it recently came up at auction. In 1999–2000 he arranged for Bill Brown, a member of the 1948 Invincibles, to present Gilchrist with his cap. Later in the season, Brett Lee received his own cap from two stalwarts of the 50s and 60s, Colin McDonald and Ian Meckiff. We always make sure we wear our caps for the first session we field in of every Test.

Some people have attributed our run at success to the quality, or lack of it, of the opposition. Other than to say one team is identifiably better than the other, it is often difficult to work out to what degree any result is due to one group of players performing especially well or the other being sub-standard. We can only beat the opponents we are thrown against. That is not to say that some teams, like the West Indies, haven't deteriorated, which is a shame for world cricket. On their day Pakistan can be sensational. We made sure they didn't have those days and showed more steel under pressure. As for New Zealand, they have become a strong unit and the margins of victory – 62 runs in Auckland and 6 wickets in Wellington and Hamilton – show that we didn't have things easy. India have a great batting side, especially in India, Sri Lanka are dangerous, but where I think we have it over most sides is our consistency.

Sometimes you have to hit rock bottom to progress – as I think was the case at Hampshire in 2000 when Rod Bransgrove, a successful businessman, took charge of the club after our disappointing season and laid down plans to mount a revival. Where West Indies are concerned I think their decline was camouflaged for a couple of years by Courtney Walsh bowling long spells and taking wickets and by Lara playing the occasional brilliant innings, such as his 182 in Adelaide.

West Indies draw enormous pride from their cricket and I felt sorry for them as the embarrassing results in 2000–01 continued. I can understand why people might have rubbed their hands and thought this was payback time after the way West Indies dominated – almost bullied – sides in the late 70s and 80s. For the sake of world cricket, though, it is important that they can bounce back and, if not become a dominant force again, then at least be competitive. If the game dies out on the islands and in Guyana that is no good for anybody who has the best interests of the game at heart. You would like to think that players of yesteryear would come and help and that the public would all encourage everyone and try some new things.

Where Australia are concerned I believe the introduction of Gilchrist and Brett Lee lifted us another cog, because they performed sensationally straight away. Gilchrist is a phenomenal batsman to have coming in at number seven. The fact that he had played a season or two in the one-day internationals before his Test debut meant he was familiar with the dressing room and could handle the nerves. Filling Ian Healy's shoes can't have been easy. From his first game against Pakistan in Brisbane, where he crashed 50 from 46 balls, he looked at home. If he was not a wicket-keeper he would probably get a game as a specialist batsman in the top six. Whether he would succeed I don't know, because the demands on him would be different, but my guess is that he would survive through his pure talent.

Whenever a fresh young player comes into the team and performs well immediately it lifts the rest of the side. Lee is a classic example. He didn't just add blinding pace, an option that, with the greatest respect to the likes of Glenn McGrath, was not there before. His sheer enthusiasm was contagious and the way he burst on to the scene reminded us all of our youth. Comparisons have started to be made between us and I have tried to help him in areas such as management, sponsorship and endorsements. Like Gilchrist, he made a sensational start, taking 5 wickets on his debut against India at Melbourne. As well as the gift to be able to bowl consistently at more than 90 mph – and I believe gift is the right word – he has the charisma and personality to attract attention from the crowds, television audiences and therefore sponsors, and he loves it.

If he stays clear of injury I think he could make fast bowling as fashionable in this decade as it was in the 1980s and as spin became in the 90s largely through Anil Kumble, Saqlain Mushtaq, Muttiah Muralitharan and Mushtaq Ahmed. Spin is no longer a dying art and it is particularly satisfying to see great slow bowlers in one-day cricket with men around the bat, genuinely attacking, when ten years ago people said there was no room for spinners in the limited overs game. All of us spin bowlers owe a lot to Abdul Qadir because he was the first leggie to be dangerous in one-day cricket. With Brett Lee and Shoaib Akhtar on the scene I can see the emphasis changing again. Let's hope that spin maintains a presence and dominates again in the 2010s.

While the contribution of Gilchrist and Lee can be measured in runs, wickets and catches, it is harder to quantify the impact of a coach on the squad. Bobby Simpson and Geoff Marsh had Test match experience. But John Buchanan, the current coach, has had no experience of international cricket – just the odd Shield game. Buchanan is from a completely different angle. He is probably the most thorough coach I have known and some of his ideas are very different and come from left-field, but they seem to be working. The coaches before him left the team in good shape and Buck has brought in new ideas with success.

Everyone is familiar with the picture of this tall, slightly awkward-looking figure with glasses hammering data into his laptop computer or scribbling on endless sheets of butcher's paper. It certainly isn't the traditional image of a cricket coach. On our activities away from cricket we split into two teams – the Julios, named after the suave, sophisticated singer, Julio Iglesias, and the Nerds. The Julios are people like Mark Waugh, Michael Slater, Brett Lee, Greg Blewett and Errol Alcott, our physio. Those are the guys who make an effort with their appearance and know one end of a blow drier from the other. The Nerds generally include Glenn McGrath, Mark Taylor, Steve Waugh and Adam Gilchrist – the ones who don't worry too much about their hairstyle or the latest fashions. Down the years Brendon Julian has been the most appropriate captain of the Julios, while Tim May led the Nerds with distinction. But, with the greatest respect, I think it is only a matter of time before our coach assumes Tim's mantle.

His ambition is to be able at the end of each day's play to give an individual disk or feedback sheet to every player containing data of his performance. To people like myself who aren't quite up to date with new technology that seems incredible. He already has an enormous amount of information stored up about our opponents. Obviously the more experienced players like the Waughs and myself are familiar with which batsmen hook compulsively, or who tends to nick to the slips or doesn't play spin so well, for example, but even then it is invaluable to have that knowledge re-inforced by tangible evidence. I still back myself to use the old brain, but if anyone is unsure or there are differences on what approach to take, the computer is a good back-up. When he took over before the Pakistan series he set up one-on-one meetings with all of us to outline his ideas, tell us what he expected of us and ask what we wanted from him. He stressed the importance of knowing us as characters as much as cricketers. He is big on setting goals.

The fact that he didn't play Test cricket is an interesting facet of his career. His track record at Queensland, coaching the side to a first ever Shield win, was superb and those who questioned his methods were in the minority. With the game becoming so much more 'professional', shall we say, I think the modern coach needs to offer more than his own experience. It is not enough these days to turn up an hour or so before the game and go through the motions with a few stretches. Although we sometimes wonder what is behind Buchanan's routines, the results show that he knows what he's doing. He has been known to have us work on juggling, as though we were about to join a circus. Sometimes we hit balls with our eyes shut. Occasionally we have been told to jog around the boundary while trying to bounce a ball up on our bats. As Mark Waugh said, it was hard to see how that particular exercise was going to help us but we gave it a go. I can only assume it was designed to improve our concentration. With Buchanan there is a reason for everything, even if it isn't obvious to us. We trust him and try to keep the whingeing to a minimum.

During 1999–2000 I think we were superior to Zimbabwe, Pakistan, India and New Zealand in every department. That was also the case the following summer against West Indies. The art of batting in a Test match has lost its way with some teams. These days a player can get sledged for taking all day to score a hundred, but five days is a long time for a game of cricket – Allan Border stressed to us to be patient – and that sort of contribution can be invaluable in difficult conditions. The growth of the one-day game has played a significant part, I think, in the trend to early Test finishes, but in Australia we are well aware of the differences between the two games. We aim to score 300 runs in a day – that is our aim, but if the opposition bowls well then we sum it up quickly.

When the run began in Harare in the third week of October 1999 I don't think any of us even knew the record for successive wins – probably not even Steve Waugh with his vast knowledge of the game's history.

We were delighted to be in Zimbabwe after a difficult series in Sri Lanka which we lost, and the one-off Test was played in a fantastic spirit. The Zimbabweans seemed to think of it as an opportunity to pick our brains and, although we won comfortably, by ten wickets, I am sure they were better for the experience. It was also something of an experience for me. In the first innings I took up the wicket-keeping position for one ball while Ian Healy stood at slip still wearing his gloves and pads. This wasn't quite as mad as it sounds. Bryan Strang was going down the wicket to Steve Waugh and missing as often as he connected. We reckoned if the ball could be taken by a fielder we would have a better chance of throwing down the wicket. It didn't work, but it made Strang think. The other memory is of Healy leading a rendition of 'Under The Southern Cross' for what proved to be the last time.

Three weeks later his illustrious Test career had finished and we were back home for what would prove an historic summer. We arrived in Brisbane to find that Buchanan had hung a banner on the dressing room wall that read: 'Today is the First Test in our journey to the Invincibles. Let's make the ride enjoyable and attainable.' Talk about setting his sights high. Maybe he knew something that we didn't.

Pakistan can be brilliant, as they showed in the World Cup in England, but they could never be described as consistent. Having reached 3 for 265, they then lost 3 wickets at the end of day one and that gave us a psychological advantage which we did not surrender. After Slater and Mark Waugh completed hundreds I thought I was on the way to a maiden hundred myself in a last-wicket stand of 86 with Scott Muller of which he scored 6. It felt particularly sweet to smash four sixes off Mushtaq Ahmed – so much for the leg-spinners' union – but Mushy took his revenge when he caught me off Wasim Akram for 86. At least a lead of 208 left us in a terrific position and, with Gilchrist taking a superb stumping off me to remove Azhar Mahmood on the final day, we managed to complete the job. On his home ground, Healy joined us for the celebrations afterwards and officially handed over the prestigious role of leading the team song to Ricky Ponting.

The Second Test in Hobart will be remembered forever for the Langer-Gilchrist partnership. I watched every ball with my pads strapped on as the next batsman in and to be in the middle when we secured the winning runs was fantastic. When Gilly made the winning hit I went to say well done – but I had forgotten to run myself. He just screamed, 'Run!' Cricketers become very superstitious when a partnership is going well and while Langer and Gilchrist gradually ran and stroked their way to the target with ever-increasing confidence and certainty the rest of us were not allowed to leave our places. I made more of a contribution in the field with 3 wickets in the first innings and 5 in the second, including Saeed Anwar, bowled when he looked dangerous on 78. The pick of them, though, must be an incredible catch at slip by Mark Waugh to dismiss Inzamam-ul-Haq. Inzamam is such a powerful bloke that even when he doesn't middle the ball it can really fly. This time he edged a full-blooded cut and saw Waugh hold on to the chance high to his right. Junior has been sensational off me all around the wicket, he is a great slip fielder.

A couple of days later a saga began which made me very angry because I was nothing more than an innocent bystander in an incident which I believe grew out of all proportion. A Channel Ten TV show called *The Panel* used some of the cricket footage from that game and fiddled with the volume levels on effects microphones that had been placed around the ground. Normally they stay in-house and nothing is ever heard. Imagine the conversations of the crowd or camera crews at a cricket game making the airwaves – the mind boggles. They picked up a phrase that has become known as 'Can't bowl, can't throw,' when Scott Muller fielded a ball that Inzamam-ul-Haq hit towards the deep square leg boundary. I was the bowler, Gilchrist was keeping wicket and Mark Waugh stood at slip.

There was no way of knowing where the voice came from, but *The Panel* decided that it belonged to an Australian cricketer. I did not watch the programme, but I managed to get a video and it could have been anybody talking. It was not me, and for people to come to the conclusion that it was, I found amazing. I think that certain people, players, public and media wanted it to be me. That is why people started saying, 'Oh, that sounds like Warnie.' No one else was questioned and no reason was put forward for who or where else it could have come from. Certain people jumped to the conclusion straight away.

Unfortunately, Scott Muller had been dropped for the next game at Perth. He was understandably disappointed. I had gone out of my way to make him feel comfortable both on his debut in Brisbane and then in Tasmania because I knew from my own experience how daunting it can be to join the Test squad for the first time. The likes of Allan Border, Geoff Marsh and David Boon were good to me when I was new to it all and I always try to be the same with any newcomer. Scott even said to me that I was the only one who went out of my way to make him feel welcome. Two and two don't equal five, do they?

The Third Test began only four days after Hobart, but when we arrived to start practising the story had already been followed up on the front and back pages of the newspapers with yours truly getting the rap from certain journalists. Almost as soon as the squad arrived at the WACA ground for the preparations I was approached by Brian Murgatroyd, our media liaison manager, who tried to speak with Scott. It seemed that Scott, too, thought that the voice sounded like me on the tape and was very angry. There was no way I wanted the matter to linger, so when I found out that Scott thought I was the culprit I rang him as soon as I could to say, first of all, bad luck about not being picked, mate, and then to add that Murgers had relayed their conversation to me. I wanted to make sure he knew that I wasn't to blame for what had been caught on tape and to point out that, in my opinion, it was just another example of media hype.

When I got Scott on the line I could tell that he was extremely upset. He fired back with a torrent of abuse that really took me by surprise.

He said that I'd pretended to act as his mate, while all along I didn't think he should have been in the team. I told him that I couldn't believe he seriously thought it was me. But, if a straight denial wasn't good enough, I said I would gather evidence and prove it.

Even then, in that first conversation, he seemed to have lost grasp of rational thought. He felt that people would close ranks to protect me.

What people don't realise is that if it had been me I would have owned up. From a team mate's point of view I was very disappointed.

By now the issue was getting ridiculous, with newspapers beginning to conduct polls to ask the public if they thought I was guilty. I realised the need to dig deeper to prove my innocence, which as a senior player and vice-captain should have been unnecessary. It wasn't, so I went on a mission to get proof. All in all this was hardly ideal preparation for a forthcoming Test match.

I spoke to Gary Burns, the director of sport at Channel Nine, to ask him to have a look at the footage, to check every single camera angle they had of the incident.

A couple of days later he told me there was a front-on shot in which my lips didn't move through the entire sequence. The microphone in the stump only picked up Inzamam calling for two runs in Urdu. Burns also found out for the first time where the words had actually originated. They came from an effects microphone somewhere around the boundary and appeared to be a cameraman saying to his mate: 'This bloke can't bowl and he can't throw.' Apparently, it is very unusual for the words of the camera crew to be picked up in this way, but now, at least, I thought there was enough for Scott Muller to deliver a not guilty verdict in my direction. How wrong I was.

Relieved that the whole business could be put to rest, I rang Scott again with the evidence, as promised. But still he didn't want to know.

'Mate, I know it's you,' he said. 'You can give me all the proof you want, but it was you.'

I suggested that this represented concrete proof and that if he still didn't believe me or wouldn't at least look at the evidence – which in my view he ought to have done in the first place rather than hang me – then it was he rather than me with the problem. The second conversation ended on no happier terms than the first. I was really disappointed and starting to get frustrated because I didn't know what else to do. Allan Border, a selector and a fellow Queenslander, spoke to Scott to try to bring him to reason. Not even AB – who has since described it as 'the biggest non-event of all time' – could get the message through. If Scott wasn't going to believe Australia's most capped player, and didn't seem to consider the evidence either, then it was a sorry state of affairs. Whatever advice he was getting, it was the wrong advice.

Channel Nine were desperately trying to track down who it came from. They also wanted to know who the guilty party was. It turned out to be one of their cameramen by the name of Joe. The situation had got so far out of hand that it could have been an episode of *The X Files*. *A Current Affair*, a programme which usually investigates issues of national and international importance, also ran a story. They unveiled the man who has become known as Cameraman Joe as though the discovery was a great victory for journalism. Joe admitted his error on national TV and apologised to Scott and myself. 'You beauty,' I thought. Finally he would say, 'Sorry, mate' and we could all get on with playing cricket.

Wishful thinking. Because even then a section of the press saw an opportunity to have another swipe. Joe had just happened to turn up wearing a Nike T-shirt and, somehow, a story went around saying that I had given it to him to gain publicity for Nike, one of my old sponsors. From there it was only a small step to suggest that Joe had been a plant all along. One other thing was that Mark Waugh and Adam Gilchrist didn't hear anything.

Meanwhile, a journalist from *The Australian* who doesn't have me on his Christmas list, had gone to a police voice specialist to try to implicate me, but the plan backfired. The facts were that it was not my voice and he had to publish the findings of the voice analyst.

Documentary programmes? Voice specialists? Aren't there more important issues troubling the world? It was all unbeliev-able to me. Anyway, the analyst confirmed that the voice could not be mine. So, for a third time, I gave Scott a ring. I was excited because now he had all the proof and I was out to get an apology from someone who doubted me.

'Look, mate,' I said, 'even this reporter who hates my guts now says it couldn't have been me. What more do you want?' Even then he wouldn't back down.

Initially I felt sorry for Scott. It wasn't a nice thing to happen. Having said that, I'm sure over the years that a lot worse things have been said. If I really said those words I would have held my hand up and been man enough to apologise and tried to shake hands on the whole business, as I told him many times. Besides which, anybody who has played sport at whatever level will have said and been subjected to far more unpleasant things on the field at some stage. Scott just wouldn't let it lie. He was like a dog with a bone. There were so many conspiracy theories. Scott had lost friends and team mates by over-reacting practically since day one. Unfortunately for me, despite being proved innocent several times over I was booed later in the 1999–2000 season during a one-day game at the Gabba. What can I say? To get booed for something I didn't do, when it was proved I hadn't done it, in my own country was something I couldn't put into words. The Gabba is my most successful ground in Australia and I love playing there.

The matter raised its head again in 2000–01 when Six & Out, the rock band made up of New South Wales cricketers, including the Lee brothers, released an album which included a song called 'Can't Bowl, Can't Throw'. There is a line in it which goes, 'Don't ask Warnie, it was Cameraman Joe.' Scott, needless to say, was furious, prompting the band to claim that the song wasn't about him at all. I don't suppose the group were deliberately trying to wind him up, but after everything that had gone before I think the subject would have been best left untouched, even if it was recorded as a bit of a laugh. At one point I was told by the Queensland Cricket Association that Scott was talking about taking legal advice. Frankly, I wish he had done, so that all the facts and video evidence would have come out. The matter could have been cleared up for good.

I'm sure the result in Hobart had a demoralising effect on Pakistan, who conceded a first-innings deficit of nearly 300 in the final match at Perth before losing comfortably. In the past we had been a little complacent at the end of series already secured but this time we were ruthless and clinical. Winning becomes a habit and should not be surrendered easily. I think that old weakness is now well and truly overcome.

With the series against India due to start less than a fortnight later, there was little time to celebrate. The international schedule rarely allows much of a break these days and after our tremendous performances against Pakistan most of us wanted to keep the momentum going in any case. We also knew that India, despite the genius of Sachin Tendulkar, struggle with the bouncy wickets in Australia. Having lost the previous series on their soil we didn't lack motivation and, while I don't think I have to prove anything to anyone, I hadn't enjoyed much success against the Indians and wanted to change that.

The First Test at Adelaide went superbly. For the second time in the summer I had a wonderful chance to reach three figures – and once again I fell on 86. The main thing was that we kept our winning streak going. But from there I bowled probably as well as I did all season. It is always important to lay down a marker early in the series and, by removing Tendulkar, Rahul Dravid and Sourav Ganguly, I like to think I dispelled any thoughts that they could take me on at will. I managed to get the left-handed Ganguly stumped with a googly, bowling from deliberately wider of the crease around the wicket. I also enjoyed the one that bowled Mannava Prasad around his legs. When I bowled in tandem with Glenn McGrath we built up a lot of pressure and set the tone. Bowling is as much about partnerships as batting, maybe more.

On a personal level the 6 wickets at Adelaide plus the 86 with the bat meant I went into the Second Test on my home ground in Melbourne needing the same again to equal Lillee's magical figure of 355. I would love to have passed the great man in front of the Victorian public at the biggest event in our cricketing calendar, the Boxing Day Test. Rain on the first day made 26 December something of an anti-climax and after another deluge twenty-four hours later, we had to re-arrange our batting order in search of quick runs and a declaration second time around to stay in the victory hunt.

In the event, I could take only a single wicket in each innings.

Brett Lee made a great debut with 7 wickets, serving notice that he intended to be on the scene for many years to come. In the second innings Tendulkar's wicket was the one we wanted and I was happy getting him with a top-spinner which dipped in and he padded up, out lbw.

So, once again we had sealed the series with a game remaining. Again, too, the opposition seemed to be demoralised and we raced to a massive innings and 141-run win inside three days in the final game at Sydney, where Justin Langer continued his outstanding form by completing a double-century.

The wicket wasn't a normal turner in Sydney. I don't know why – it was more a seamer's wicket.

On reflection, being so close to the record probably affected me. I strained too hard to snatch wickets instead of working on batsmen and gradually luring them towards danger. I was trying to take wickets every ball. I even forgot the advice I give to young bowlers by going for too many variations too quickly. Fortunately, with Glenn McGrath and Lee again scything through the India batsmen my own moderate performance in this match did not have a bearing on the result.

My appearances in the subsequent Carlton & United series were restricted by a muscle tear in my side, but I did return for the finals against Pakistan. From there it was on to New Zealand for our final commitment of the summer with me still 4 wickets short of equalling the record.

Before then, I was inadvertently involved in a misunderstanding that caused no little embarrassment to all of us and Adam Gilchrist in particular. The tour social committee of Gilchrist, Matthew Hayden and myself devised a game where each member of the party had to buy a shirt for one of the others on a bad-taste theme to be worn on the next night out. We all had a bit of fun scouring the charity and bargain basement shops in Dunedin – that is until the local paper ran a serious story about cross-dressing in the Australia team when a reporter spotted poor Gilchrist showing unusual enthusiasm in buying a frilly blouse. There were a few ribald comments when we arrived at the ground and again when we turned up at a pub dressed in our new costumes. It was all a little bit of fun.

In contrast, another incident early in the tour was no fun at all. We were playing a one-day international at a brand new stadium in Wellington which had been declared smoke-free. More than that, there was a $10,000 fine for anybody caught smoking. Quietly, however, an official from New Zealand Cricket told us we would be all right to light up in the privacy of the dressing room. During a rain break, while Ian Harvey, Michael Bevan, Steve Bernard, the team manager, and myself were playing cards, I had a cigarette. This was in front of our dressing room. Suddenly, as in the Caribbean less than a year earlier, I saw a camera flash. I turned round to see two kids of about fifteen or sixteen, laughing to each other and looking altogether a great deal too pleased with themselves.

One of them kept saying: 'We've got a picture, we've got a picture.' My instant reaction was to let the matter pass, so I did for a while. Then when the card school finished I went over to ask why they were so interested in taking a photograph of me smoking. 'We just wanted to keep a picture of you,' one of them said. But they only took a few and I just happened to be smoking. It was common knowledge that I was having a few smokes. It really isn't a matter of national importance, but the media kept harping on about it. My concern was over the conflict that might face the security people who had said that we could smoke in a non-smoking stadium.

So I decided to offer a compromise to the kids. If they gave me the disposable camera I would develop it and send on all of the prints except the snapshot of myself. They said they wanted to hang around to take some pictures of the New

Zealand team. I could understand that and didn't have a problem. Eventually we agreed that at the end of the game they would give the film over to Bernard with their names and addresses and I would stick to my side of the deal. Everything was okay. I trusted them and assumed they trusted me. Not wanting anyone to get into trouble, I thought this would work out.

Difficulties began to arise after the game was abandoned an hour or so later. I sought out the lads, asked for the camera only for one of them to claim it had been stolen. The rest of the group were giggling in the background. It was perfectly clear they were either trying to wind me up and take the mickey or intending to try and do something with the photograph itself. The idea that at this particular time somebody just happened to have taken the camera was ridiculous. As if to try to remove these suspicions, one of them offered – I stress, offered – his bag for me to look through. To no huge surprise the camera was not there.

By this stage I wanted the matter brought to an end. 'Okay,' I said, 'how about if I keep this bag until the camera turns up.' One of them still kept insisting the camera had been taken, with no conviction at all. Then, seemingly from nowhere, an adult appeared and told me to give the bag back to the kid. I said that he gave it to me to look through and that I was minding it until the camera turned up. I thought the matter was under control, but then it got way, way out of hand, for the man then went to get the police. Now the police asked me what had happened. I told them the story. After my explanation one of the policemen told me to give back the bag. I did as he asked and waited for the camera to be handed to me, but instead I listened incredulously as he told the kids they could go.

'Well,' I said, 'that really got to the bottom of things, didn't it?'

He asked what the kids had done wrong. While I acknowledged they might not have broken any actual laws I said that people could get into trouble if they sold the picture to a newspaper, and that a certain common sense should prevail. The kids said they wanted it for their personal collection at this stage and were not going to sell it. But so often with officialdom they look for common sense in the rule book when it isn't there. Had the police not weighed in the kids would have given me the film and more than likely the matter would have been closed.

To this, the policeman replied: 'Why don't you have another cigarette and I'll take a picture as well,' in a very sarcastic and smart-arse way.

I couldn't believe the guy's attitude, and told him what I thought. Bernard, who had been listening, suggested that I let it drop. I agreed, although I couldn't believe it. As I walked away I was still annoyed at their approach. Looking back I probably should have left it alone, but I didn't want anyone to lose their job or pay a fine.

It was only a matter of time before the newspapers picked up the story – or a very partial version of it. One of the policemen decided to try and make a name for himself. Yet again the issue was blown up out of all proportion. Where I had tried, reasonably, to sort out a minor problem, I was now being portrayed as a common crook. The kids even went on television in New Zealand and Australia saying that Shane Warne used to be their hero and describing how he had gone right down in their estimations. I could have written their script myself it was so predictable. The first stories, blown-up with big headlines, are usually the most damaging and once again my reputation had suffered before the truth emerged, but sometimes mud sticks, and people once again have to make up their minds about what really happened.

As a gesture of friendship I helped to arrange for the kids to come to a day of the Test and have a chat when we returned to Wellington in March. When we met again they were sorry for what happened. They said that they had not wanted the incident to reach the media and complained that the newspapers had hounded them at school.

'So why did you talk to them then?' I asked. 'Why didn't you let the matter drop?'

One of them said that he thought it was just a small matter. I pointed out that it was until they talked to TV and the newspapers. In the end we agreed that perhaps we could all have handled things differently. So what happened next? They went straight to the TV cameras saying that I hadn't been apologetic at all. But I had. And for my part, I'm now known in New Zealand as the player who snatches kids' bags. Interestingly enough, the ACB, who knew exactly what happened and all of the facts, didn't do anything.

Because of our Test run the fact that we also set a record for successive one-day wins has been overlooked. We actually went to fourteen games without defeat, thirteen in succession, stretching back to a C&U game against India, before finally losing to New Zealand in Auckland when we had secured an unassailable four–nil lead in the series. At this point we decided to experiment with the batting order and, apart from Damien Martyn's hundred, the rest didn't really perform. Given the vagaries of the one-day game, the way that any single batsmen can swing away with all the luck in the world on any given day, I think to go for so long without losing is incredible. I am convinced we have a great chance of becoming the first side since the West Indies in 1979 to retain the World Cup when it takes place in South Africa in 2003.

Much as I enjoy the limited overs game, I could hardly wait

for the Test series to begin to have another crack at passing Lillee and to keep the team record going. Auckland has not traditionally been a lucky ground for Australia but, with my wife, parents and brother all in town expecting something to happen, I really wanted to achieve the milestone that eluded me in Australia. In the end – and without bowling at anywhere near my best – I finally reached the landmark. It turned out to be a thrilling game. We secured a lead of 51 on first-innings and managed to extend that by 229 second time round as Dan Vettori, the young left-arm spinner, added 7 wickets to his earlier 5. At 6 for 195, with Craig McMillan and Adam Parore beginning to look set, they certainly had a chance before losing the last 4 wickets for 23. Our experience of winning from tight situations carried us through.

I had taken my tally to 354 in their first innings but then struggled for consistency. Perhaps because of nerves and trying too hard it just wasn't happening. Finally, I turned one enough to bowl Nathan Astle around his legs to equal the record, but when I was pulled out of the attack soon afterwards I thought the magic wicket would have to wait until the next game at Wellington a fortnight later. However, with Paul Wiseman and Simon Doull starting to post something of a stand for the last wicket, Steve Waugh decided to bring me back into the attack. Wiseman attempted to sweep and the ball ballooned off his glove for Gilchrist to take a comfortable catch. I had practically started to appeal when I saw him shape to play the stroke.

Walking off to a guard of honour generously formed by the boys was among the most exhilarating moments of my life. My proudest moment was walking on to the ground at Sydney for my Test debut, when I looked at the electronic scoreboard which read: 'Congratulations, Shane Warne – 350th Test cricketer to play for Australia.' I never imagined I would play for my country and once I had a taste of international cricket I knew that this was my goal in life.

When I had finally taken the record I also felt a certain relief. I don't play for milestones, but I could not help but know about this one and the more I tried to forget it, the more anxious I became. Once again, I knew deep down I had tried too hard and just needed to relax. Back in Auckland, the congratulatory messages soon started to flood in. One of them I valued in particular came from Lillee himself. He pointed out that he'd taken the record from a leg-spinner (Richie Benaud) and now seen the dose repeated on him. Faxes and telegrams came from all over the world – from India, Pakistan, New Zealand and England, from friends and players alike. As much as for myself I felt pleased for my family and all the people who had stuck by me through some difficult times. The fact that Simone and my family were there made it even better. Jason and my dad came into the dressing room to share the beer and champagne. And for the only time in my career I was invited to sing the team song, with Steve Waugh, in the absence of Ponting. That night I went to a restaurant with my parents – unfortunately Simone had to stay in the hotel room with the kids – before joining the team later on. What a night, my brother Jason and our friend Fin joined us as well and we had a great time.

After that I wanted to get to Wellington for the Second Test as quickly as possible so that I could relax and bowl as well as I knew I could. I felt far more comfortable there and took 7 wickets including Astle with a dream flipper and then McMillan first ball. I was also happier in the final game at Hamilton, where Langer, still considered little more than a blocker by those who don't know his game, struck the third fastest hundred in Australian Test history to round off a memorable campaign. Some people tried to read a lot into the way Chris Cairns took me on, but I always felt I had a chance against him. When he's allowed to play well, he hits some amazing shots – some of the sweeps he played were extraordinary. Spin bowlers get hit every now and then – it is an occupational hazard. We secured another three–nil series win.

As we closed in on the West Indies' record of eleven wins people began to ask whether we were, indeed, the greatest side to have played. A question like that is impossible to answer because it comes down to a matter of opinion.

I would love to have bowled against the West Indies side of 1983–84 – Gordon Greenidge, Desmond Haynes, Viv Richards, Larry Gomes, Richie Richardson and Clive Lloyd. I might have been carted all over the park, but I would have relished the challenge. Whether I would have fancied trying to bat against Malcolm Marshall, Joel Garner and Michael Holding is another matter.

It is interesting to compare the two sides, just as it is to imagine how we might have fared against Bradman's 1948 side or the 1972 team of Ian Chappell. Frankly, I think suggesting one is better than the other is unfair to everybody.

A great player in one era would have been great in any other. Arthur Morris would have adapted to the modern game just as Steve Waugh would have fitted in fifty years ago. And I like to think I wouldn't have fared too badly bowling on those uncovered pitches. Later in the book I pick my best Australian side from those I have played with since breaking into the team in 1991–92. There is even a case for saying that the 1993 side under Allan Border, including David Boon, Merv Hughes and Ian Healy at his absolute best, might have beaten the 2000 bunch. Now there's one to raise a few heckles.

In total we used twenty players during the twelve Tests on the way to breaking the record. Interestingly, the West Indies only needed fifteen in 1983–84. That statistic underlines our tremendous strength in depth and perhaps the most amazing fact is that we couldn't field what I guess was our strongest team. By the time that Jason Gillespie recovered from injuries to feature against West Indies, I had broken my finger. Here is a short insight into each of the players and personalities who helped to make history.

Stephen Waugh (captain, 12 Tests)

There isn't much more to say about Stephen. He has been up there among the best batsmen in the world for the last five or six years and is our most consistent player. The number of times he has dug us out of trouble is uncanny and that knack of surviving is a credit to his discipline, toughness, motivation and sheer will-power. Our friendship has survived some tough times together. He has always been there for me in the past and I would like to think I have helped him too. Stories that he doesn't spend much time with Mark are true. As they both often state, after sharing the same bedroom for fifteen or sixteen years there isn't much left to say to each other. The household must have been ultra-competitive. When one of them used to borrow their dad's car he would fill it with just enough petrol for the trip and to get home – meaning that the next one often had to push it to the service station to refuel. Steve is fascinated by the history of the game and takes a great interest in the places we visit – he is always out with his notebook and camera. He loves getting out there and having a look at the country. He told us one story about a Maths exam when a question asked for the circumference of a circle. Thinking this was simple, he plucked a hair from his scalp, stretched it over the diagram, measured the distance with his ruler and came up with the answer. Fortunately he has a better grasp of batting and leading the team on the field. Nicknamed Tugga.

Justin Langer (12)

He was around the side for a long while without playing a lot of Test cricket but cemented his place as successor to David Boon at number three during the 1999–2000 season when he really blossomed. His great work ethic helps him when he does hit a bad trough, but I think because people focus on that dedication they overlook the fact that he is also a quality stroke-maker. One of the guys at the hub of the team and very unselfish. Also a keen writer for his web site. Nicknamed Lang, Alfie (after the rugby league player Alfie Langer) or Mini Tugga, because he copies Steve Waugh.

Glenn McGrath (12)

He has shown what is possible by bowling a consistent line and length and just doing a little bit off the pitch. There is nothing spectacular about him, but he has already established himself as a legend in the game. Away from cricket he has started a charity for breast cancer following his wife Jane's illness. They are a smashing couple who have been through more than most of us can imagine together already. In the dressing room he has succeeded Merv Hughes as the pest, always throwing things at you or moving your gear. Despite the evidence of years and years of low scores he still fancies himself as a batsman. When he comes back in after yet another duck he slams his bat down shouting: 'Glenn, why do you bother?' to himself. He is improving, but at a snail's pace. Deep down, despite his aggressive appearance when he bowls, he is one of the gentlest characters in the side who likes nothing more than heading back to the Bush for a spell of fishing or shooting. Nicknamed Pigeon.

Michael Slater (12)

An instinctive player who wears his heart on his sleeve. That enthusiasm rubs off on us all, which means he is important as a character as well as being one of the best opening batsmen in the world who can get us off to a flying start. He has been around for a while now and is so explosive with the bat that he can set up a game or allow us to blow away the opposition in the first session. Nicknamed Slats or Sybil (because he takes on a different personality after a couple of drinks).

Mark Waugh (12)

His laid-back approach and very dry sense of humour have stood him in good stead when his place has been under threat. He has great hand-eye co-ordination and must be one of the most naturally gifted sportsmen – let alone cricketers – in the world today. He is also one of my best mates in cricket and we used to share a room in the days before the ACB gave us single rooms. We share a common taste for a punt, though Mark is more into the horses, while I prefer the casino. He has shown his consistency and longevity over a ten-year period which shows he has a great attitude and adaptability. Nick-named Junior.

Adam Gilchrist (11)

As I have said, one of the key figures behind our success. He has brought a new dimension to the position of wicket-keeper/ batsman and I'm sure over time he will be one of the best ever. His batting really is dynamic and great to watch. A Julio in a Nerd's body. Nicknamed Gilly.

Shane Warne (10)

I guess you know something about me by now. Nicknames include Warney, Suicide (after the INXS song, 'Suicide Blonde'), Factor (The Warne Factor), Hollywood, Truman.

Greg Blewett (9)

Made a magnificent start to his Test career against England but has been in and out since and hasn't really cemented a place, although he has a lot of the attributes needed to be a top-class batsman. Along with Ricky Ponting, he is a fine player of short-pitched bowling. I hope he gets another chance because he is a fantastic player and his innings of 214 against a really good South Africa pace attack in Johannesburg in 1996–97 is one of the best I've seen. But the fact is that with Australian cricket being as strong as it is any opportunities need to be seized. A really good golfer with a four-handicap. Nicknamed Blewey or Blueboy.

Ricky Ponting (9)

He was sixteen when Rod Marsh described him as the best young batsman he had seen. Since then he has become a great young batsman with the potential to get even better. Most of his family play golf in single figures, so there is obviously enormous talent in the genes. Ricky plays to scratch or one regularly. His fielding has been important. It is often overlooked as a major reason for our success. He really understands the way a game is going and has that ability to concentrate for long periods. I think his bowling is under-used. When he came back into the side after suspension against Sri Lanka in the Carlton & United series in 1999, I decided to give him 10 overs with the ball to get him in the game early and he thrived on the responsibility. Showed similar powers of recovery in 1999–2000 when he responded to three successive ducks against Pakistan by scoring three hundreds in the next four Tests. Owns and trains greyhounds in his spare time. Nicknamed Punter – another one with a fondness for a flutter.

Damien Fleming (7)

His ability to swing the ball is up there with the best in the world. In my experience only David Saker, from Victoria, has the ability to generate as much movement through the air. I'm sure he would be hugely effective in England. Likes heavy metal in a big, big way. It is always bad news when he gets hold of the music box in the dressing room. A very witty and inquisitive man who will go into the streets when we are abroad and start interviewing the general public with his video camera. Nicknamed Flem or Ace (as in *Ace Ventura,* one of the Jim Carrey films he watches over and over again).

Brett Lee (7)

Loves the international scene, and why not? The enjoyment is visible in everything he does and it keeps the rest of us enthused. If he stays injury-free there is no reason why he shouldn't be successful for many more years. When an increasing number of commitments allow he still goes to work in a suit shop. He also plays guitar in a band called Six & Out made up of New South Wales players which has been known to perform in pubs. There is no chance of success going to his head – he has a very level head on his shoulders. Nicknamed Binger.

Colin Miller (4)

Something of a journeyman who played for three state sides and appeared to have tried everything else in the game before turning his hand to off-spin at the age of thirty-two. He made his Australia debut two years later. His versatility makes him a really handy bloke to have in a squad – sometimes he even bowls seam to one batsman and twirl to the other in the same over. His spin is improving at a good rate and the pace of his off-breaks makes it difficult for batsmen to use their feet. Away from the field he is happy sitting by a poker machine with a rum and Coke for hours on end, just thinking to himself and getting quietly drunk. That is his laid-back nature. In the off-season, when most of us are sick to death of airports, he will put together an itinerary that takes him all over the world seeing the sights and experiencing different cultures. Nick-named Funky.

Matthew Hayden (3)

Works hard to develop his game. Once he gets in he possesses all the shots, as he showed in the last tour of India. A very thoughtful person with a strong religious faith who is always off finding the nearest Catholic church wherever we are. An extremely hard worker who really does enjoy other people's success and a good bloke to have around and a guy you really want to do well. Nicknamed Haydos or Dustus.

Damien Martyn (3)

He and I were the young punks of the side in the early 90s, the first graduates from the Academy to make the full Test team. He went through a heck of a lot early in his career and, if he is honest, he will look back and realise he might have handled things differently. I think he has learnt from his mistakes and matured into a very good cricketer people expected him to become maybe five or six years ago. He is a dominating player and, once set, there are few better batsmen to watch today. In some ways I feel sorry for him because when he has come into the side he has taken the opportunity to impress, but still had to step back down when the likes of Ricky Ponting and Steve Waugh return. When he gets a chance at a full-time situation then look out because he is pure class. Nicknamed Marto.

Michael Kasprowicz (2)

Contrary to the image fast bowlers have of being hard-nosed, in-your-face characters, Mike is a real gentleman. If anything he is probably too nice, but he has also enjoyed some deserved success at Test level. His 7 for 37 against England at the Oval in 1997 was a superb piece of bowling when we really needed it and it showed he has the potential to be genuine world-class. A big man who could have made the grade in rugby, and also a talented cartoonist with an eye for a smart caption. His efforts leading the attack in India in 1997–98 were inspirational to us all. Nicknamed Kasper.

Stuart MacGill (2)

Has a huge ability to bowl leg-spin and at times he has found being number two or three frustrating. He desperately wants to establish himself as Australia's top spin bowler, just as much as I intend to make him wait. He is a couple of years younger than me so his chance will come. Maybe we will be able to bowl in tandem – who knows? – as we did in West Indies in 1998–99. People speculate about rivalry between us but, other than on a professional level, I don't sense there is anything there except friendly competition. He has said a few things in the past, but that's okay. We help each other with certain points of technique, just as I believe spinners all over the world should work together. Loves a glass of wine and gets through a huge number of books on tour. Nicknamed Stewie or MacGilla.

Scott Muller (2)

Played two Tests.

Andy Bichel (1)

A really good tourist who has never complained about being twelfth man and deserved his opportunities against West Indies when we equalled and broke the record. A real 100 per cent man who runs in whatever the state of the pitch and can be a dangerous player in helpful conditions. Nicknamed Bick or Andre Bichelle, a great bloke whom everyone wants to see do well.

Jason Gillespie (1)

Very similar to Justin Langer in his commitment to hard work, which makes it even sadder that injuries have restricted his number of Test appearances. Otherwise he would have been a permanent fixture for three or four years and nobody in the side begrudged him success against West Indies in 2000–2001. His efforts in India were inspirational. The broken leg he sustained in collision with Steve Waugh in Sri Lanka was probably the most horrific injury I have seen on a cricket field. An inspiration to kids everywhere for his courage. Another of the good guys in the game. He works hard and does some funny things, like leaving messages on PA systems in lounges (like 'Teresa Green, please come to the front desk'). Has a good sense of humour and is always looking for something to make us laugh. Nicknamed Dizzy.

Ian Healy (1)

Along with Darren Berry from Victoria he is the best gloveman up to the stumps I have seen, and he is also one of the hardest triers. We had a great rapport as a bowler/keeper combination. He would make lots of suggestions about batsmen and the way I should work on them. The wicket-keeper is in the best position to be able to look into the batsman's eyes and identify any fear or uncertainty there. Ian was usually a pretty good judge. He was also a very handy lower-order batsman himself and I'm glad he played in the game against Zimbabwe in 1999–2000 so he could be part of the record-breaking run. In the end Gilchrist just offered more of a package in the selectors' eyes and if he plays as often I'm sure he, too, will be recognised as one of the all-time greats of Australian cricket, like Healy. His work ethic was second to none. A good team man and his practice of throwing a golf ball against the basement walls is legendary. Nicknamed Heals.

The back-up

The support staff have been unbelievable. Errol Alcott, the physio, has been around for a long time, I don't know where I would be without him. And the same could be said for Patrick Farhart who shares the physio duties these days. Errol is also the person everybody goes to, to get things off their chests. Steve Bernard, the manager, has a good cricket background as a player/selector. He knows what it is all about and always thinks of the player first, which is important. He is also my 500 partner in cards and is a very good player. David Misson, our fitness man, knows when to push us and when to back off. His place was taken by Jock Campbell when Misso went to the Sydney Swans. Mike Walsh, our scorer and assistant manager, does a great job and has been involved with the Australian team since 1989. He loves Aussie Rules football and Essendon is his side, so when the great Kevin Sheedy has addressed the team Walsh has been like a kid in a lolly store.

14

WHO RUNS
THE GAME?

I GUESS THAT in any organisation there will be a certain suspicion between employer and employee, but the relationship between players and administrators in Australia is probably better now than ever before and probably the best in the world. As with captaincy, the key is to have good, open lines of communication. Following the dispute in 1997–98, which almost led to a players' strike, those are now in place. I still believe, however, that some members of the ACB still pay too much attention to the media. While the Australia Cricket Board obviously runs the game here, the media has a more influential role in shaping policy than many people realise.

As I have said elsewhere, the media played an enormous part in the decision to remove me as vice-captain in 2000 after we had won ten consecutive Tests and were on the way to an all-time record. I wonder if the fourteen directors of the ACB, the people who really carry authority, thought through the implications of their actions on that occasion when they went against the wishes of the selectors themselves. They have now set a precedent.

Dad suggested that the ACB might want to speak to me, but even then I couldn't imagine it would reach those proportions. As I said before, the matter was private. He said that the story about the telephone conversations with the girl had generated more interest than I realised and was gaining momentum. By then Australian journalists in England had begun to follow me around and were hanging around our home and the cricket grounds for the summer, trying to get a comment so they could sensationalise it.

Stories can become exaggerated when they happen on the other side of the world. It is almost like a game of Chinese whispers. A cat might cross the road, but after the tale has passed around thirty people that same cat has gone twice round the block and stopped off for a pizza and a beer as well. I found it interesting that the English tabloid newspapers, with their reputation for sleaze, chose not to follow up the story. It was an issue in one paper for one day, coming and going with no real reaction at all. The English media treated me so much better than the Australian press. The only place where it ran and ran was in Australia. Journalists clearly saw this as the big opportunity to nail me once and for all and some people launched an assassination of my character which was to generate so much momentum that certain members of the ACB felt they had no other option and sacked me as vice-captain.

A lot of people who played for Australia were asked to comment about the situation, as well as many who hadn't. They were all invited to join in the debate. Some did and some didn't, but it surprised me that so many people wanted to comment. Austin Robertson, my manager at the time, was in England but my brother, Jason, faxed all the stories over from home and kept me informed about what was being said on television and the radio. I couldn't believe what was happening. It was a mistake, yes, but it was a private matter and had nothing to do with cricket. Explicit talk on the telephone did not mean that all of a sudden I'd lost my flipper or forgotten how to set a field.

I feel that the ACB should have acted firmly as soon as the first journalist raised the question of the vice-captaincy. In my opinion the ACB should have come out straight away and said the incident had nothing to do with cricket and was simply a matter between myself and my wife.

By coincidence, Malcolm Speed, the chief executive of the ACB, was due to come over to England for the International Cricket Council's annual meeting in July, shortly before the usual meeting to decide a captain and vice-captain for the coming season. He suggested that we meet up in London so that he could let me know how the directors of the ACB were thinking. That seemed like a good idea.

More than a month after the initial story the papers in Australia were still speculating about what might happen and running the rule over my possible successors. Although my brother had been keeping me abreast of the publicity back home, it was not until Speed, at our meeting, presented me with a book of cuttings stretching back to the original stories that I realised just how much attention it had been getting. I will swear that his book ran to hundreds of sheets of paper.

The meeting itself I thought was very positive. Speed was completely frank. He listened to my version of events, some of which he didn't know about and which surprised him, and to my thoughts on the vice-captaincy issue. He seemed to agree that it had been blown out of proportion. He understood the situation, but pointed out that I was being scrutinised as a public figure. The Board is made up of fourteen directors and he said that a few of them had telephoned to say they were not happy. I found that disappointing because they had not contacted me for my side of the story or even waited for Speed to convey it to them, following our meeting, before making their judgement. They had already formed an opinion.

'How many people are we talking about?' I asked. 'Are we

looking at one, two, half of them, all of them? What do the selectors think? Am I in trouble with the vice-captaincy?'

His reply came as a real shock. 'It's looking that way,' he said.

I asked where the selectors stood, thinking that they were the people who knew the team and what was best for it. They had feedback from Steve Waugh and John Buchanan. I thought they decided who should be the captain, vice-captain and the composition of the team. I didn't really know that the fourteen directors decided what happens in everything. I was surprised to discover that, while the selectors made recommendations, it was the directors who had the final say. Now I could see which way the wind was blowing. It seemed a ridiculous state of affairs when the selectors, people who had played the game at the highest level, with Allan Border, Trevor Hohns, Andrew Hilditch and Geoff March (since replaced by David Boon) could be over-ruled on a cricketing matter when that is what their job is, to pick the team and its leaders.

I have expanded on that side of the business elsewhere in the book, because I think the Board decision could have implications for the future of Australian cricket. Suffice to say here that I had been vice-captain to Steve Waugh on a winning run of ten Tests and led the side pretty well in the eyes of most observers when I filled in as captain in one-day cricket – eleven games, ten wins. I rang Hohns, the chairman of selectors, a week or so after my meeting with Speed, just to clarify in my own mind what the selectors were thinking. As far as they were concerned I had done a great job and they thought I was the best man to continue as Stephen's deputy. I was very relieved and thought that everything was going to be okay.

By that stage, though, the decision had effectively become a fait accompli. Speed said that he would pass on my story – the truth – to the directors. True to his word, Speed called me as soon as the decision had been made. It was 2.15 am in England and I was asleep at the hotel in Derby where I was staying with Hampshire. The conversation was short and to the point. He said that I had lost the vice-captaincy and that Adam Gilchrist had been chosen as the new vice-captain.

'Thanks for the call, Malcolm,' I said, 'and goodnight.' With that I put down the receiver and rang Simone straight away. Even she was disappointed. Then I turned back on to my side and tried to go back to sleep.

Only time will tell whether I captain Australia in a Test match or not, whatever will be will be. It is an honour that I would deeply treasure. Denis Rogers, the Board chairman, has told me – and the public – that I am not necessarily out of contention in the future. If I am the best man available when Steve Waugh decides to hang up his boots then I might still be appointed. If it happens, it happens, but if it gets to the stage where I am too old and not at my best I suspect they are more likely to go for a younger man and rightly so. You have to make your decision at the time when it has to be made.

People might think I was responsible for my own downfall. At least, now, I have given my side of the story. I made a few mistakes along the way, but all in all it has been an enjoyable journey that is not over yet. It is an easy thing to say that we all learn from our mistakes. But in this case, I have – and become a better person for it. I am a cricketer and a human being.

There is a wealth of experience in the selectoral panel of Trevor Hohns, Andrew Hilditch, Allan Border and David Boon, who recently took over from Geoff Marsh. Marsh had been involved with the side as coach less than twelve months before joining the selectors, while Border's record of 156 Test appearances may never be broken. The directors, in contrast, are enthusiasts who, most of the time, do a great job, but on this occasion I think they got it wrong. Hohns told me when the media campaign was at its height that the selectors would recommend that I stayed in the post. I would like to think, too, that Steve Waugh, the captain, and John Buchanan, the coach, were favourable to my continuing. The fact that the Board didn't seem to take any account of what the selectors thought was best for the side really hurt.

I have given my heart and soul to Australian cricket and I like to think I've earned the respect of the ACB. I have helped to put a few backsides on seats and made spin bowling more interesting. I play in an aggressive, animated, emotional way which reflects the pride I take in representing my country. That should have counted for something, I would have thought.

We need to be careful that the captain and vice-captain are the best people for the job and not appointed simply because they are squeaky clean and do all the right things. Please don't get me wrong. I'm not saying anything against our current leaders. We just have to be careful that in the future the best people get the job. We do not want a Richie Cunningham figure in charge unless he is the best person. He was the character in *Happy Days* who was always polite and well-mannered, who said the right things at the right times, but relied on the Fonz, a more confident, streetwise figure, to overcome his problems in the real world. Cricket can be a colourful game and has a rich history of interesting players. Sometimes a captain needs to put a few noses out of joint. We don't want robots in charge of players or teams.

It amazed me that certain people think I have something against Adam Gilchrist, my successor. What a load of rubbish! He possesses a good, clear mind and has made a fantastic start to what I hope should be a long Test career.

When we assembled in Brisbane for the indoor one-day tournament against South Africa for the first time after the Board's

Glenn McGrath at Lord's in 1997, where he took 8 for 38.

Jason Gillespie is a vital member of the Australia side, whenever fit.

Matthew Elliott, one of the 1997 Ashes stars, on his way to 199 in the Fourth Test at Headingley.

Contemplating the Ashes series to come at a press conference in England, 1997.

In England in 1997 – spin bowlers need to look after their fingers.

Jacques Kallis of South Africa becomes my 300th Test wicket, Sydney, January 1998.

Starting to unwind with Ian Healy, man of the match at Trent Bridge, knowing that the Ashes are secured.

More runs for Mark Waugh in our 1999 World Cup game against Zimbabwe.

Delight in the green and gold as Allan Donald's run-out takes us to the 1999 World Cup final.

Celebrating our World Cup final win, to the disapproval of MCC members, it seems.

Steve Waugh and I share the privilege of meeting the Queen during a World Cup reception at Buckingham Palace.

The 1999 World Cup winning squad with Steve Waugh and myself holding the trophy.

Above Justin Langer and Adam Gilchrist pulled off a spectacular success against Pakistan at Hobart, November 1999.

Right Fitness permitting, Brett Lee has the potential to be one of the all-time greats.

Below A familiar feeling as Sachin Tendulkar works me away for runs. I don't think I've bowled to a better batsman.

Above Raising a glass with my brother and dad after passing Lillee's record.

Left Paul Wiseman of New Zealand caught by Adam Gilchrist in Auckland, March 2000. This was my 356th Test wicket, breaking Dennis Lillee's Australian record.

Below Receiving my Hampshire cap along with Alan Mullally at Southampton, 2000. Brian Ford (the Hampshire chairman), David Robinson (cricket chairman) and Robin Smith (captain) make the presentation.

decision I made a point of shaking his hand and saying congratu-lations. As if I am going to hold it against him, he's my team mate. I was disappointed at some suggestions that I might nurse a grudge. He was not involved in the decision. He said after being appointed that these weren't the ideal circumstances to gain the vice-captaincy, but what was he meant to do?

My concern is what might happen a few years down the track, because the directors have set a precedent. What happens in the future if an outstanding player comes through the ranks, a great cricketer who would make a natural leader but who committed some bad deed off the field? Alternatively, I wonder what might happen if the backgrounds of the fourteen directors themselves were investigated. If the same rules apply, as they should, then they, too, must have led unblemished lives or they are not fit to do their jobs.

Where the selectors are concerned, they have a tough job selecting and trying to squeeze everybody in, but it is better that way than not having people to pick. People have had a fair chance but with so much depth in Australian cricket there is always somebody else ready to step in if a place becomes available.

When a player comes in to replace a regular player they must grab their chance. Most often they do. It is a big help that the domestic competitions are so strong and competitive that the jump to Test cricket is not as great as it is in England, for example.

The selectors have not been afraid to make difficult decisions. There was an example in 1999 when Gilchrist replaced Ian Healy, even though Heals wanted to play a final Test in front of his home crowd at the Gabba. Dropping Healy, hastening his planned retirement, was a brave move, but Gilchrist immediately kept wicket tidily and scored 81 in our 10-wicket win against Pakistan.

I know that Heals thought it was a harsh decision at the time and nobody would have criticised the selectors for sticking with one of the all-time greats in those circumstances just for one more Test. I'm sure that Healy would have done an equally steady job, but the way Gilchrist had taken to Test cricket showed he was ready.

Even though I disagreed with my own omission for the Fourth Test against West Indies in 1998–99, I could understand the reasoning. I would like to think I have repaid the selectors' faith in me earlier in my career.

The views of the captain have to be taken into consideration because he, after all, is the man who takes the players on to the field and he needs to have confidence in his team. Matters are different on tour because the selectors do not travel with the party. Maybe one should, who knows? I think we have it right, the captain has a major say in conjunction with the selectors.

Knowing when to step down is a difficult call when it has been your life for so long but, deep down, players know when their time is up. Now that the rewards for international players are greater than ever before it might be tempting to go on even for just one or two games too many and place the selectors in a difficult situation. I don't think any of the Aussie team would do that.

Players of standing should know their games well enough to be able to look at themselves and work out if they are holding back someone or the rest of the team, or not doing themselves justice. When they reach that point they should make it easy for the selectors by stepping down voluntarily. Having been dropped, I don't want my own career to end that way. There is no way I will do that. I will retire when my enjoyment has gone and when my bowling is no longer good enough at that level. Or I suppose I might not have any say in the matter.

The selectors could just say: 'Sorry, mate, your time's up.' Experienced players have gut feelings. I can also understand the temptation to go out on a high after considering my own future following the World Cup win in 1999. On reflection I thought I had something to offer to the Aussie team.

I played my early cricket for Australia with Border and Marsh, who later became a very popular and effective coach. I played with Hilditch in grade cricket at Glenelg and, although I never faced Hohns, I followed his progress when he was on the 1989 Ashes tour from club duties in England. I have found him a very open and honest chairman who has always been available to the players. The days when we had to read the papers or listen to the radio to find out if we had been picked are thankfully over. I remember discovering I was going to England in 1993 by turning on the wireless at the home of Simone's mum and dad. It was a nervous time because the names were read out alphabetically and I was trying to keep a count of the players until the announcer reached the three Ws: Warne, M. Waugh, S. Waugh.

Contrary to some of the publicity during the 1997–98 dispute, the players have never wanted to run the game. All we wanted was an input and a fair slice of the pie, and I think now the balance is right. Through Tim May, the Cricketers' Association (ACA) works constructively with the ACB, particularly with Steve Bernard, the team manager, and Richard Watson, the operations manager, along with James Sutherland from the ACB on a day-to-day basis.

When there was talk about a strike it was just so the ACB would listen to us. We just wanted a fair hearing, that's all. It was for the state players as well as the international players, for every first-class cricketer in Australia. The state players were being expected to dedicate years of their lives for relatively small reward and even less security. These days there is far more to playing for Victoria than turning up on the morning of a match and maybe practising a couple of times a week. We felt that if more was being expected in the way of training camps, coaching clinics, fitness sessions and 2nd XI fixtures, then the reward should be there. All up it comes to about seven or eight months a year. Whether that is a good or bad thing is another story. From being on around $25,000 less tax each year a regular state player can now earn up to $80,000 as a contracted player. He now has the security to organise a mortgage or a loan, instead of having to worry from week to week, and our domestic game is more professional as a result, which is the way it should be.

Our campaign got serious towards the end of the England tour in 1997 when we voted to appoint Graham Halbish, the former ACB chief executive, and James Erskine, a highly respected figure in the marketing world, to help our campaign. The decision to use Halbish, with his knowledge, antagonised the Board, but showed we were more serious than trying to gain the odd, relatively minor concession for a few of us fortunate enough to have reached the top. Cricket had become a big business and has continued to grow ever since with the latest TV deal for the next two World Cups.

We were not being greedy, simply making sure we were receiving a fair share compared to other sports; and trying to find out what was a fair share. Although cricket was the most successful national sport, we discovered we were the lowest paid as a percentage of revenue. We did not think it unreasonable for the players to receive 20 per cent of the cake. Of that 20 per cent the split was 55 per cent going to ACB contracted players (the Australia squad, in effect) and 45 per cent to the state cricketers. When we began negotiations we started at a figure closer to 30 per cent and compromised from there.

Unfortunately the media concentrated on the earnings of the top few players. They were getting some figures that were uncannily accurate, but which included endorsements and sponsorships. I'm not sure where the information came from. It was dirty pool.

Gradually through the 1997–98 season our resolve hardened. As the ACA treasurer I was heavily involved. None of us really wanted to strike, we just wanted to be heard. I am not a political animal, but I felt there was something really worth fighting for here and helping in a small way to improve the lot of state cricketers now and in the future ranks as a proud achievement. At that time May was the president, Steve Waugh the secretary and Greg Matthews and Tony Dodemaide made up the committee as former players. It was a very interesting time and one that was important to all of us.

As relations between the players and officials deteriorated matters threatened to come to a head during the Test series against New Zealand, this despite our calling a truce ahead of the first game in Brisbane. A ballot among state cricketers revealed unanimous support for a strike if need be. That meant that if the national team went on strike, the ACB would not be able to pick eleven other players, because the ACA had unanimous support from all the players. It was a stalemate. The situation became further complicated when Taylor, thinking he should take the initiative as the national captain, entered into talks with Denis Rogers, the ACB chairman, and came back with what he thought was a solution. We discussed this as a team during the Second Test at Perth.

Then we put it to a secret ballot of the twelve players in Perth with the votes being placed in a cap and me writing down the votes on a board as they were pulled out one by one. The final tally was 11–1 against the solution as put by Rogers to Taylor, and in favour of talks with May. There was no question that we would strike if need be, even though, deep down, nobody wanted to. The fact is that, if the Board had refused to talk and compromise, we would have had no other course of action except to strike. We were looking towards the subsequent one-day series against New Zealand and South Africa as the time to withdraw, knowing that the state players would not be prepared to step in.

Thankfully we did not have to strike, and all of us were very happy. We managed to get a verbal agreement that the ACB would talk to us – meaning May – between the Test and the one-day series and from then on it was a case of both sides playing give and take. It should never have been thought of as a matter of winners and losers because we all wanted the best for Australian cricket. Unpleasant words were exchanged at times and tempers lost, but I think it is something that had to happen given the changing nature of the game. At the end of it all both sides emerged the wiser and we have all gone from strength to strength. It is now a win-win situation for the ACB and the ACA. It works very well now.

Despite all of the meetings, we still managed to beat New Zealand by an innings in Perth, when no dressing room conversation was complete without some reference to the on-going dispute. Mark Taylor must have been going through hell and a real tough time as captain and I was very happy that we won and the dispute was over. Everyone was relieved. I think it said much for the commitment of the players overall that we beat an improving New Zealand side two–nil.

It is only because cricketers were relatively so poorly paid in the past that the figures we get paid now seem so high, but compared to other sports they are around average or just above. Ex-players coming out of the woodwork and saying they only earned x amount to play hurt because times have changed, the marketing side has been developed and cricket is big business rather than a game. Television has brought cricket huge exposure and commercial success. At the start of the financial year the Board now estimates how much revenue it expects to bring in and the players benefit from anything beyond that figure. In 1999–2000, for example, when we strung together six successive wins at home and also took the one-day series against India and Pakistan, that meant quite a windfall for all international and state players.

The incident in my career that I regret the most came during the First Test against South Africa in Johannesburg in 1993–94. To this day I have no idea why I abused Andrew Hudson, probably one of the nicest guys ever to have played the game. The reaction back home provided my first taste of bad publicity and I had to work hard to redeem my character and show that success hadn't gone to my head, which it never has.

It was my first taste of South Africa and I found it hard to come to terms with the demands of some of the people. There was a lot of attention on us from the moment we landed. Wherever we went people wanted autographs – which is fine, we always try to oblige – but I did not like the way that some people, which seemed to be a large number of adults, would almost demand signatures in an aggressive way, without thinking to say please or thank you. They wouldn't worry about jostling each other or pushing through kids to make sure they got what they wanted. Worse than that, I also received calls in my room at the hotel from people who just wanted to be abusive – some of them in the middle of the night.

The Wanderers ground is not known as the Bull Ring simply because of its high circular stands. The home crowd generates an intimidating atmosphere and the walk from the dressing room on to the field can be quite scary as it passes through a grassed area where the players are protected from the public only by low fencing. When I fielded on the boundary I tried to have some fun with the crowd – just the usual tricks, like looking down my trousers when somebody asked me to show them my mystery ball. But when I was suddenly hit on the back by an orange, and then turned round to see the security guards laughing, I could feel myself getting more and more angry. I thought that was unfair.

Coming on to bowl in the forty-fourth over I was like a bomb waiting to explode. I bowled Hudson around his legs and almost immediately it felt as though somebody had pulled the pin from a grenade. I started shouting and swearing at the poor batsman before being restrained. Every time I see the clip now I cringe. I just lost it. David Shepherd, one of the umpires, immediately called over Allan Border and asked him to calm me down. I knew I was in the wrong in a big way and accepted the fine of 1,000 Rand (around $400) levied by Donald Carr, the match referee, after a meeting that night with Allan Border and Cam Battersby, the manager, who had also witnessed everything that happened. On the way back to our dressing room I sought out Hudson to apologise and explain the situation. Like the man he is he accepted the apology and we even managed to share a joke about what had happened with the whole South Africa team.

What annoyed me the most was the way the ACB then felt I needed to be punished a second time – worse, they fined me $4,000 without any right of appeal, which goes against all natural justice. They made their decision without hearing my version of events. Unless they had been at the Bull Ring that day and followed the growing levels of intimidation through the early weeks of the tour they could not have made a balanced judgement. Their decision followed criticism of my behaviour from the media, some of whom were writing and broadcasting from the comfort of their offices in Australia, unbelievable stuff. Merv Hughes suffered the same fate after being found guilty of sledging. He was fined by Carr and then again by the ACB.

From Johannesburg we had gone to nearby Sun City holiday resort, supposedly to chill out for a few days, but with so many television crews having decided to follow Merv and me to keep the story moving, it wasn't easy to relax. Fortunately, my dad, a man I deeply respect, had arrived on a pre-arranged trip and he encouraged me to try to forget the problem and effectively start again. In the end, I went to visit Border in his room at Stellenbosch, with Merv, to see what he thought of the whole situation. Although he was sympathetic and agreed that the ACB had mishandled the situation, he said the best response was to make sure we put all our efforts into winning the Second Test. The subsequent victory in that game at Cape Town was very satisfying. AB had a lot on his plate but he always found the time for you. That was one of his greatest strengths.

Since then, as I have explained earlier, the relationship between the players and the ACB has improved remarkably which is great for everyone concerned. I don't know whether the repercussions of a similar incident would be the same today now that better lines of communication are open. I like to think that at the very least somebody would have asked for my side of the story.

At that time the Board was very sensitive to criticism that we were becoming too aggressive on the field. This might have been the opportunity the directors wanted for them to be seen as being tough and they used us as an example. The shame is that such a great Australian cricketer as Merv didn't play again for his country after that. Cape Town was his last Test.

Having ex-players involved in cricket administration makes a lot of sense, to my way of thinking. I hate the way that politics and vested interests get in the way of sport, especially cricket. It really disappoints me that people should pretend to be on your side one minute and then word gets back that they have said the opposite to somebody else. Saying one thing to your face and another behind your back is really weak, and those people are the worst kind. If you have a problem with anyone you should confront them straight away and sort it out.

I am pleased that the ICC are trying to take firm action on the general issue of match-fixing. Cricket needs to have a strong, worldwide governing body with full responsibility for the game. Unfortunately, that is not the case at the moment because power still lies in the hands of the home boards. They need to work in conjunction with each other. The game is expanding, with more and more money coming in and, encouragingly, development projects are in place all over the world. It should not be run according to the interests of a single country or a single power bloc.

The ICC should be aiming to recruit the right calibre of personnel. I believe the senior figures should be a combination of proven business people, the sort who have not been afraid to make difficult decisions and have a history of hard work and generating profits, former players and other cricket people who have worked at a good level, not just been stalwarts of their local club for year after year and are appointed as a reward. I'd be the first to recognise that without the stalwarts a lot of things would not happen. They are valuable and likeable people. What I'm saying is that running cricket at the highest level shouldn't be done on a 'you scratch my back, I'll scratch yours' basis. The approach has to be professional and thorough and with willingness to learn. I think we're all trying to improve and it is slowly happening. Two of the major issues they need to sort out are the chucking process and the standard of umpiring. There needs to be a better process for bowlers with suspect actions. On umpiring, anyone who has played first-class cricket should be fast-tracked.

15

THE ART OF LEG-SPIN

I CANNOT LOOK at cricket in isolation from the rest of my life. That is why my family, who have been the biggest influence on my life, are also the biggest on my career – my mum, dad, brother and Simone, my wife. The four of them have been terrific. When I was young, my parents offered all the encouragement in the world to my brother and me, even on the many occasions when we must have driven them to distraction. These days Brigitte, my mother, calls herself 'the coach' when she rings before a game to wish me luck. Jason, my brother, has also been one of my best friends, and my dad – well, he's just been a great father.

Simone is the biggest stabilising influence in my life today. She tends to cop my bad moods when things haven't gone well on the field. There are some things about me that only she knows. Fortunately, I don't get angry very often. If it's a problem with someone then I will confront them straight away, but if it is something only I can sort out I probably bottle it up too much. Simone has become my shoulder to lean on and the children have been a great leveller to both of us. They help us to keep things in perspective.

For the first few years in international cricket I couldn't really do much wrong. I have often wondered what made the situation change. Perhaps there was a bit of jealousy. I can't put my finger on it.

Since then the criticism has become hugely personal. I have lost count of the digs about my weight, the car I drive, my hair, where I live, what I've done wrong and what I'm worth, which are often thrown into articles gratuitously. There might be an element of the Tall Poppy syndrome here. Who knows?

The media frenzy began after the Melbourne Test against West Indies in 1992 when I took 7 wickets in the second innings, and hit fever pitch after the Gatting Ball in England a few months later.

That was when people really wanted to know everything about me on and off the field, particularly details of my hobbies, my eating habits, my background at the Academy, my school-days and – most important, it seemed – my ex-girlfriends.

From being an inexperienced state player and fringe Test bowler I was suddenly seen not just as the great white hope for Australian cricket but as the guy who was making leg-spin bowling fashionable.

I was twenty-three, still very naive, and, however it looked publicly, everything was happening so fast. All of a sudden I was followed in cars by cameramen and snapped at every opportunity. Journalists wanted to find new angles all the time and were prepared to encroach on to my private time with Simone. I struggled to come to grips with it at times, because it was all new to me.

Bus tours used to come past our house to see where I live and take photographs. I remember one occasion when Simone and I were walking around in Bristol soon after our engagement in 1993 and were followed by a photographer who waited until we started to tuck in to a bucket of chips before taking his snaps. That was the time when newspapers started paying ex-girlfriends to reveal my past. Even during the World Cup in

1999 somebody came out of the woodwork from a long time ago. It upsets me when people are prepared to make themselves look so cheap in that way for money.

The worst case of press intrusion was probably when a reporter for the *Melbourne Age* wanted to do a story about my mum and dad in 1994. At the time I was writing a column for the paper myself, so I put it to my parents who said straight away that they weren't keen on the idea. I passed that back on. That should have been the end of the matter. However, the journalist decided to do some investigating and find out where they lived. The newspaper printed the address of our house. Three days later we were burgled. That was totally out of order. Sometimes those people ruin it for the cricket guys who have to cover the sport day in, day out. There is no excuse for that. My parents suffered enormously and that wasn't fair.

Where does my public life end and my private life begin? It is a difficult one to answer and a very fine line. But there should be a line – unfortunately there is not. One of the nicknames I had for a while was Truman, as in *The Truman Show*, the film starring Jim Carrey in which the character's life is filmed twenty-four hours a day. Ian Healy nicknamed me Elvis, after Elvis Presley, in South Africa in 1994. Earlier, in my football career, Trevor Barker called me Hollywood. On a number of occasions I have described my life as being like a soap opera at times – a series of apparently unbelievable events chained together.

I accept that sportsmen and women are role models and that is why the public are interested in our lives, but we are also human beings. I find it rewarding beyond description to see kids flipping leggies to each other in a park and thinking that I might have played a part and had something to do with it. The problem is that it's hard to reach agreement, to compromise. What would you do if the media decided they wanted a photograph of your new baby and you did not want that to happen? Believe me, it isn't enough to say no. Photographers hang around outside the house and try to see through the windows with their long lenses – it's amazing what lengths some of them go to. You draw the curtains and black out the car windows but still they persevere. The result is that eventually you allow a staged photograph – which you didn't want in the first place – otherwise you have to put up with it every day.

On the playing side itself I think Allan Border, Terry Jenner and Ian Chappell have been the men to help me most. Border was my first captain of Australia. He was the guy who really showed me what it takes to play international cricket and how much it means to play for Australia. Jenner, to my eyes, is the guru of spin bowling. He has given me a deeper insight than anybody else into the art of that leg-spin. What I admire most about Terry is that he doesn't impose his ideas. For a coach he listens as much as he talks, although when he does talk there is no time wasted in pleasantries before he arrives at his point. He is a direct, forthright bloke who has strong opinions.

There is no doubt that meeting Jenner was the highpoint of those difficult months at the AIS Academy. I think even then he recognised I was a little bit different. In the twelve years since, our relationship has developed to the point where we teach each other. Until we started working together he had never bowled a flipper, even though he played for Australia and had a great record for South Australia. From what people say, he would have played far more regularly for his country if only he possessed more self-belief. I think we were good for each other. Ian Healy christened him the Spin Doctor and the name has stuck. It is the perfect description.

He is always encouraging me to try something different in the nets, but accepts that not everything will work. I remember when he asked me to bowl a different line, outside off stump, instead of my usual middle and leg or leg. I pointed out that it was not my style, but eventually I gave it a go and promptly pulled three or four down short. In that case he accepted that it just wasn't going to happen. These days we have a very informal arrangement where we speak to each other every few weeks during the Australian season. He will ring me if he spots something on television, or I will get in touch with him if I feel something isn't quite working. The relationship works because we get on well as people. We are both pretty down to earth people who enjoy a beer and a chat. Both of us have been described as non-conformists in our time, which may or may not be true.

As an example, when I came back into the side after my first operation on my spinning finger in 1996–97 it took time for my confidence to return. Confidence is one of those immeasurable factors that affects every part of your game, and because I wasn't certain of myself I could not seem to fizz the ball the way I had done almost routinely before surgery. Terry was in Sydney commentating before the Second Test against the West Indies and corrected the matter very simply by getting me to bowl from a standing start and spin the ball purely from my hand. He had noticed from replays during the previous game in Brisbane that I was putting the ball on the spot rather than spinning it there.

One tip of his I've employed is to bowl a wrong-un when a batsman first comes in. Yes, you are bowling the ball for him, not the batsman who is on strike. It doesn't matter if the batsman on strike picks it. The idea is that the new guy at the non-striker's end knows I can spin the ball both ways so that when he gets to the striker's end he immediately starts to look for the one that goes the other way. Thinking it will only be a matter of time before I send down a wrong-un, he becomes more and more confused the longer I leave it, looking for something that might not be there.

Terry has also taught me about using different angles at the crease when I go over the wicket, and helped me over my over-spinner. I managed to develop a ball that goes more slowly through the air but bounces a little more than the leg-break. Carl Hooper of the West Indies has fallen for this one a few times. But Terry is shrewd enough to appreciate that my biggest weapon is the ripping leg-break and has never compromised that for the sake of variety.

Richie Benaud is another guy who has given enormous help. I wonder how many young viewers of Channel Nine in Australia and Channel Four in England realise he was a great leg-spin bowler and very intelligent captain, one of the best. He is not a man to volunteer information because he does not like to impose on players, but anybody who asks is guaranteed a friendly reception. All of his work for television over many years has helped to make him a superb analyst and his position high up behind the bowler's arm means he always has one of the best seats in the house, backed up by replays. I know he loves watching leg-spin bowling. Every now and then I will ask whether he has noticed anything about my action or delivery stride, knowing that if there is anything to see then Richie will have spotted it.

Few people in my experience speak such good, clear sense as Ian Chappell. We were introduced by Jenner while I was at the Academy and have grown to become good friends. With his terrific knowledge of the game, he is a fantastic bloke to grab for a chat over a beer. He has helped me through some difficult times and been there to share some of my happiest moments. What always impresses me about Chappell is his upbeat and positive outlook, no matter how stressful the situation. There is always wisdom in what he says and he speaks logically without over-complicating a subject. Of all past Australia captains he is the one I would most like to have played under. Clearly, he was a masterful tactician and a fierce competitor who always backed his players, no matter what.

It was Chappell who taught me the importance of knowing myself and backing my own judgement. He said that no two players were the same when it comes to preparing to play. If I wanted a few beers to relax on the eve of the game, then why not? We became close during the 1996 US Masters golf tournament in Augusta. He was commentating for Channel Nine and I had gone along to learn the ropes. As a result of one of many conversations he invited me to a batting clinic he was about to run at the Academy back home. This came about after a couple of beers at the end of a day's play at the golf. We were just chatting about batting and the West Indies who were coming out that summer. I had just had an operation on the spinning finger and thought that it could be a target, so why not get some practice against short-pitched bowling? It was fantastic and I felt confident after spending some time with Ian in Adelaide.

My first coach for Australia, Bobby Simpson, was another guy absolutely committed to Australia and the good of the game worldwide. He has gone on to do a lot of work for the ICC. It helped from my point of view that he was a part-time leg-spinner himself, even though he is better remembered for his batting. Simpson showed me that bowling around the wicket could be an aggressive rather than a negative approach. I remember being twelfth man for the Perth Test against India in 1991–92 when we started chatting about spin. I didn't believe him at first because I couldn't see anything positive in what he was saying. It just seemed to be a way of keeping the runs down rather than taking wickets. I had never really given it much thought. But then at the close of play he took me to the nets and told me to strap on my pads before proving his point. During that session he must have had me out stumped three or four times. Clearly he had something worth taking on board, or at least thinking about. I mentioned it to Jenner who was open-minded, as always, and decided to set about practising. I soon realised he had a point and since then some of my favourite wickets have been taken around the wicket, including my three-hundredth in Tests, Jacques Kallis, bowled with a top-spinner which he tried to pad away. Thanks, Simmo!

Simpson passed on another theory, that around the wicket is a way of making sure the action is working properly. Very often since then I have gone around the wicket for a few balls and felt better immediately after switching back. He encouraged me and showed me what I could do and helped me to be the best I could. That's what coaching is all about.

It is difficult to say how many different balls I have in my armoury now, because each one has small variations. I have two wrong-uns for example, one designed to spin more than the other. Then I have the basic leg-break with overspin or side spin and a straight ball that looks like a leg-break but just goes on with the arm. The zooter is like a back-spinner, and then there is the flipper, a ball that has served me especially well. The other delivery is natural variation off the wicket! In all cases I can control the amount of spin I try to impart, vary the wrist position slightly and use a rounder arm or higher action. But what a bowler cannot control is the variation in the wickets.

There are so many combinations, but in essence a wrist-spinner can reach Test status with one single ball – as long as it is a really good leg-break. That is worth any number of wrong-uns, flippers or zooters because it is the ball that consistently causes batsmen difficulties, right- or left-handed. Anything beyond that is a bonus as long as it can be controlled.

What matters is not always how many deliveries you possess, but how many the batsman thinks you have. Half of the battle is sowing doubt in his mind. If he is looking out for the wrong-un, it makes no difference whether you can actually bowl it or not. There is so much truth in the old saying – if a batsman thinks the pitch is spinning, then it's spinning.

So much improvement comes with practice, experience and developing a plan. I have learnt to think of three words all the time – what, when and why. That means always knowing what I am going to bowl, when I am going to bowl it and to be clear why I have chosen that option. When I was younger I just sent down the biggest leg-breaks I could and slipped in a wrong-un or a flipper every so often just because it was a long time since the last. There was no long-term strategy. I knew the what, but not the when and the why. Sometimes I wonder if I have gone too far the other way, whether I have too many choices and have forgotten to keep things simple. I think these are the times when I haven't bowled well. If I am in any doubt I send down a leg-break. That will always be my bread and butter.

I generally decide what to bowl as I walk back to my mark after the previous ball, then pause to be absolutely clear in my mind. If I am not sure, the pause is a bit longer than usual. Once my mind is clear and I start to walk in, there is no time for a change of plan. Leg-spin bowlers start to get into trouble if they have second thoughts. In fact, I would guess it is one of the most common reasons for bowling a bad ball. Either the ball becomes stuck in the hand or the bowler fails to complete the action.

A lot of wrist-spinners hold the ball tightly, but I prefer a very loose grip. That way I feel more relaxed in my approach. I have tried the more traditional method, but it has always made me too tense as I walk in. From experience I have also dragged more balls down short with the tighter grip. By loose, I meant that I like to be able to pull the ball out of my hand with the other easily. As with so many aspects of bowling, though, there is no right or wrong. I would never persuade a youngster to grip tightly. I do not think it is the role of the coach to impose himself on somebody who has a natural aptitude for turning the ball. Paul Adams of South Africa has an extraordinary action, but somehow it works for him.

Equally, a young bowler should always be prepared to listen. It doesn't cost anything. I have been fortunate down the years to receive help from the likes of Jenner, Benaud, Jim Higgs, Ashley Mallett, Border, Bob Paulsen and Simpson, all of whom have bowled spin. The best advice I can give to aspiring leggies – or any budding cricketers for that matter – is to think of yourself as a human sponge and try to absorb every bit of advice that is out there. If you think the guy is talking rubbish, then be polite by saying thank you, and quietly ignore it. But if you keep an open mind, you might be fortunate occasionally to pick up a real beauty. Try it, and if it doesn't work then try the next thing, because that one might. The key then is to practise, practise, practise. Wrist-spin is not easy to get right. It takes hours and hours of hard work. Although I make jokes about my lifestyle and diet, about the beer and pizza, I also spend hours trying to fine-tune my game. I was brought up to work hard during the day and then enjoy myself after hours. Success is so much nicer when you know it has been earned.

Other than being able to turn the leg-break and possessing a strong work ethic, a wrist spinner must have patience. Without it there isn't much point bothering, because batsmen just don't give their wickets away as a token of respect for a good ball. As bowlers we have one important psychological advantage. If we make a mistake, we always get another chance.

No matter how far the batsman hits the ball it always comes back. All right, I will re-phrase that. Sometimes it is a different ball if he has hit the first one out of the ground, but the point is that we can turn back to our mark for another opportunity. If the batsman doesn't quite get everything right only once, then his game is over for a while.

I own a good collection of footage of myself bowling down the years and my action has changed slightly for no particular purpose or reason. This happens to most bowlers. As we get older and suffer with injuries alterations creep in subconsciously. Bowling is a strenuous occupation and we have to learn how to survive with a few niggles. I would guess that it is a luxury for any experienced bowler to be completely 100 per cent fit at any time. When my shoulder was really hurting during the 1994–95 Ashes series I crept into one bad habit. Initially, when Terry Jenner told me he'd spotted a problem, I felt sceptical because I had taken 20 wickets, including a hat-trick, in the first two Tests but, as usual, there was something in his words and I rectified the problem by the end of the campaign. I wasn't following through and my arm wasn't coming across my body.

Generally, when I am not bowling well it is because I am falling away at the crease, not following through or pushing the ball out of my hand rather than spinning it. These are the three key areas I think about first if I don't feel right and, with experience, I have learnt how to solve the problem almost immediately. Over the years some of my best 'coaches' on the field have been, firstly, Ian Healy because he has the best view behind the wicket, then Mark Taylor and Mark Waugh at first slip. I will occasionally ask how I look every few overs as a matter of course. Terry taught me the phrase 'Think high, spin up.' In the early days my arm was quite low which made it difficult to bowl the wrong-un or over-spinner. I concentrate on making sure my action is not too round-arm or too high and, again, that I spin the ball instead of just putting the ball on the spot.

By coincidence, when I broke my finger in 2000–01 I was spending some time with Giles White, an opening batsman with Hampshire who had come to Australia during the English winter to work on his game. Giles was basically a top-order batsman who bowled a bit of wrist-spin. He had never really devoted much time to spin but clearly had the ability to bowl. Helping Giles made me go back to basics myself and for the first time in years I started to think seriously about how everything worked again. When I came back for Victoria, and then against West Indies in the one-day series, my action felt smooth and I turned the ball sharply almost from day one. It was great to have Chalkie and his wife Sam stay with us, they are a lovely couple.

There is a great brotherhood among leg-spin bowlers. For a time it seemed that the art might be lost and I think we all realise the need to make sure as much knowledge of the craft stays within the game. One of my happiest memories is meeting Abdul Qadir at his house in Pakistan. Qadir is one of the true greats and before long we were sitting on his living room floor flicking leg-breaks and flippers across the room to each other. Back then, in 1994, many locals thought he should still be in the Pakistan team. I would go further and say he is probably good enough to play Test cricket even now in his mid-forties. There is no fat on him and he still has great enthusiasm for the game and leg-spin in particular.

Qadir reiterated to me the importance of being patient in the fourth innings when spin is expected to come into its own and there is pressure to take wickets. He pointed out that whatever the target, half of those runs will have to come off me because I will bowl half of the overs. If I am more patient than the batsman and he is trying to win the game – not save it – by chasing a target, that gives me a good chance. He wanted to see how I bowled my flipper and he showed me his wrong-un in turn. I thought his wrong-un was fantastic. Our actions were different – he would come bouncing in with a quick, whippy action, whereas I walk to the crease. But our mindsets turned out to be quite similar. We both think very aggressively.

It is impossible to put a price on an evening like that. The game owes a great debt to Qadir for effectively keeping wrist-spin alive single-handed through the late 70s and 80s. Fast bowling dominated and any spin in one-day cricket was of the negative variety or a last resort. I like to think I have played a part in making spin fashionable again, but I hope people don't forget the part played by Qadir in the history of cricket. Fortunately, Australia has a tradition of great leg-spin going back to the likes of Clarrie Grimmett and Bill O'Reilly before the war and Richie Benaud afterwards. That is why I received encouragement from the likes of Jenner and Jack Potter at the Academy, when in other countries I might not have even made the first-class game.

The wrist-spinners who gave me most pleasure during the 90s were Anil Kumble and Mushtaq Ahmed. If he was not a hero to India already then Kumble set himself up for life that day in Delhi in February 1999 when he took all 10 Pakistan wickets in an innings. To do that is incredible because, by definition, if wickets are not falling at the other end there ought not to be too many problems with the pitch. It is one of the all-time great bowling performances, unbelievable stuff.

The two of us have had dinner a few times and, despite our different backgrounds, always get on like old buddies. Spin bowling is an international language in itself and whenever two exponents get together we chat about our methods. It is no different from a couple of used car salesmen bumping into each other – they will pass on a few tricks about deceiving customers, while we talk about deceiving batsmen. Kumble's strengths are his longevity and consistency. He rarely gives anything to hit, and because of his high action he generates good bounce. By the final day on an up and down pitch he can be lethal. Australia's method over the years has been to treat him as a medium-pace inswing bowler.

He has shown me his flipper and I showed him how I bowl my big leg-break. In truth I don't think we have mastered each other's delivery yet. I went away and practised and I still try occasionally. I know what to do, but it doesn't quite seem to work. That might be because our actions are completely different.

There is another lesson here for any kids – if something works for you, then don't change because your mate does it differently. Kumble is a thorough gentleman off the field but extremely competitive on it.

Mushtaq has the same temperament. He has clearly based his action on Qadir and, while he might not be in quite the same class, he has been a good bowler for Pakistan. I really enjoy watching Mushtaq bowl because of his sheer zest. He always expects a wicket. His leg-break doesn't turn much except from wide outside off stump. Australia's method has been to play him like an off-spinner and use our feet.

Some time in the mid-90s I gave Mushtaq my flipper and he showed me his wrong-un. I thought that was a pretty good trade-off. He proved a quick learner and suddenly took a lot of our wickets in the 1995–96 series. More than one Australian batsman asked me what I had done. They seemed to overlook the fact that I happened to be taking a few wickets myself as well.

Navjot Sidhu is a player who was hard to bowl to because he was so quick on his feet. Laxman on the 2001 tour to India was unbelievable, dancing down the wicket hitting leg breaks out of the rough through midwicket for 4.

Some people have said that my duel with Sachin Tendulkar in India in 1997–98 was the most compelling Test cricket they have ever seen, but there is no doubt he enjoyed the better of the exchanges. He has played me better than anybody. Most Indian batsmen pick the length very quickly, even when it is flighted above the eyeline, but Tendulkar moved into position even earlier than the likes of Mohammad Azharuddin and Rahul Dravid.

His footwork is immaculate – he would either go right forward or all the way back – and he has the confidence to go for his strokes. I suppose I would be confident too if I batted as well as Tendulkar.

Although my statistics in that series don't make happy reading, I am still prepared to say it was a pleasure to bowl to him. The only comparable batsman would be Brian Lara in the Caribbean in 1999. No player can ever win a game on his own, but Lara came close in Jamaica and Barbados. He is an exciting batsman and, if his mind is right, he is very hard to bowl to.

Much has been said and written about the best way to play me, particularly the merits or otherwise of the sweep shot. It is interesting that the players I have mentioned as being successful – Tendulkar and Lara – hardly employed the shot. Lara has used it in one-day cricket, but that's all. I am always happier to see batsmen sweep. The stroke can generate runs, but it also carries a high risk because it is so hard to control.

I always back myself over time to either bowl the batsman behind his legs or get a top edge or lbw. If the ball is the right length to sweep it can usually be driven just as easily and with far less jeopardy.

In contrast, I hate to see batsmen pad me away. It is the one thing guaranteed to frustrate me and I don't think it is very attractive to watch for the spectators. I would much rather batsmen tried to take me on, even if I concede a few more runs. At least that way I have a chance of taking a wicket. If a batsman decides he is just going to kick everything away it is quite difficult to get him out. There is the possibility of one bouncing a little more and maybe hitting the glove or perhaps getting a nick if the ball really rips, but waiting for that to happen can be a lengthy process.

For a bit of fun I wondered how I would try to play my own bowling. The honest answer is that I would struggle. I'm a sucker for anything flighted, so I would run down the pitch to try to hit the ball over the top. As a bowler I think that patience is one of my biggest strengths, but as a batsman I just want to hit the ball as far, as hard and as often as I can. I don't worry too much about actually building an innings. On a good day I'd back S. K. Warne the batsman to clout S. K. Warne the bowler for 30 or 40, but it would still be a brief innings. How out? Either caught at long off or stumped (and I don't think the square leg umpire would need to call for a TV replay). Can't imagine why that maiden hundred is proving so elusive . . .

Leg-spin is fun and I have enjoyed the battles with the best players in the world over the last ten years. It is exciting and hard work but, with practice, there are wickets there to be had.

16

SLEDGING

S LEDGING is a form of gamesmanship or in the words of the great Merv Hughes 'verbal pressure'. It is a way of raising the chances of forcing an error by trying to put the batsman off his game in order to pick up a wicket or irritate a bowler into losing his line and length. If I can get a batsman out by saying something that affects his game so much, then why not? That is a chink in his mental armoury. The word derives from the simile 'As subtle as a sledgehammer' – which says it all. It should not become too nasty or personal.

Fast bowlers generally sledge out of frustration. Darren Berry and Greg Matthews are two of the more refined exponents of the art. When I hear Glenn McGrath shouting something like 'I'm going to hit you on the head, buddy' to a Test batsman who has just hit him to the boundary, it is frustration, but it does put doubt into the mind of the player. McGrath some-times comes out with a few clangers, but he does intimidate some batsmen.

For some reason Australia have acquired the reputation of being the worst sledgers in the world, but I think New Zealand should hold that mantle. Whether they just reserve it for us because of the geographical rivalry I don't know, but sometimes it feels like being in an aviary full of twittering birds.

Most of the time they are not particularly nasty, just silly comments. I think Adam Parore is the worst, but most of the keepers say a lot and I remember an occasion when Mark Waugh had enough of Parore's constant verbals. They both use equipment from the same company and eventually Mark turned round to Parore and said: 'How much do you have to pay for your bats cost price?' Any slight on his ability tends to keep Parore quiet for an over or two and that nice one-liner kept him quiet – unfortunately only temporarily.

Compared to the Australia side I joined in the early 90s the team of today is relatively quiet, even with McGrath in our ranks. Merv Hughes led the way. He claimed in his book that a quarter of all his wickets were down to sledging. Merv was a fine bowler and he intimidated a lot of batsmen. With his stare, sweat and handlebar moustache he did have a certain aura about him. His words were funnier rather than anything else, and that is the trick of putting a batsman off or breaking his concentration. It just didn't look that way when he stared at a batsman. With a face like that he didn't really need words, but they add to his image and his act.

Dean Jones used to have plenty to say and David Boon used to mumble a few remarks from under his helmet at short leg. Both of the Waughs were quick to join in with their one-liners and Ian Healy believed that contributing more than the odd word came as part of the wicket-keeper's job. But I think the cleverest sledger was probably Greg Matthews. He was very intelligent with his choice of phraseology and genuinely annoyed batsmen with his comments. Matthews really showed there could be an art in sledging. He did his homework.

Part of the trick is recognising who might be vulnerable and who is best left alone. Although Border used to be quick to let his opponents know what he thought of them in the middle, he was the last person it was advisable to sledge in return. Those who did put in a word usually regretted it, because he simply became more determined to preserve his wicket. Some days he would say to a fielder who happened to be walking past, 'What are you looking at,' just to try to provoke a response to fire himself up. He was looking for that element of confrontation to help him focus on the task ahead.

Border taught me the usefulness of sledging in raising my own game. If things were not happening for me, he suggested, then it was probably worth having a word with the batsman – not for the sake of having a go, but to switch myself on for the contest.

Cricket isn't an easy game, but it is a great leveller sometimes. Fortunately, I have learnt it is far more effective to make the odd comment here and there than to maintain a continual flow. I have seen too many batsmen step up a level when they have been sledged. You have to pick your mark. Suddenly the guy can have 30 or 40 runs to his name and be well set for a major innings, while the bowler has wasted all his energy.

I wonder how the Aussie sides of yesteryear would cope with the game today. There is so much television coverage that you have to accept that a lens will be on you all the way through, though you forget this sometimes in the heat of battle. Whatever is said out there can be replayed, even words that slip out in frustration. People can lip-read. There is no point wondering whether or not this has become too intrusive because cameras are as much a part of modern international cricket as the stumps and bails. Nowadays you might wait until the end of an over just to be a bit subtle. It is possible to make a point when you bend down to pick up a ball or walk past the batsmen when they are having a chat in the middle of the pitch. As I said, if it helps the prospects of picking up a wicket without transgressing the laws, then why not?

Certain batsmen are definitely vulnerable – Daryll Cullinan more than most. We have had a lot of success against him before the South Africans toured Australia in 1997–98. Just before the start of that series there was a double-page feature in an Australian newspaper in which he revealed how he had seen a psychiatrist to help him overcome Shane Warne and the Aussies. I couldn't believe it. I knew that Daryll was a bit fragile at times, but never imagined he would go to a shrink to learn how to read a googly. The First Test at Melbourne finally dawned. Adam Bacher fell to a fine slip catch by Mark Taylor and my old mate walked out gingerly. I let him take guard before saying, 'Daryll, I've waited so long for this moment and I'm going to send you straight back to that leather couch.' A couple of balls later I bowled him for a duck. He was more embarrassed than anything else, but those words had clearly unsettled him, and he didn't take any further part in the Test series.

Usually when I give him a serve he just looks down at the ground. Perhaps the funniest moment involving Cullinan, though, came when he actually bowled to me. He got me out and I'm sure he enjoyed that moment and so he should.

His mates in the South Africa team became increasingly worried about what seemed to be Daryll's phobia and a few of them thought that it was going a bit too far. In January 1998 on the day before our Test in Sydney, Dave Richardson and Pat Symcox approached Mark Taylor and myself to try to persuade us to have a chat with him to sort out the problem. There had been a few verbals between us, but why should I want to sort anything out when I had the upper hand? If Daryll had any sense he would have come into our dressing room at the close of a day's play, shared a beer and just got to know us all a little better. There are no mates out on a cricket field. We all play to win, but we are not monsters and never rub it in any more than we have to. The first time I had what you could really classify as a proper chat with Daryll was after the

World Cup semi-final at Edgbaston. It was a bit uneasy. As we exchanged shirts he said: 'I expect this will take pride of place in the bunny's section.' I just laughed with him and said it would go on the wall with the others. I would never humiliate a guy and if you look at Daryll's record against other countries he is a very talented batsman. Once you get to know him he is okay.

The South Africans play the game hard in the middle, nobody more so than Brian McMillan. He could be a really intimidating figure if you showed him any sign of weakness. During our first series after they were re-admitted into international cricket he was batting with Peter Kirsten when Kirsten nicked one off me for what I assumed would be 3. They ran 2, but McMillan stumbled and went through the 'Yes, no, stay' business so that he was back at my end. 'Looks like you don't fancy it very much, Depardieu,' I suggested. We had christened him Depardieu because of his resemblance to the French actor, which McMillan didn't seem to take as much of a compliment.

'Listen,' he said, 'a lot of people go missing every day in South Africa and one more won't be noticed.' A couple of overs later he had another go. 'Next time you're in South Africa I will take you fishing,' he said, 'and I will use you as bait for the sharks.' I thought nothing of it – until we actually went to South Africa. It was lunch at Johannesburg and we were starting to tuck in when McMillan stormed into the room brandishing an AK47 pistol, shouting: 'Right, I've had enough of you Australians.' It was a scary moment for a second or two, then we all laughed. Brian is a fantastic fellow and we have shared a few beers over the years and got to know him. He is a character; the game needs them.

There is a good relationship between the two countries. We have had some great battles down the years and we mix a lot after games. On the other hand, the West Indies tend to keep to themselves. They don't say much to the opposition. Occasionally they come up with some funny ones, such as 'Perform the operation,' to Courtney Walsh. But they are usually content to play the game, put their headphones on and go back to their hotel. On the pitch they try to get under you with those hard, long stares rather than words. Desmond Haynes was an exception. He used to wind up the fast bowlers from bat-pad. Allan Border told me that Haynes's trick was to walk up to the likes of Joel Garner and say, 'Did you hear what that batsman called you?' Of course the poor batsman had not said anything, but there was no point wasting breath in pleading innocence. And then the batsmen would face some thunder-bolts from their four fast bowlers. A few others are: 'C'mon Amby, you're in the basement, man, get up on the top floor,' or 'I think he wants to hook – help him out!'

England have generally begun each series against us with plenty to say for themselves. The problem is that if you start sledging without being able to back up your words with per-formances then it soon loses its effect. There is no point threat-ening this and that if you are going to be rissoled inside three days. The Poms have had their opportunities but we have usu-ally been able to get on top of them. Merv Hughes in particular relished the Ashes contests and usually reserved a special word for Graeme Hick. In my four series they have just said the odd word here and there.

On the other hand, I believe they can be susceptible them-selves. My dismissal of Nasser Hussain in the first Carlton & United final match at Sydney in 1999 springs to mind. England needed less than 50 to win with 6 wickets in hand and 10 overs remaining and Hussain was going pretty well. He has the reputation of being a little on the fiery side and I decided the only way we could win from that position was to tempt him into doing something silly. At that stage he was not a regular feature of their one-day side so I tried to goad him by talking him through the game. I would say things like, 'This is where it's crucial not to get out, Nass,' or, 'Don't let your team mates down now, mate.' This went on for a couple of overs and he said a bit back, so it was game on. When he ran down the pitch and hit me over the top I clapped him and said: 'Great stuff, Nass, that's the way to do it.' At the end of the over his face was red and you could almost see the steam coming out of his ears. I knew then that the ploy might work. Lo and behold, in the next over he ran down the track and was stumped by Adam Gilchrist about three yards out of his ground off my bowling. With new batsmen in we had a chance. Adam Hollioake followed next ball and we ended up winning the game. It was one of the few occasions sledging worked – remember, pick your moment.

I could have been made to look like an idiot, but Nasser fell hook, line and sinker. There was nothing personal, but I just needed to do something to change the situation. A few days later I was chatting to Alan Mullally, who told me that the guys in the England dressing room could see what was happening and were praying that Nasser would not start answering back.

Of the Asian countries Pakistan have the most to say for themselves – except, not unreasonably I suppose, they speak in their own language. That in itself can be unsettling – just as when Allan Donald starts growling in Afrikaans – because you are not quite sure what is being plotted. So far the one little bit of Urdu we have managed to get our heads round is 'Shabash, shabash,' but then only because Moin Khan uses it to encourage his bowlers six times an over. It means 'Very good'. The Indians are much the same and Sri Lanka prefer to use the stare.

We have our own few words of code that we use to try to get under a batsman. Sometimes Mark Waugh will shout at me from slip, 'He's wearing little pads, mate.' This comes from what we used to think was a trick of Nasser Hussain's. We reckoned he deliberately wore youth pads to try to con the umpire, when the ball hit him above the knee roll, that it would pass over the stumps, when really it should have been lbw. Nowadays, Mark makes this remark when he thinks I can bowl a batsman round his legs – in other words there is not enough pad to be able to kick me away if I pitch it outside leg stump. I remember getting Jacques Kallis out in this fashion exactly as Mark predicted in Johannesburg. Mark has a very good cricket brain and is a funny man with his one-liners. Whatever he says is generally on the money.

Some of the most aggressive sledging occurs between teams in Australia, as I quickly discovered. Like most aspiring players, I would guess, I came in for special treatment in a very early game for St Kilda, my club side. It happened in 1989–90 when we played against Waverley, who happened to include Rodney Hogg. He was still pretty sharp in those days and had a great reputation. He also had these very, very light blue eyes which seemed to pierce through you like a laser beam.

He must have detected that I was not entirely at ease because when I took guard there was hardly a fielder in front of the wicket. They were all under my nose. The first ball fizzed past and I looked up to see Hoggy almost face to face, snarling: 'I'm going to kill you.' That might not affect me now, but as a nineteen-year-old, a kid trying to bat against a legend, I don't mind saying that it brought a lump in my, shall I say, throat. Somehow I managed to block the next ball, but unfortunately it hit the bat-pad man on the nose and started to trickle blood. 'C'mon, boys,' Hogg said, 'he's hurt one of us, let's make sure we hurt him back.' At this point I forgot all of my ambitions and just wanted to get away from the crease as quickly as I could. Needless to say, I did not last much longer.

Overall, though, I must have made a good impression on Hogg. During my spell to him he turned to Shaun Graf, who was fielding at slip, and told him: 'This bloke should be playing Test cricket.' In those days he also wrote a column called 'The whole Hogg' in *The Truth* newspaper, which is noted for its form guide. In it he suggested that an unknown kid by the name of Shane Warne who had just reached First Grade would one day take 500 Test wickets. Marbles upstairs, everyone thought. I hope he is right because that would be fantastic. Apparently, he stopped writing for them not long afterwards because the editor thought he didn't know what he was on about.

By the time I made my Sheffield Shield debut for Victoria against Western Australia in the season on 1990–91 I was a bit more clued up in the whys and wherefores of men's cricket, but not much. I was still very nervous, though, and I copped a stream of abuse from Tim Zoehrer because I took my time to assess the field when I went out to bat – though the way he played the game he would have found any excuse for a few words. 'Any chance of facing up, biscuit?' he said. Biscuit? I did not have a clue what he meant. But all through the innings he kept it up. Biscuit this, biscuit that. Back in the pavilion I asked my team mates what was going on. It turned out that this was his favourite term – stop using your face as gorilla biscuits. In other words, you're an ugly so-and-so. I must admit that it went over my head.

It is part of the induction to cricket in Australia to receive a few words as the young player and you generally cop it from the senior players in the opposition. More than anything I think players are curious about whether a rookie will respond, to find out what he's made of. But the verbals are not completely reserved for newcomers. The atmosphere out in the middle for some of the games between Victoria and New South Wales over the years can be more fierce than a Test match and I can remember one contest when I was beginning to make my comeback after the shoulder operation. You would not have known that most of us were mates in the Australia team.

Michael Slater was batting and Darren Berry and I were trying to get under him. We took it in turns to go 'tick' then 'tock', letting Slater know that we thought he was a time bomb about to explode any minute. He was furious and had a go back. It calmed down and he and Mark Waugh won the battle, as they both made runs. Remember, pick your mark! At the other end Mark suggested I was taking things a bit too far. He was probably right, but I threw in: 'Go and blow dry your hair, mate.' Now Mark is one of my best mates in the game. I had even flown from Melbourne to Sydney for his birthday not long before. The emotion sometimes get the better of us.

In conclusion there have been many fun situations, there were also times when we went a little bit too far. It is all a learning curve, life, cricket, everything, but it has been fun. I don't say much any more, only when we really need to change the game. Generally now I try and let the ball do the talking.

17

SPONSORSHIP

MORE MONEY is coming in to the game today than ever before from sponsorship and television deals. In Australia we are very lucky to get well paid for representing our country and with further income available to some players from personal endorsements we are fortunate to be able to afford a comfortable lifestyle. Sponsorship is a win-win situation for all parties – but only as long as we all remember the good of the game has to come first. As a cricketer it was drilled in to me very early that earnings come from performances, not the other way round. I take the view that if I do the business on the field then, with good management behind me, the financial side will look after itself. Some young players want big dollars before they have performed in the big league.

I believe it is the right of every person to be able to endorse a product if the opportunity arises. We know what we can and cannot do, what is reasonable and when we might be crossing the line. I remember when Coca-Cola sponsored an Australia tour to India, Pepsi approached my management to back their own drink. They offered $150,000 US for a commercial in India, but in that situation I knew there was no way I could accept, even though each player's share from Coca-Cola was only a fraction of what I could have earned from Pepsi. The fact that two huge multi-national companies are prepared to use cricket as a battleground underlines the massive popularity of the game in India and I suspect Pepsi made the approach simply to try and stoke up publicity.

Over the last five years I would guess that our contracts simply for playing the game have quadrupled in value. The improvements reflect Australia's recent success. Crowds for the West Indies series in 2000–01 were enormous and the marketing and corporate sides are more professionally run than ever. There is a better relationship between players and officials now. We play exciting, attractive cricket, but in the world generally today you see fewer drawn games than even two or three years ago. Some people might argue this is because batting techniques are looser as a result of one-day cricket. Whatever, the paying public does not seem to mind, and without them we would not have a professional game at all. Thankfully, there appears to be no evidence that the match-fixing issue, the most serious since World Series Cricket more than twenty years earlier, has dented confidence in our sport.

One of the most important decisions facing an international player today is to find a good manager, a guy who can be trusted to think of the best interests of his client at all times. Austin Robertson, a very shrewd, experienced guy was recommended to me by Allan Border. Signing with Austin was one of the best moves I made. He got 20 per cent of my salary from endorsements but it was money well spent. People would still come to me directly with a proposition, using the line that it would save the agent's commission, but I always referred them to Austin. To play cricket successfully demands complete concentration and I do not want to have to worry about business deals on the field. I'm lucky also in having a fantastic agent in the UK. Michael Cohen's involvement and friendship have been wonderful. It is a pleasure to be associated with him.

The days when eleven blokes just turned up at a cricket ground and played are long gone. There are so many obligations now that we have to report four days before the start of the first test of the season. Part of this is taken up with meetings to go through any new ICC regulations, playing conditions for the series, racial vilification issues and to check our new gear for the summer. Then we have to sign cricket bats and shirts for the team sponsors and make sure our own equipment is in order. None of this is particularly demanding physically, but it consumes more time than people on the outside can imagine and these commitments cannot be left so late that they impinge on the actual cricket.

What really hurts is when I hear players from the past say that we no longer play for the love of the game or that we are only in it for the money. The fact is that beyond the very basics of trying to score runs and take wickets – which will be there for ever – cricket has changed beyond recognition. It has become an industry in its own right. We could not hold down a full-time job outside the game even if we wanted to. With one or two exceptions, no employer is going to take on somebody just because he happens to be a Test cricketer, because he knows that he can't dedicate the time.

Other than the odd day here and there the period between September to late February or March can be written off straight away. Increasingly, too, games are being scheduled in what is recognised as being our off-season. As I write, the ACB is looking at the possibility of staging matches in Darwin and Cairns next July or August. On top of that I anticipate more indoor series, such as the successful one-day tournament against South Africa in Melbourne in 2000. Surely it is a good thing that our best young players today are able to forge a full-time career in cricket, rather than having to weigh that up against work outside the game, or being forced to pull out of tours because their boss simply can't afford to give more time off or he might lose his job.

Don't get me wrong. Most former players in Australia are fantastic. It has been a privilege to meet people like Arthur Morris, Bill Brown and Sir Donald Bradman, to name but a few. I genuinely think they are pleased for the success we are enjoying and the lucrative opportunities that have come our way.

I appreciate that not everybody is fortunate enough to be able to do something he or she loves on a full-time basis and get well paid for it. But even though we are well rewarded that doesn't mean we feel any less for the game than the stars of yesteryear. The fact that in the past players were not treated as well as they deserved does not mean we should suffer too.

The dispute in 1997–98 was all about discovering whether we were getting a fair slice of the cake and, if not, to make sure we received our due reward. If cricket continues to grow as it has done over the past decade, which I hope and expect will be the case, then tomorrow's players have the potential to make even more from their skills. I, for one, will not begrudge them a penny.

At a rough guess, around 70 per cent of my income these days comes from sponsorship and other commercial enterprises. The market place revolves around supply and demand. When I broke on to the scene I was something a little bit different as a leg-spinner. With the help and advice of Austin I have tried to go with companies that fit in with the image I want to portray. I take a genuine interest in the likes of Nike and Just Jeans and have made a number of good friends through my association with them.

I feel I should explain the deal I had with Nicorette. My smoking habit was well known and in January 1999 Nicorette approached me to ask if I would consider endorsing their product, a chewing gum with nicotine which is designed to wean people off cigarettes. Simone, my wife, doesn't like smoking and, with a second child due within the next five months, I wanted to try to give up. I did not get any enjoyment from standing in the rain outside our house in Melbourne to have a cigarette. It is something I should have put my mind to years earlier but now, after some fourteen years as a smoker and with my lungs in a dreadful state, I decided to give it a go.

My arrangement with Nicorette was to endorse the product. Contrary to certain reports, there was no clause in the contract that said I must go a certain time without a cigarette or must have stopped completely by such-and-such a date. They did have counsellors and other people to talk to if I was struggling at any stage. At my initial meeting with their representatives they could not have made the difficulties clearer. A lot of people don't even manage to crush the habit after two, three or four attempts and some never manage at all. The experts told me that it is very hard and that 80 per cent of people don't give up at the first attempt. Smoking is very addictive. I said that I was pretty strong-willed and, without making promises, I would give it my very best shot. On that understanding we shook hands.

The starting date was 1 January 1999, and the final Test of the summer in Sydney began the following day. It was my comeback game after the major shoulder operation, so I was anxious and nervous, but got through the game without a cigarette. After our victory the beer was flowing and a few of the boys were having a smoke and asking whether I wanted one. My reply was always, 'Thanks, but no thanks.'

I was making good progress and when the occasional craving came along I managed to resist it. The gum was working.

In the West Indies it was harder. I had returned to the side after surgery sooner than I probably should have, and lost my place for the first time in eight years for the final Test in Antigua. I was still the vice-captain and being dropped represented a big shock, but I accepted it. Simone, being pregnant, preferred not to join the rest of the players' wives in Barbados at the end of the tour before we moved on to the World Cup in England. I missed her company. Steve Waugh was in the same boat, but I was disappointed at the way things had fallen. Stephen and I had been friends for nearly ten years so it was a bit awkward at times, I felt under the pump and couldn't feel free.

Finally, after nearly four months and a few drinks to celebrate keeping the Frank Worrell Trophy, my resolve broke and I accepted a cigarette. Some guy happened to be there with a camera and decided to take a photograph. He immediately started jumping around, shouting: 'I'm going to sell this, I'm going to sell this.'

'Well,' I replied, 'if you want to be an idiot that's up to you.'

Next morning I rang Austin Robertson, my manager, and he explained the situation to Nicorette. I said what had happened, that I had a smoke for the first time and that some guy I had never seen before had captured the moment on film. They were fine about the whole business. They repeated that giving up is hard, asked if I wanted any help and whether I was going to try again. There was no way I intended to let my efforts of the previous months go to waste just like that for one weak moment, so I confirmed I would keep trying.

The news – if it can be described as news – broke that I was smoking again and that I had reneged on the deal. The insinuation was that I had taken the money but never really tried. It just wasn't true. What people also didn't know was that I donated a decent portion of my contract to charity. I did it privately because I wanted to – not as a way of getting good

PR. I had not sought publicity, just as I do not seek publicity when I visit hospitals. Sometimes it is a very difficult and sad situation and for the kids to be hassled by the media is hard sometimes. I just want to go and have a chat and hope to help in some small way.

A month or so later, unfortunately, I lapsed again. As I say elsewhere in the chapter about the World Cup, I felt under pressure for all sorts of reasons in England and, this time, one cigarette led to another. I did not intend to mislead Nicorette, who had been very good to me, so I told them I was having the occasional cigarette. The good thing is that I am down from forty to forty-five a day to about twenty, so I think it has worked. They were obviously disappointed, but understood and said that if and when I decided to stop again they would supply me with more chewing gum. One day I might take them up on the offer. These are the facts.

One offer I remember turning down was to pose in just a jockstrap, holding my cricket bat, in some nets in England during the 1993 tour. A newspaper was prepared to pay £25,000 for the shot, but I just thought that was going too far – and I'm not sure the eventual shot would have been as pleasant for their readers as they expected. The old adage 'Less is more' holds particularly true as far as I am concerned in the world of advertising. I like to think I have given every commitment my full attention.

The deal with Just Jeans is an interesting example of the way sponsors and sportsmen can work well together. When I signed a deal in 1994 I was the new young face of Australian cricket. Just as people would expect, I wore jeans and smart, casual tops away from the game. Craig Kimberley, the owner of Just Jeans, thought I would relate to potential customers and I modelled for their catalogues and on television and appeared at a few store openings. Now I am a more mature person in my thirties with a wife and a couple of kids. While my profile has changed the market remains the same and it was a mutual agreement not to renew the deal. I spent a very enjoyable six years with them.

One of the most nerve-racking experiences of my life came when I took part in a fashion parade in Melbourne – and shared a catwalk with the supermodel Helena Christiansen. I tried to strike up a conversation with her as we started to show off the clothes, only for her to say firmly but politely that we were supposed to walk without talking. The idea was that I undid a button on my jacket at regular intervals before whipping it open and spinning round at the end. But I forgot to undo the last button and couldn't get the jacket off, much to the amusement of the audience.

Meeting people from different walks of life is an attractive spin-off from sponsorship deals themselves. Cricket can become insular at times. Through my association with Nike I have come across Michael Jordan, Andre Agassi and Bo Jackson and gained a fascinating insight into the way they prepare. I joined Nike in 1994 and they stuck by me through thick and thin. I have been over to places like Los Angeles to shoot commercials for them. Unfortunately we have now parted company.

Loyalty should be important in any business relationship. In 1994 I had a lucrative offer to wear Bolle sunglasses, but I stuck with Oakley because their lenses are the best. They have supported me right from the start of my career and I also have friendships from within the company. Once again, it was a case of endorsing a commodity that I believe in. I need sunglasses, just as I need clothes and sportswear. The same goes for equipment, an area of the game which I find particularly interesting. Advances in technology and research continue to produce lighter and more effective protective gear. One reason why I switched from Gunn and Moore to the County-owned Gray Nicholls in 1999–2000 was because they gave me an input into some of the designs. It has been more professional at Grays because they are always open to suggestions and improvements.

A deal with Crown Casino involves handing over prizes to big winners – a task I always perform with a mixture of jealousy, admiration and hope that one day I might be on the other side of the handshake. The reason the relationship works and carries conviction is because people know I like a bet myself. A few years ago Austin tried to strike up a deal with one of the leading pizza companies. Unfortunately, the parties couldn't quite agree when it came to number-crunching. I thought there would be some good material in that because of my early days as a delivery boy. A commercial could have been real fun.

More and more players are involved with the media these days, either writing for a newspaper, working with television, or both. I enjoy the media work, and having my own column means I can put the record straight on certain issues and share my opinions. It is the one occasion where I control the context as well as the words. Recently I have written for *The Times* in England and the response has been terrific. Almost every week while I was at Hampshire somebody would approach me to say how much he or she liked the column or agreed with my opinion. My job is to give an insight into whatever the issue of the day happens to be, from a player's viewpoint.

My work for Channel Nine has involved presenting and commentary. I enjoyed working with Richie Benaud and all the team while I was recovering from injury during the West Indies series. To see the professionalism of guys like Richie is always an eye-opener. The key is to speak economically and to add to the picture. People can see what is going on; our role is to explain why, and maybe suggest what could happen next.

Much as the Channel Four coverage in England impressed me while I was over there in 2000, I still think our own Channel Nine leads the way in television coverage of cricket.

As an indication of the work that goes in before agreeing to a deal, I can give the example of promotional work I have done for the Moscow Circus when it comes over to Australia. The issue of animal rights is extremely sensitive and initially I received a lot of critical letters – some of them sadly using language I would not want my kids to hear – which asked if I was aware of the way the creatures were treated. Well, yes, I was. I can't abide cruelty and I checked out the facts before giving the circus my backing. The management showed me how they look after the animals and I was happy that everything was in order.

All my sponsors have been fantastic – Just Jeans, Sony, Foxtel, CH9, Onetel, Crown, Nike, County, Oakley, SPC – and without their help over the years I wouldn't be in the position I am now.

One thing that has given me great satisfaction is a spinner's kit which I brought out. I receive so many letters from kids wanting to know how to bowl leggies that it is hard to find the time to respond with more than a few words in each case – and I do try because I know how much it means. So I helped to put together a video and produce a ball which shows exactly where the fingers need to be placed for the different deliveries. It was a good venture at an affordable price, another consideration where kids are concerned. I like to think it helped to point a few children in the right direction.

Very few players are still competing at the highest level in their late thirties. In my case the peroxide blond with the earring has gone. As you get older your priorities change. Cricket has always been my number one, but now my family comes first and I am lucky to have done well enough to ensure they can enjoy a nice way of life. I have also been fortunate in another area – my dad happens to be a financial adviser. Somebody up there must like me.

18

CAPTAINCY

ALL THREE of the captains I have played under for Australia have been something special. Allan Border inherited an almost impossible situation not long after the retirement of Greg Chappell, Rod Marsh and Dennis Lillee, and Kim Hughes's emotional resignation with the West Indies at their peak. The game was low at home, yet AB managed to mould a generation of players into winners by instilling the values of sheer hard work and determination. He led by example and showed all of us how to play the game and what it meant to represent your country. Mark Taylor inherited a very good team and stamped his own authority. Under his leadership we grew with experience to leapfrog West Indies and become the best in the world. Then Steve Waugh accepted the baton and led us to a record-breaking sequence of Test and one-day victories. Statistically, at least, we can claim to be the greatest Test team at the moment. That is a great testimony to all these captains.

It is hard to overstate Border's part in this and in my own development. He is one of the biggest influences of my career, if not the biggest. When I used to play with my brother, Jason, in the back garden as a kid, Border was one of the players I pretended to be with his little bob before the ball was bowled. But for the trust he placed in me I might not have played more than three or four times for Australia. He has become a close

Above Terry Brewer, the dressing-room attendant, rings the bell for the last time at Northlands Road. Unfortunately, it tolled for Hampshire as we were relegated from Division one.

Right The Northlands Road ground – my home for 2000.

Below An emotional day for Hampshire on the final morning of championship cricket at Northlands Road. The county moved to new headquarters for the 2001 season.

Above John Buchanan, typically deep in thought, has taken Australia to new heights as coach.

Above left Terry Jenner, the Spin Doctor, illustrates a point in England in 1997.

Left Talking tactics with Bobby Simpson, my first Australia coach, at The Oval in 1993.

Below left A minute's silence after the death of Sir Donald Bradman, before the First Test in Mumbai, 2001.

Below A rare, quiet moment in India as I catch up with Sachin Tendulkar

ormer Indian captain Mohammad Azharuddin
I was surprised when he was implicated in
e corruption affair.

Salim Malik – he tried to bribe me to
under-perform in Pakistan in 1994.

he strain shows on Hansie Cronje at a press conference in the early days of the match-fixing
andal, April 2000.

Bowling for my state, Victoria, in the Mercantile Mutual Cup.

Wide World of Sports team – back row (*left to right*): Simon O'Donnell, Ian Botham, Tony Greig, Bill Lawry, Ian Healy, Michael Slater; front row: Shane Warne, Ian Chappell, Richie Benaud, Mark Taylor, Steve Waugh.

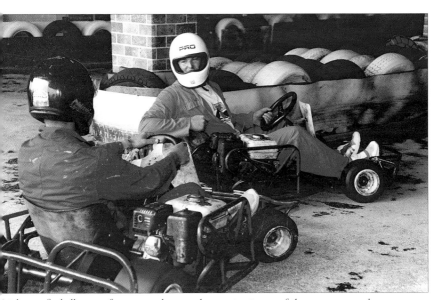

Cricketers find all sorts of ways to relax – go-kart racing is one of the more unusual.

At the casino with one of my best buddies, 'Beefy' Botham.

My dad with his grandchildren, Brooke and Jackson.

There's nothing better than being at home with the kids.

Right A chip off the old block? Proud dad with son Jackson, born during the 1999 World Cup.

Below 'The coach' – advice from my mum always welcome.

The happiest day of my life – getting married to Simone.

personal friend and even now, years after his retirement, I still turn to him for advice. I would back his judgement without question.

Coming from New South Wales, Border had a great under-standing of spin bowling. He recognised that wrist-spinners in particular had a role to play in international cricket. He also knew from his own occasional slow left-arm how it feels to be put to the sword on a flat pitch. Despite his experience and sheer ability he was a good listener. He would suggest fielding positions but let me make up my own mind. He made me believe that what I said genuinely mattered, even though I was still a young player.

Although he played with intensity, some of his wisest words were saved for the bar, where he would hold court for hours discussing the game. Even towards the end of his career, when I came into the side, he remained a magnificent, gritty batsman who put a high price on his own wicket. It was a great example to the rest of us. He was almost as competitive in the nets, encouraging me to bowl as though we were in a match situation and telling me to set imaginary fields as I tried to prise him out.

Border did not really suffer from a serious loss of form during his spell in charge. Mark Taylor had some initial problems with a pair in his first game as skipper, so Border's consistency was remarkable really. Captaincy, especially at that level, can be all-consuming, with the meetings and form-filling that come as part of the job. Taylor liked to do everything himself and I remember AB telling him to make sure he concentrated on sorting out his own game because that can suffer when you first start out as captain. The only question ever asked about AB's place in the side was the position he should bat.

I don't think it is coincidence that both Taylor and Steve Waugh learnt the ropes under Border. They are different characters, but they all share that deep desire to be successful. Waugh, in particular, leads by example in the same way as AB, batting with that defiance. Taylor was more of a talker than AB or Tugga. He would make a conscious effort to canvass opinions before making his decisions and would sort out problems as they arose over a chat. I am not suggesting that the other pair didn't, but Taylor did everything himself where Tugga and AB used Bobby Simpson and John Buchanan, the coaches, more. As with much of captaincy, there is no right or wrong about it, just a slight difference in approach.

I had already played under Taylor on a 2nd XI tour to Zimbabwe before he succeeded AB three years later. By the time he took over I was an established player, the self-doubts had gone and, if anything, I needed a calming influence. Taylor helped me to handle success. He was always there to listen and tell me what I needed to hear or just be there so I could get things off my chest. I remember a long chat on the bus in Johannesburg when he was vice-captain when I had been fined after the Andrew Hudson incident and could not work out why I had become so aggressive. Then during the 1997 Ashes series, when I felt I was beginning to lose some of my edge, we had another conversation and he put things in perspective. Under Taylor we beat West Indies twice, defeated South Africa home and away and retained the Ashes. Captains bear the brunt of criticism and sometimes lose their jobs when matters go wrong, so they are quite entitled to take some of the credit for success.

Having said that, captaincy is almost impossible to evaluate. Taylor has rightly been heralded as one of the best men to lead Australia. The debate about any captain centres around the ability of the side. Yes, we did have a great team, but Mark was a very, very good captain. It must be easier to lead a side including the Waughs, Slater, Ponting, McGrath and the like than some of the teams AB was given in the mid-80s. I wonder if he would have taken so many risks as captain had he come into a side that was unsuccessful. Border was more likely to play the percentages. I am not demeaning any of Taylor's achievements, because the captain still has to blend the players into a unit and to create a relaxed environment in which the talent can flourish.

There are plenty of examples of decisions that many people thought were wrong at the time – such as electing to bat on a greentop at Old Trafford in 1997 – but which turned out to be an inspired hunch. He was the right man for the job and combined good leadership with a good Australia side to make us a strong unit.

To his absolute credit his captaincy remained unaffected by a slump in form that would have unsettled a lot of captains. As the 1997 Ashes tour approached we all desperately wanted Tubs to find form and beat England, the captain more than anybody. We were all fully behind him and waiting for him to do well, but at times it was inevitable to wonder where the runs were going to come from. But we all knew they would. At his best he was the finest around, sometimes an attractive player and when he was out of form he could look awful at the crease but still score runs – a sign of a great player. But he had plenty of guts and was good to watch on song. The fact is, however, that despite going for twenty-one innings without a 50 we had still beaten Sri Lanka, West Indies and South Africa and were red hot favourites to overcome England for the fifth time in succession. That is a sign of good teams – you can carry one or two while still winning and his captaincy did not suffer.

I think he deserved every opportunity the selectors gave him. He definitely enjoyed an extended run because his captaincy was deemed to be of the highest order, which it was. In effect he was seen as an all-rounder.

Reflecting on that year, the senior players, myself included, perhaps should have offered more support. I don't mean in public, because whenever the question arose, which was increasingly regularly, we stressed that he remained the man to do the job – and we believed it – and that he was sure to come good in the near future. But away from the spotlight he might have needed a few more arms around the shoulder. I would say, 'Keep going, Tubs' now and then, but never really sought him out for a longer chat. He was always there for us, and maybe we could have given a little more back. It is always hard to know what to do but I think we all let him down a bit.

Tubs was generally an outward-going guy who was happy with a glass or two in his hand. Once he was appointed vice-captain to Border he toned down his act but was still an affable, open bloke.

The reaction when he finally reached three figures in the second innings of the First Test at Edgbaston showed just what a man he was. His pride, determination and sheer guts shone through on his face as he overcame all of the uncertainty and self-doubt that must have burnt within and the standing ovation from the crowd underlined his popularity in the game overall. Once he scored that hundred he became something like the Mark Taylor of old, as a batsman with shots all around the ground and pulling anything a little short. Although I was not on the tour, his unbeaten 334 against Pakistan at Peshawar in the 1998–99 series which equalled Sir Donald Bradman's highest score for Australia must have been a monumental effort.

Following somebody as successful as Taylor could have been a burden. One reason Stephen has done so well is because he has not automatically reproduced Taylor's methods. He is his own man. When the captaincy came up for grabs there were three main candidates, the two Waughs and myself. Stephen got it and I received the vice-captaincy. I was interviewed by Malcolm Speed, the chief executive and thought I acquitted myself pretty well. But I was nowhere near as disappointed at missing out as I was to have the vice-captaincy removed some time later.

I was excited and honoured to be named vice-captain to Stephen in the first instance. I thought we made a great team. Stephen had played for longer and become a good friend. He deserved the job and has done tremendously well ever since. As the vice-captain to Taylor he was the obvious choice to step up and I knew he would value my input.

I think he needed a few months to grow into the job. At the start, while he was feeling his way, he wanted to make sure everybody knew he was going to be a good captain. He is a man capable of making difficult decisions. We worked closely and pretty well during our all-too-brief partnership and he has continued to enjoy a run of results that eluded even Border and Taylor. I was number two for the first ten games of the record-breaking run in 1999–2000, the 2000–01 run and also the World Cup win. With so many great players in the side, and with newcomers like Adam Gilchrist and Brett Lee hitting their straps immediately, we have formed a great side.

Waugh and Buchanan gel well together. They both work assiduously in their own way. Stephen is known for his great sense of history and recognises what playing for Australia is all about. He is at his toughest out in the middle where he relishes a fight. His best innings have been played under pressure, which is a sign of a great player.

I would love the chance to be able to captain Australia in a Test match, having led my country in a fill-in role in one-day cricket. It is largely a question of when Waugh decides to step down, but it is not a position that I am chasing. There are several younger candidates who would make able captains.

Ricky Ponting has an imaginative cricket brain and has established himself as one of the best batsmen in the world. Adam Gilchrist is also an obvious choice, but we just have to be careful that his duties don't get too much. We don't want to dull his effectiveness as a keeper and powerful batsman. He would make a good vice-captain. The dark horse could be Simon Katich, from Western Australia. He has a level head on his shoulders and just strikes me as a player who bats in a smart, intelligent way. It was revealing that he scored well for Durham when he played in England in 2000, while I was at Hampshire. The pitches are notoriously difficult in the north-east and completely different from anything he would have experienced before, but he quickly adapted his game. As somebody who wants to learn and is prepared to listen I think he has a big future.

Comparing captains of different countries is almost impossible. It must be far more difficult to lead New Zealand or England than Australia because of the players available. If the quality is there then a leader can blossom and his job must be easier. For a country like Zimbabwe, though, a captain could make all the right decisions and play brilliantly himself but still lose series after series. You have to look beyond results and work out which countries are making progress, which are falling behind and how much of that can be attributed to the guy in charge. He has to get the team together and that is what AB, Tubby and Tugga have done in their own ways.

Wasim Akram is somebody who has impressed me overall, despite making a few errors in the 1999–2000 series in Australia. I liked his confidence and willingness towards his spin bowlers. Politics plays such a part in Pakistan cricket that in many ways it is an impossible job. He coped as well as anybody has managed in my time. The best players do not always make the best leaders, but he managed to lift the youngsters in the same way that Imran Khan lifted him in his early career. To keep those players pulling in roughly the same direction is no easy task. Wasim managed to do so fantastically during the 1999 World Cup to reach the final. The likes of Saqlain Mushtaq and Abdur Razzaq clearly wanted to play for him.

Opting for the leading player is usually the safest selectoral option. While the team should comprise of the best eleven players available, not all of them are ever captaincy material. Some players are happy to concentrate on their own game. They can be intense and selfish, which is fine up to a point, but a captain has to be able to see the full picture and understand how his players are feeling individually. One of the interesting captains was Mike Atherton. He came in at a tough time and I think he did an okay job from what I saw, but the one thing that I thought let him down was his body language.

When you turn up at a ground midway through a game it should be impossible to tell from the body language whether the fielding team is on top or behind. You should have to look at the scoreboard, not see it on the field. The tone in the field is set by the wicket-keeper and the captain and Atherton sent out the wrong signals. I appreciate that his back gives him pain during long sessions but he could hardly expect his team to look enthusiastic when his own shoulders were hunched forward when they weren't on top and his hands were stuck in his pockets. However, he is a thoroughly likeable guy.

Jimmy Adams has been the best West Indies captain of recent years. He is such a lovely guy that players feel bad about letting him down, a loyal man who deserves and generally receives that same loyalty in return. For Brian Lara I think the job was too much of a burden. He seemed to covet the position too openly for the liking of some people, but didn't appear to be temperamentally suited. Although West Indies managed to draw our last series in the Caribbean, in 1998–99, that had much to do with Lara the batsman rather than the captain. The recent series in Australia would have really hurt Adams.

One man I rate extremely highly is Stephen Fleming of New Zealand. The side has had all sorts of problems bonding and suffered run-ins with coaches down the years, but Fleming has helped to bring them together and pull in the same direction. Like a good captain he gels the team. Until he took charge we always felt they were content simply to compete against us. Under Fleming they have developed a more ruthless streak, set their sights that bit higher and are genuinely annoyed if they don't win.

I always enjoyed filling in for Steve Waugh, and leading Victoria. It came as a real disappointment when I was removed as captain of my state in 1999. There was a fair amount of disharmony in the side when I took over from Dean Jones. The selectors decided they wanted two of the most respected players to take charge in an attempt to bring about stability. I thought it worked pretty well with myself as captain and Tony Dodemaide standing in when I went away to play for Australia, and then when Darren Berry, our wicket-keeper, took over as my deputy after Dodders retired. In 1998–99, my final year at the helm, we won the Mercantile Mutual Cup and climbed from fifth to third in the Sheffield Shield. I thought that Berry, John Scholes, the coach, and myself managed to restore morale in the side. Everyone knew the situation and was happy with it, I thought. It was the most successful season we had in years. And the Shield final was a real chance. History shows we were on the right wavelength.

Before the start of the next season the state selectors decided they wanted a captain who would be able to do the job for the whole campaign instead of taking charge for the odd game in between the growing schedule of international commitments. I could understand the logic behind this argument but, the team having done so well in 1998–99, I thought there was a case for keeping the Warne/Berry partnership intact. The selectors knew I would be away for most of the time, hopefully, when they appointed me in the first place and I couldn't understand why the parameters should suddenly have changed. I felt a lot of sympathy for Berry, who certainly would have been available for the whole summer. He has given everything to Victoria cricket and been a good mate to me personally down the years, as well as an exceptional wicket-keeper who could have played many times for Australia but for the presence of Ian Healy.

The selectors appointed Paul Reiffel as captain and Berry as vice-captain. It seemed a bit of a strange choice, because Reiffel had always kept himself to himself, had not said much and had never been thought of as captaincy material. He also didn't have much experience of it, but Victoria made further improvements in 1999–2000, reaching the Pura Milk final with our new captain taking 59 wickets himself. He might be the best choice. I wish him well and I hope he keeps it up.

So far my fill-in captaincy for Australia has been restricted to one-day games. Tactically, I always tried to break those matches down to three sections – the first 15 overs, the middle 25 and the last 10. I think as a bowler I saw things a little differently. I still think there is a place to attack in limited overs cricket. The games can become a bit predictable so I am all for bringing the fielders in and forcing batsmen to hit boundaries over the top to score runs. Some captains would disagree with this and are happy to concede singles as long as the boundaries don't follow. But I know the importance of being able to probe at a batsman and if shots that would normally gain an easy single go straight to a fielder instead, then it puts him under pressure to produce the big hits that carry a heavy risk factor. Even in the 50-over games I like to bowl with a slip and a silly mid off occasionally. Alec Stewart paid me a big compliment after we won the Carlton & United series in Australia in 1998–99 when he said that he'd learnt a great deal from what he described as my positive captaincy.

It comes down to reading a situation and being prepared to gamble if need be. Sometimes you have to buy a wicket just as you would in the Test arena. Really it is nothing more scientific than following a gut feeling. The more you play, the more those instincts are honed, although I remember an idea that seemed to come from way left field paying off in my first game in charge for Victoria against New South Wales. They were going well and Shane Lee had started to hit the ball like a dream, so I turned to Matthew Elliott, our opening batsman who bowled occasional slow left-arm. I knew that Shane would feel duty-bound to make use of a short leg side boundary at the SCG but would also feel slightly apprehensive about getting out and suffering the ribbing that would follow. His concentration seemed to go and he was caught in two minds between having a go and making sure Matty did not get him out. In the end he was stumped. Matty was spewing when I then took him off, but he had done his job, and he got another wicket later. Whatever people thought of my captaincy, nobody could ever say that games I was involved in just drifted along.

Communication is absolutely vital, probably the most important factor. Everybody needs to know his role. Every single cricketer has been omitted at some state to accommodate the balance, but whenever I was in charge I made a point of always giving a reason for the decision.

Allan Border told me early in my Australia career to put myself in the captain's position all the time. It is a way of improving concentration and feeling involved at all times. I used to try to second-guess Border's next move to think about the odd fielding change and work out who might be able to break a partnership. With experience I gradually used to make a few suggestions, even before becoming vice-captain. It is important to know the minds of every one of your side but still not lose sight of your own game. When I filled in for Stephen I enjoyed grabbing the ball and trying to lead the way by example, just as Border, Taylor and Waugh did with the bat. It didn't always work, but it was fun trying.

Captaincy did not change my outlook on the game. I thought it was important to remember I had been chosen because of who I was and for the way I played. I always tried to build somebody up if I thought he was down in the dumps and give a colleague a pat on the back after doing something well. I wanted everybody to feel a vital member of the team. When I threw the ball to somebody I wanted him to know I genuinely thought he was the best bet to take a wicket. As I discovered in Sri Lanka under Border, it is amazing what can be achieved when you feel you have the absolute confidence of the man in charge. Dreams are free and just maybe I might get a chance down the line. You don't know what the future holds.

19

DREAM TEAMS

NOTHING IS MORE LIKELY to start an argument than picking a cricket team, either for real or as a bit of fun. Being a selector is a difficult task. Those guys are on a hiding to nothing. They get much of the blame when things go wrong but virtually no praise when things work out perfectly. There is no right or wrong, just a matter of judgement. This is something the Australian selectors have done very well. Differences of opinion are inevitable. In fact, if a hundred people wrote down their all-time great Australia side, I'd be surprised if there were too many the same.

All of us like playing at being a selector. Sometimes a few of us in the dressing room might find a pencil, a few scraps of paper and cook up our dream teams. This time, I've given the matter a bit more thought than usual. I've also decided to pick twelve rather than eleven for my Australia and Rest of the World sides in Test and one-day cricket. The only criterion is that I must have played with the Aussies or against the Rest in a full international. That, unfortunately, rules out one of my all-time favourites, Ian Botham. Beefy was the greatest all-rounder along with Sir Garfield Sobers, and has become such a good mate. It is one of my regrets not ever bowling to him, or Viv Richards, in an international game. Whether or not we won the games, we'd be guaranteed some fun afterwards. And Boony would never be short of a drinking mate!

AUSTRALIA TEST 12

1 Mark Taylor

For his determination at the top of the order. Sometimes he could look really ugly at the crease but he would always put a high price on his wicket and once he got in he could take to the attack. His catching at first slip was extraordinary – he took fifty-one catches off me, the best ever fielder-bowler combination.

2 Michael Slater

The first session of a Test match is always so important and Slater is capable of destroying the opposition's plans in that time. He has every shot in the book and could have 70 or 80 on the board himself before lunch, to leave the other side demoralised. If he plays through the first two hours you know Australia are going to be on top.

3 David Boon

The most reliable number three I have played with, and also the most consistent over a long period of time. I can't remember him having a run of low scores. He was the bloke who set the standards for the rest of us to follow. Didn't say much, but when he did say something he was on the money. He was also the best bat-pad fielder I have seen.

4 Mark Waugh

Such a graceful player, he is one you would love to watch in full flow. He has a lovely, laid-back attitude and could make batting look easy. My ideal fielding team around the bat was always Taylor, Boon, and then Junior close in on the off side. With those three any half-chance would be snaffled.

5 Steve Waugh

A man for every occasion and perhaps the most ruthless cricketer I've played with. If the chips are down then Stephen is the man you want walking out to bat. He was also a handy bowler in his younger days.

6 Allan Border (captain)

This is the man who taught me how to play Test cricket. Not just me – all but Brett Lee of my Australia dream twelve learnt the ropes under AB. He told and showed us what it means to play for our country and was my easiest choice for the side – a great batsman, great man, and underrated left-arm spin bowler.

7 Ian Healy

His work behind the stumps to Tim May and myself during the Ashes tour in 1993 was immaculate. Also a determined batsman and a real fighter in any situation, a good man to have on the field or in the dressing room. Adam Gilchrist has made an unbelievable start to his career but it is too early yet to compare him with Heals.

8 Shane Warne

Only so I can bat ahead of Merv Hughes. Otherwise, my spinner would be Tim May, and if the Test is taking place at Sydney then we would both be in the starting XI. Maysie was great fun and a real prankster. I would back our record in tandem against most other pairs.

9 Merv Hughes

He taught me so much about life and cricket and has become one of my best mates. When I came into the side he went out of his way to make me feel welcome. Sometimes his ability to bowl got lost as people concentrated on his charismatic style, but those of us who played with him realised he was a fantastic fast bowler. Although people might consider him a pest, he was very good at gauging the mood in the dressing room. He knew when to be serious and when to crack a joke.

10 Brett Lee

If he stays fit Binga could break all the records in the book. His sheer pace adds another dimension and he is also a handy batsman to have down the order. His youthful enthusiasm lifts the side and he also has a very good head on his shoulders.

11 Glenn McGrath

With his consistency, his ability to hit the right line and length to right and left-handed batsmen alike, he is a must in this side. He always has the batsmen under pressure and does the basics very well. He is a pest in the changing room but is good value.

12 Bruce Reid

But for persistent injury he would have been one of the all-time greats. His height meant he gained steep bounce and he would also supply variety being a left-armer. Also a formidable drinker and a great bloke.

Ricky Ponting, in time, might force his way into the middle order, but at the moment the combination of Boon, Border and the Waughs looks formidable. I found it far harder to pick four pace bowlers from a field of seven or eight. Craig McDermott, with 291 Test wickets, Jason Gillespie and Damien Fleming have also put in match-winning performances. But I just think Brett Lee deserves a place for the way he has created a new dimension in the side.

The toughest decision was to choose a captain between Border, Taylor and Steve Waugh. They have all shown great leadership qualities, but in the end I went for AB simply because he showed the other two the ropes. He started the ball rolling and made life easier for his successors.

REST OF THE WORLD TEST 12

1   Saeed Anwar (Pakistan)

Has all the shots in the book against both pace and spin. His footwork is impeccable and he is an accurate judge of a single. Anything short and wide will race to the boundary – a quality batsman in all conditions.

2   Graham Gooch (England)

Just squeezes in ahead of another fine player, Desmond Haynes. Gooch was one of the toughest openers I played against. It was always a real effort to get him out, especially in the 1993 Ashes series when he scored two hundreds against a really good attack. Led from the front, but always a good bloke to have a beer with afterwards.

3   Brian Lara (West Indies)

A lot of flair with his high backlift and on his day the most entertaining batsman in the world who can tear an attack to ribbons. When his eye is in and his mind is switched on, there isn't much point setting a field because he is good enough to penetrate it.

4 Sachin Tendulkar (India, vice-captain)

The best batsman I've played against by a distance. What makes him the best in my eyes is the way he judges the length faster than any other player and rocks on to the front or back foot almost as soon as the ball has left your hand. He does not settle for 60s or 70s but goes on to score big hundreds. At his present rate he could even score a hundred hundreds in international cricket. Has a phenomenal range of shots against spin. His bat might weigh 3lb 2oz, but his timing is still first-class.

5 Martin Crowe (New Zealand, captain)

A very graceful player who carried a massive responsibility in a struggling side towards the end of his career, much like Allan Border in parts of his. Punched out runs consistently and always looked to sweep against spin. I saw bowling to Crowe as a real challenge but hugely enjoyable, also the skipper.

6 Jacques Kallis (South Africa)

When I first saw him I couldn't work out what all the fuss was about, but over the last three years he has developed into a high-quality all-rounder. That shows his determination, dedication and passion for the game. He has become a solid, dependable batsman who will continue to improve and is now a genuinely hostile bowler with a fast outswinger.

7 Chris Cairns (New Zealand)

I'm not sure at the moment whether Cairns or Kallis is the best all-rounder in the world, but they are definitely the top two. He has matured enormously over the last two or three years, having taken time to fulfil his potential. One of the most destructive batsmen in the world who can change a game in a session. He hit Brett Lee for two sixes at Wellington, one hook and one straight over his head, which were truly amazing.

8   Moin Khan (Pakistan)

As good as anyone when it comes to keeping wicket to spin. Also a great encourager with his cries of 'Shabash, shabash.' A team's energy in the field is largely dictated by the wicket-keeper. Moin is also a good batsman who has gone in at number six for Pakistan.

9   Wasim Akram (Pakistan)

His record speaks for itself. He can bounce people out, or pitch it up and generate swing and then reverse swing to deadly effect. A lot of bowlers have one weapon or the other but few possess both. Also a very handy lower-order slogger with a Test double-hundred to his credit.

10   Saqlain Mushtaq (Pakistan)

He was taken off-spin bowling to another dimension with his mystery ball, the off-break that turns away from the right-hander. Even after four years not many batsmen can read it. I would love to bowl in tandem with Saqlain.

11   Curtly Ambrose (West Indies)

Quite simply the best bowler I have seen through my career, either pace or spin. Like a Ferrari, he has that extra sixth gear which he slips into when his team really needs it. Otherwise, his accuracy makes him almost impossible to score off. His spell against us at Perth in 1992–3 of 7 wickets for 1 run was absolutely awesome and won West Indies the match and the series.

12   Brian McMillan (South Africa)

A tough character and a great team man, the best all-rounder in the world in the first half of the 1990s.

As well as Botham, I just missed playing against Gordon Greenidge and Viv Richards, otherwise I guess they would have come into the top order. The hard part was again leaving out world-class bowlers. Shaun Pollock came close, but I have gone for two specialist bowlers and Wasim's variety swung it (literally) in his favour. I don't think Pollock's batting puts him in the class of Cairns and Kallis as an all-rounder. Allan Donald is another who almost made it. As for the spin department, I chose Saqlain rather than Muttiah Muralitharan because he has given something new to the game.

   The game itself would be a real thriller and certainly very hard-fought. Overall, though, I'd back Australia to win if we were playing at home. Anywhere else in the world it would be anyone's game – but Australia would probably win.

AUSTRALIA ONE-DAY 12

1   Mark Waugh

A free-flowing stroke-maker who can mix the ones and twos with powerful hits, and is also brilliant anywhere in the field.

2   Adam Gilchrist

Capable of striking fours and sixes practically from the first ball and a solid wicket-keeper. Also sets up a left/right combination with Junior.

3   Dean Jones

One of the all-time great one-day batsmen who took running between the wickets to a new level. It would be worth the admission to watch Jones and Michael Bevan turn ones into twos and twos into threes.

4   Steve Waugh

I think Stephen has actually improved as a one-day batsman in his mid-thirties, which says much for the sheer determination of the guy. He was also a fine bowler with a great slower ball and yorker, before being restricted by injuries. In those days he was known in the side as the 'Ice man' because of his ability to bowl at the death.

5   Allan Border (captain)

Can bat according to any situation. Whether the innings needs quick runs at the end or rebuilding after the loss of a couple of quick wickets, AB will produce the goods. His left-arm spin was underestimated and he was also a brilliant midwicket fielder. His background in baseball meant he hit the stumps with uncanny regularity.

6   Michael Bevan

Phenomenal ability to hit the ball into gaps, which is just what you want in the middle order. Also paces an innings magnificently. He sums up one-day match situations better than anyone I know out in the middle. We always reckon that if Bevo is in at the end of an innings then we have won the match.

7 Darren Lehmann

This choice might surprise a lot of people, but I rate Lehmann the best improvising batsman I have seen – just what you need in the final overs. He can somehow squeeze a yorker behind point or tickle it to fine leg. A special talent who is unlucky not to have played far more international cricket. Along with Mark Waugh, the best player of spin in the country.

8 Tom Moody

A very handy player who could come in and hit boundaries straight away or put on the brakes with his deceptive medium-pace.

9 Shane Warne

It's my book.

10 Brett Lee

With his raw pace and ability to swing the ball in he can clean up at the end of an innings if he gets his line right. Cricket is a simple game – if you bowl straight at his pace there's a great chance of wickets. A sensational prospect.

11 Glenn McGrath

A model of consistency, McGrath is the banker for economical figures, although I would give him the new ball and back him to dismiss the openers early.

12 Ricky Ponting

Along with Jonty Rhodes, Punter is the best fielder in the world in the crucial backward point area. I think he actually hits the stumps more often than Jonty. The ideal man to come on if one of the older players conveniently tweaks a hamstring.

What I like about this side is the depth of batting and variety of bowling options. Only Dean Jones cannot actually bowl (he throws) and if we needed a tenth man to join the attack then it would probably be too late anyway. There is also a good balance between the hitters like Moody and Gilchrist and the accumulators, with AB and Steve Waugh there in the middle who can go either way. This side is picked in the same way as the Tests, from the players I have played with at international level when they were at their best.

REST OF THE WORLD ONE-DAY 12

1   Saeed Anwar (Pakistan)

Can play either the aggressive or supporting role in the opening stages.

2   Sachin Tendulkar (India)

Capable of dominating from the first ball.

3   Jacques Kallis (South Africa)

Promoted to number three to underpin the innings. Great ability to hit through point and cover off the back foot, an important shot to play in the first 15 overs. Also plays swing bowling well and delivers a good fast-medium pace.

4   Brian Lara (West Indies)

Just a brilliant, match-winning batsman. Imagine him coming in after a great start.

5 Jonty Rhodes (South Africa)

Whatever he picks up with the bat you can add on another 20 for the runs he saves in the field with his brilliant diving stops at backward point and sheer presence. Batsmen daren't take a single to Jonty. Only Bevo matches his running between the wickets in the game today. He has perfected the art of turning for a second or third. Also a great energiser in the field. He's always the one running to give the bowler's cap or jumper to the umpire and geeing up the team. A fantastic all-round guy.

6 Chris Cairns (New Zealand)

No ground in the world is big enough to stop Cairns lifting the ball over the ropes. He and Mark Waugh are the furthest hitters I've seen.

7 Lance Klusener (South Africa)

Cracks the ball harder than anybody in the world today with his spectacular baseball-style swing. Rescued South Africa so often in the 1999 World Cup, almost taking them into the final at our expense. Strong character and clever bowler who varies his pace intelligently.

8 Moin Khan (Pakistan)

Can get the total up from 250 to 280 in a couple of overs to push it beyond limits.

9 Wasim Akram (Pakistan)

In certain conditions, such as the 1992 World Cup final against England in Melbourne, he is almost unplayable with the white ball.

10   Saqlain Mushtaq (Pakistan)

I can't remember seeing anyone take him on successfully at the end of an innings. Those who try to go down the track are usually undone by the one that goes away. Particularly useful in running through the lower order.

11   Curtly Ambrose (West Indies)

Would take the new ball and probably not go for more than a couple per over.

12   Darren Gough (England)

Has become as good as anybody in the world at reverse swing which makes him a good man to have in the closing overs. A real winner.

It is probably quite revealing that nine of my one-day side are also in the Test squad. There is a place for limited overs specialists, but from experience I think that great players are great players whatever the form of the game. People of this quality are good enough to adapt to any situation.

20

2001 TESTS

AFTER THE SEASON with Hampshire and a minor knee operation, I could barely wait to resume my Test career in Australia. We had home Tests against the West Indies before going to India and England in 2001 – different challenges, but each one enthralling in its own way. Unfortunately, a freak injury sustained during a game between Victoria and New South Wales put paid to any chance of taking part in that first series.

I stood underneath one of the simplest catches you could imagine at slip after Mark Waugh misjudged a slog/sweep off Colin Miller. The wind took it away at the last minute and, instead of landing between my palms, the ball struck the end of my spinning finger and bounced a couple of metres in the air before I caught it second time. Phew, I thought – and only then did I feel a surge of pain. I looked down and saw the end of the finger pointing left from the knuckle. It had been broken in three places and the surgeon had to pin it in two areas to straighten it again.

I could only watch from the commentary box as the boys completed a 5–0 rout and try to comprehend how the once great West Indians had fallen so far. It wasn't just that they underperformed; the absence of fight really surprised me. The quicks would routinely leave them at 50 for 3 or 4, giving the change bowlers the opportunity to clean up the middle to lower order.

Unfortunately, compensation for missing the home series did not arrive in India. People have described the series there as being one of the greatest of all time, and I have certainly never played in a contest where fortunes changed so dramatically. Everything hinged around a fantastic innings of 281 by V.V.S. Laxman in the Second Test at Calcutta. But for that, we would have taken a 2–0 lead and, I'm convinced, have gone on to complete a clean sweep in Madras.

Without making excuses or being disrespectful, I will be very surprised if Laxman plays a similar innings again. I don't mean that he is not capable of scoring as many runs in a Test match. In fact, I hope he goes on to make 300 because he's a nice guy and a good player. I just don't think he could do it in the same way. Some of his shots on this occasion defied belief. For most of the time I thought we bowled well at him. I went around the wicket, but he just kept stepping away to hit the ball through cover, or against the spin through midwicket. History shows that you can't play like that for long without getting out. Maybe Sir Donald Bradman was an exception, and perhaps Brian Lara has batted in a similar fashion once or twice. For this one innings, Laxman joined that élite class.

The story of the match was that we led by 274 on first innings and had India 115 for 3 in the second, with Tendulkar back in the shed. Sourav Ganguly then put on 117 with Laxman before the fifth-wicket stand of 376 with Rahul Dravid. We have generally had the wood on Dravid, me in particular. Basically, our plan is that when he comes in, I come on. But you could see him growing in confidence as Laxman went about his shots. You had to take off your hat to the pair of them.

When somebody is batting as well as Laxman, my first thought is to cut off the boundaries, but it was nearly imposs-

ible. The quicks tried everything to no avail. I decided to switch
and bowl in to the footmarks outside leg stump from over the
wicket to try to dry him up, knowing that Indian batsmen
hardly ever sweep. Probably because there was nothing to lose
– nobody expected them to recover – Laxman decided it was
going to be him or me. I tried everything, even a couple of
bouncers and hip-high full tosses, to catch him by surprise. In
one over I bowled six flippers but he had an answer for everything. Before Calcutta, he averaged around the 25 mark. We
just happened to cop him on the one day of his life when he
batted like a dream.

Having spent so long in the field, trying to save the game on
the final day represented a huge challenge, let alone reaching
a target of 383. We lost by 171 runs as our record-winning run
came to an end at number sixteen. That wasn't something we
dwelt upon. It is an old cliché, but we really do take it one
game at a time. We had never focused on anything more than
winning the game immediately in front of us, and so we hardly
talked about the sequence. Beaten in Calcutta, we set our minds
to the decider in Madras and, we hoped, the beginning of
another run.

That was not to be. Despite a fantastic 203 from Matthew
Hayden and a first-innings total of 391, we lost by 2 wickets.
We gave India a few scares as they chased 155 to win.
Harbhajan Singh took 15 wickets in the match to add to his
13 in Calcutta, yet we didn't really think of him as much of a
threat. He bowled off spin quite well, and that was that. In
the First Test he went for 132 in 30 overs, admittedly taking
4 wickets, and I think he gained confidence from Calcutta. He
had not enjoyed that much success before then, and hasn't
ripped through teams since. He also took a hat-trick – I was
his third wicket. There was a lot of doubt about the catch and
the third umpire gave it out.

Batsmen can always have problems against spin in India because the conditions are so different from Australia. After a couple of catches at bat/pad, it is easy to dry up. But it was Laxman, not Harbhajan, who changed the series. Another guy I thought deserved a lot of credit was John Wright, their coach. He instilled a real fighting spirit, which I felt they lacked in the past. I admired Wright as a determined opening batsman for New Zealand and his attitude clearly rubbed off.

From our point of view the biggest positive factor was the re-emergence of Hayden, who scored 549 runs (more than Laxman) and averaged over 100 through the series. A significant reason for his success was the way he threw himself in to the Indian way of life. He went out of his way to see the sights, to learn about the way people live and to chat to as many folk as he could. I remember him having long conversations with retired spinners such as Bishen Bedi and Maninder Singh about how to play slow bowling on those pitches. He is a very strong man anyway and he also worked hard on his fitness. The reward came in Madras where he achieved one of his lifelong ambitions of batting through a complete day in a Test match for Australia. He showed what can be achieved with the right attitude, a willingness to work hard and a plan.

At the start of the tour we decided to keep the whingeometer low. We tried to mix as much as security would allow and I can honestly say, in spite of the result, that it was a very enjoyable tour. A personal highlight was a visit to the Tendulkars' house on the outskirts of Mumbai. Sachin and I have become good friends and it is always interesting to talk to him, not just about cricket, but about life in general.

India has become more westernised in recent years. There are good restaurants and bars in practically every city. The players who toured thirty or forty years ago would probably be amazed at the transformation of the place. For the likes of the three Ws – Waugh, Waugh and Warne – the experienced members of the side, we have won everywhere except here. It remains unconquered territory and we would love to have one last chance to win a series in India. But there is no place for nostalgia in the game, and there is no guarantee of getting another crack. Even so, I will still remember India as being a fantastic place to tour. No cricketing education is complete without a trip to that part of the world.

I thought I bowled quite well at the start of the tour and took 5 wickets in the First Test. Deep down, though, I knew I was being camouflaged by the way the team was playing. Whatever people thought when they watched me bowl, my confidence was not as high as it should have been. At times I wondered whether my spinning finger would ever be as good as it was before. In the middle, you have to exude self-belief and should never allow your body language to say anything other than 'I'm in control.' What you think inside can be entirely different.

It didn't help when coach John Buchanan decided to go public after Calcutta in questioning whether I had the fitness – mental or physical – to cope with back-to-back Tests. He said that I looked 'distressed' at the end of the Second Test. That was the last thing I needed and I took up the issue with him. He said that he was trying to fire me up. Fair enough, but why, I asked, did he have to do it in public. If he thought that was the way to motivate me, he couldn't know me that well. Without wanting to sound paranoid, I am an easy target for certain sections of the media. To give ammunition like that was effectively writing their headlines for them. The three of us – Buck, Stephen Waugh and myself – decided that problems with anybody in the future would be resolved privately, as should always be the case. Buck acknowledged his mistake, apologised, and we moved on. There is no grudge on my part.

The six weeks between returning from India and flying out to England did me a world of good. Ashes tours have always been, and will continue to be, special. If this was to be my last, I wanted it to be a big one. I worked harder on my fitness than ever before. Some journalists thought that Stuart MacGill should have taken the spinner's place ahead of me. He bowled well against the West Indies and I wasn't at my best in India, so it wasn't unexpected. However, there is a world of difference between bowling to a dispirited West Indies team and against India in India. If I felt there was something to prove in England it was only to show myself that I could still be the same bowler I was on my first visit eight years earlier.

The triangular one-day series before the Tests received a stack of bad publicity because of crowd problems, culminating in the presentation ceremony after the final at Lord's when Michael Bevan was struck on the side of the head with a beer can. Earlier in the tournament, at Trent Bridge, we left the field after a firework narrowly missed Brett Lee on the boundary edge. There had been difficulties during the World Cup in England two years earlier and the authorities did not appear to have made much progress in dealing with the situation. You wonder what it will take before something is finally done. It really is a shame because the families who go along want to watch their heroes and enjoy the day. A few idiots can ruin it for everybody.

More positively, Australia won the tournament in relative comfort. We decided that in the first 15 overs we would try to bowl as though it was a Test match. If you aim to hit the top of off stump it is hard to score against and there is every chance of taking a wicket. We backed that up with aggressive field settings. At one point during a day-night game at Old Trafford we had four slips and two gullies in place, with Glenn McGrath and Jason Gillespie beating the bat time and time again.

That particular match sticks in my mind – and not only because we skittled out England for 86. We had decided we wanted to nail them ahead of the Tests and try to re-open the old psychological scars. They had won four successive series against Zimbabwe, West Indies, Pakistan and Sri Lanka, and there was talk about the Waughs and myself perhaps being over the hill. But we didn't think the English confidence ran as deeply as people thought. I am convinced that we seized the initiative for the whole summer that night in Manchester.

We set up a tactical group comprising Stephen, Buck, McGrath, Adam Gilchrist and me to formulate plans through the tour to present at team meetings. Even though I was no longer vice-captain, it made me feel involved and a lot of the discussions were extremely stimulating. Some of the suggestions did not come to fruition and I dare say a few of them never will, but most of the things we tried during the series worked.

When I start a spell, I generally like to land a few regulation balls in the right area before trying anything more extravagant. This Test series was different. I had enjoyed success in England in the past and I wanted to create fresh doubt in the minds of their batsmen from the start. In my first over of the First Test at Edgbaston I threw in a googly, a top-spinner and a leg-break and gained immediate reward when Mark Butcher popped one up and Ricky Ponting held a screamer just before lunch.

It turned out to be a fantastic day's cricket. Alec Stewart and Andrew Caddick staged something of a recovery for the last English wicket, but Michael Slater took the bull by the horns by smashing 18 in Darren Gough's first over. Although we wanted to get on top as soon as we could, we didn't anticipate anything like that. Even by Slater's explosive standards this came as a rare onslaught as he punished Gough for bowling short and wide. That's the beauty of Michael Slater.

Steve Waugh, Damien Martyn and Gilchrist completed hundreds and we went on to win by an innings and 118 runs. My match figures of 8 for 100 ended any suggestion that I was fortunate to make the trip. Before the game I surprised a few English journalists by talking about my new role in the side. They thought it was kidology, but I wasn't trying to pull the wool over anybody's eyes. Under Allan Border and Mark Taylor we would always bat first if we won the toss. These days, with the sheer quality of McGrath, Gillespie and Brett Lee, Stephen is happy to insert the opposition to exploit early moisture and back the batsmen to chase a small target in the fourth innings.

My job now is to tie up an end during the first couple of days and perhaps attack a little more in the second innings. There is clearly less wear and tear on the pitch at that stage than I had been used to on the final day and the bounce is generally more even. As a team, though, we have continued to be successful. The only statistics that matter are wins against losses.

Lord's, the venue for the Second Test, is always a special place. I sat in my usual corner in the dressing room and watched the action unfurl as we scored 401 in the first innings on the way to an 8 wicket win. McGrath and Gillespie enjoyed it as much as any of us, bowling superbly in taking 15 wickets between them. It was a great game for Mark Waugh, who scored 108 and also took the 158th catch of his Test career to set a new world record. As the bloke who tends to stand next to him in the slips, I am well positioned to say he has an amazing pair of hands.

We needed merely to draw the Third Test at Trent Bridge to retain the Ashes. Before the game the media had a field day when a copy of one of Buck's memos fell in to their hands. It was based, I'm told, on the thoughts of an old Chinese philosopher and warrior called Sun Tzu. This isn't everyday preparation for a Test match, but then Buck isn't your average coach. I must admit that I glanced at the first sheet and wondered what it was. I didn't look at it again. I'm no expert on cricket history, but I don't remember too many leg-spinners hailing from Beijing. During the course of a series, Buck hands out all sorts of papers. Some players devour every word religiously, others pick and choose. I'm all for anything that might improve performance and Buck is exploring new areas to just that purpose. It is uncanny, though, how often his handouts fall in to the wrong hands.

The game itself is one that I will always remember. My figures of 6–33 in the second innings were my best in a Test outside Australia (although I improved on them again at the Oval later in the month) and came at a crucial period after England restricted us to a 5 run lead at the halfway stage. The wicket that really turned the game was that of Mark Ramprakash. Having been 115 for 2, England lost Mike Atherton and Alec Stewart in quick succession. They needed to consolidate but, instead, Ramprakash charged down the pitch to me, missed completely and gave Gilchrist a routine stumping. I couldn't believe what had happened. It wasn't so much the charge itself as the timing of it. There were six overs left and it exposed Craig White, who soon followed. From then on it was a question of maintaining concentration. Errors of judgement like that can be so costly in Test cricket, and I speak as somebody who rates Ramprakash as a batsman. We went on to win by 7 wickets, the series-clinching victory tarnished only by the absence of Steve Waugh who had gone to hospital after being stretchered from the crease having torn a calf muscle.

With an unassailable 3–0 lead behind us, we might have taken our foot off the pedal at Headingley. That is not to take anything away from Mark Butcher, whose match-winning 173 will go down as a great Ashes innings. Like Laxman in the previous series, he chanced his arm and deserved his success. The fact is that rain chopped more than a full day off the game. Had the weather not been so bad we would have extended our second innings and set the kind of target that has never been reached in Test history instead of the 315 England were left to chase. Gilchrist won a lot of admiration for keeping the game alive, but he was more disappointed than anyone to lose in his second game in charge. The target was attainable, as Butcher proved, and our performance in the field was some way below our best.

All in all there was a new determination going in to the final Test at the Oval. For some of us it could be our last game in England. I'm sure that contributed to the phenomenal effort put in by Steve Waugh to recover in time. He also wanted to make a point that success at this level is not achieved without occasionally having to go through the pain barrier. Our physio, Errol Alcott, was amazing in getting him back on the park. England suffered a number of injuries through the series and we just wondered how much some of them really wanted to play. It seemed that they lacked the self-belief to put themselves on the line in case they failed.

Our selectors decided to recall Justin Langer in place of Slater. I've been a good mate of Slater for the best part of a decade and he took the decision on the chin, even though he was disappointed. I spent a lot of time trying to console him and drew on my own experience in the West Indies a couple of years earlier. I told him that it doesn't suddenly mean you are a bad player. Langer went on to prove that it is possible not only to win back your place, but to keep it. Few players work as assiduously as Langer and we were all delighted when he marked his return with a hundred.

For the old guard, the game couldn't have gone any better. The Waughs scored a century apiece, in Stephen's case despite hobbling towards three figures with another injury. It was not the prettiest hundred I have ever seen, but it might have been the most determined. As for myself, I took 7 wickets in the first innings and 4 when England followed on, to earn a second man of the match award in the series. I will cherish most the moment when Gilchrist held a thin edge off Stewart, making him my 400th victim. Overall I don't think I have ever bowled better than in this game. My confidence had grown through the series. I was ripping the leg-break as sharply as I had on my first tour, but with the experience of ten years in Test cricket I also knew which weapon to use, and when.

At the fall of the ninth wicket in England's second innings, McGrath pointed out that we were both on 31 for the series. With Phil Tufnell the last man it would not be long before one of us reached 32. McGrath has an incredible memory for all of his wickets – he knows every one in the right order. I don't have a head for figures and hadn't realised we were so close. Tuffers duly nicked the last ball of the over and it came so easily to me at slip that I couldn't put it down without raising suspicions! We all had a laugh and a joke, but I was more than happy with my contribution towards the 4–1 success.

As we have held the Ashes since 1989 I do not see why the MCC refuse to allow us to bring home the prize. Our case was falling on deaf ears so we decided to create our own trophy. Back in the dressing room at the Oval, we placed the bails that had been used in the game in a metal container with some kerosene and taped up the smoke alarms. It took a long time before they burnt properly, but a few of us eventually managed to light cigars from the embers with the song 'Disco Inferno' playing in the background. Colin Miller collected the new ashes in a little jar and the last I heard he was still trying to find a more appropriate container for them. Then it was back to the hotel for the real celebrations. Unfortunately, those plans were scuppered when a bomb scare forced us to evacuate the premises for more than an hour. Nobody felt like partying after that; we were all shattered.

Looking back at the series, the scoreline did not reflect the difference between the teams. The first three games could have gone either way. England made mistakes at the wrong time and dropped important catches. Put another way, we just coped better under pressure. We had the belief to carry us through. But I still believe that England are on the right track. One reason is the captaincy of Nasser Hussain. He has always had that aggressive streak and a positive outlook. He has shown faith in his team and the players have responded. Injuries notwithstanding, there was far less chopping and changing by the selectors than I remembered from previous visits. Hussain's biggest problem is as a batsman. His technique has not changed and we were able to exploit the fact that he gets squared up by good length balls on the off stump.

From our viewpoint there were so many plus points. As a team we bonded straight away. We set out to entertain, to score 300 runs in a day, and I don't think anybody who bought a ticket went home disappointed. McGrath and Gillespie showed that they are the finest new-ball pairing in the world, Mark Waugh batted as fluently as ever and Gilchrist always threatened to take the game from England at number seven. Given his chance at last, Damien Martyn showed what a fine, technically solid player he has become. And as for yours truly, the struggles in India seemed to be years rather than months past. Life felt good. Once again I reflected on how special Ashes tours are. I spent time with my friends from Hampshire and Bristol, my wife, kids and mum and dad. That was great. I can't wait for the next one – whether that's as a player or spectator!

21

THE FUTURE

IF MISFORTUNE STRUCK TODAY and I was unable to bowl another ball I would still be able to reflect with no real regrets on an incredible career and a sometimes unbelievable one. But the fact is that I would like to play on for a few more years yet. Fingers crossed that I'm injury-free and form stays excellent. Rarely a day passes without somebody asking how long I will continue, and the honest answer is that I don't know. My goal is to play in the 2003 World Cup and weigh it up from there. I just cannot say how long I will be able to do myself justice and maintain my enthusiasm. Anything you do in life is about enjoyment and as soon as that goes so should you. I am very lucky to do something that I enjoy and get well paid for it. I will guarantee, though, that I will not hang around for the sake of it. Mind you, the selectors can always make the decision for you. I have set myself high standards and when I do eventually announce my retirement I don't want people thinking thank goodness for that – although some of them might.

I still have ambitions in the game. I would love to score a first-class hundred. I reached 99 against New Zealand in Perth in 2001 but, agonisingly, fell that one run short. Another is to captain Australia in a Test match, having enjoyed the occasions when I led my country in one-day cricket. I think the captaincy brought out the best in me, but if time has slipped me by then so be it. There is so much international cricket being played now that records are being pushed back all the time. Maybe I can reach 500, who knows? Milestones don't make me tick but you do pat yourself on the back when you reach those sort. But I think it is unwise to set a target. My philosophy is quite simple. I want to take as many wickets as possible in both forms of the game.

So much will depend on fitness and injury. I have had two major operations on my spinning finger, one on my shoulder and one on my knee, and managed to come back each time. Despite missing the 2000–01 series against the West Indies through injury, I felt from my comeback for Victoria against Western Australia, when I took nine wickets, that the golden years might still lie ahead. I like to think those thoughts were vindicated on the Ashes tour a few months later. Like any bowler with a few scalps under his belt, I can't wait for the next challenge.

Wear and tear caused the problems which resulted in having to undergo surgery on the first two occasions. The more I looked into the matter, the more I realised the difficulties bowling leg-spin causes, because it is such an unusual occupation and the body has not evolved sufficiently to stand up to so much strain on the fingers and shoulder. The cavemen obviously didn't spend much time worrying about flippers and googlies. It is no coincidence that Paul Strang and Anil Kumble have also required surgery on their shoulders and fingers in recent times. Farther back, the problem effectively caused Richie Benaud to retire.

The main thing you need to play for a long time is mental toughness and inner strength, with a bit of luck. I am generally able to bowl without any pain. Having had the operation in 1998, my shoulder now is almost as good as new. Like the engine in a car, I had to run it in gently at the start but now, more than two years on, I feel I can bowl with absolute confidence. Without the help of Debbie Benger and Lynn Watson, my physios and friends, and the great job done by Greg Hoy, the surgeon, my career would be over.

People have said that I don't rip the ball as viciously as I did in my early days. I disagree. The fact that I no longer bowl huge leg-breaks every time is not the same as losing the weapon. There are times when I impart big spin on the ball, such as the delivery that removed Herschelle Gibbs in the World Cup semi-final in England. These days, I don't employ that ripper as a stock ball. I believe I bowl with more variety now, and the strategy includes regulating the amount of turn on each leg-break. I think I've become a smarter bowler. Maybe I outsmart myself now, who knows? I use the big one as a shock ball; it's my wicket-taking ball. But it does not always need to deviate a foot or eighteen inches to take the edge.

To a degree it is possible to legislate for wear and tear problems, to schedule an operation out of season and minimise the effects. Unfortunately, though, injury can also occur at the least expected, most inconvenient moments. There is always the danger of a freak setback, such as the one that happened at the start of the 2000–01 season. What should have been a simple catch at slip resulted in a broken spinning finger. Then there was the horrific collision between Steve Waugh and Jason Gillespie in Sri Lanka the previous winter. I don't want to tempt fate by planning too far ahead. You never know what's around the corner, so I just try to enjoy the moment.

Looking ahead more positively, the ideal situation will be to go out on my terms, probably after an Ashes series in Australia. I would also like to play in one more World Cup, if I have the opportunity. I hope people won't put two and two together and interpret this as meaning I intend to step down in 2003 after the competition in South Africa which itself follows the next home series against England.

When I do retire from the international game I would like to play for another couple of years with Victoria and try to fulfil another ambition of featuring in a Pura Cup final. I can also see myself returning to Hampshire at the new ground in Southampton, if they will have me back. I want to be able to help younger players and pass on my knowledge, especially to young spinners.

The biggest consideration in any decision will be the wishes of my family. I haven't seen anywhere near as much of Brooke, Jackson and Summer as I would have wished and I don't want to miss out as they develop. But we all have to make sacrifices and my wife and I have made a lot, so I intend to make up for them soon. I want to be around when they need me. In fact, if I thought it was best for Simone and myself and the children I would walk away from the game tomorrow.

I suppose the next question is what I will do when I stop playing. I would like to think there will be a few opportunities. The idea of spending six months relaxing at home, maybe with a holiday somewhere along the line, is very appealing. Being brought up near the beach as a kid made me realise how easy it is to relax. There is something about the water that is relaxing. Sometimes it feels as though I have spent the last ten years continuously playing cricket and I think it might do me good to get away from the game and spend some quality time with my family for a while and simply monitor events via television and a few days out with my mates.

Having said that, I would like to stay involved in the longer term. I have been contracted to Channel Nine since 1993 and really enjoy sitting behind the microphone with all the team trying to give an insight into what is happening outside. The feedback has been quite encouraging, so I hope it might develop into a full time situation. One man who is interesting to watch is Bill Lawry. He is such a funny guy and the highlight of the day is sometimes just sitting next to him off-camera. I think he has been successful because of his excitement, his sheer passion for the game. I also like the idea of presenting a chat show, either on radio or television, where I can interview sportsmen and women and other stars and try to give the listener an insight into what it takes to reach the top and what goes on behind the scenes. Having my own sporting company would be enjoyable, too.

Being a full-time coach or cricket manager is not something that has really interested me, but times change. I love helping kids and I believe that all international cricketers have a duty to put something back into the game. Maybe the answer would be to set up a leg-spin academy along the lines of the Dennis Lillee clinic for fast bowlers, where young spinners from all over the world could come along for fine-tuning or the equivalent of a service. Alternatively, I might be able to help out Rod Marsh at the AIS Academy in Adelaide in the same way that Ian Chappell goes along to help out with some simple techniques and ideas about playing spin and short-pitched bowling. Much coaching, of course, is done informally – just the odd word between a couple of leggies when they happen to meet.

Maybe another option would be to put my name up as a selector. I like to believe I can spot a player who might be able to cut it at international level and I would take it as a privilege to be asked. I just want to stay away from making difficult decisions about people I have played with and who have become mates. So maybe down the track. It is not just about picking guys who happen to be making runs or taking wickets. The knack is to look at when a player performs and how well he appears to cope in pressure situations. Once a guy has been identified as having potential it then becomes a matter of waiting until he hits form – so that he goes into the side with confidence – and an opportunity becomes vacant.

Taking the game as a whole, I sense there is still massive interest, despite the slur brought about by match-fixing allegations. The only way to show that the game is completely above board is to let the ICC investigative department do their job and get to the bottom of it and then get rid of the people who have been involved. For world cricket it is important that England, South Africa and West Indies, as well as ourselves, are all doing well because passion in the sub-continent will always be enormous.

The West Indies Cricket Board needs to pull its socks up quickly. Officials have a responsibility to the game worldwide, not only in the Caribbean. Unfortunately, there doesn't seem to have been much foresight in the 1980s when they were winning series after series in comfort and fast bowlers seemed to be falling off a conveyor belt, which can happen and sometimes you need to hit the bottom before you can reach the top again. They made the mistake of thinking that would continue naturally, but the rest of the world caught up and West Indies had no system of any substance on which to fall back. If they lose Courtney Walsh, Brian Lara and Jimmy Adams in the space of a few years they could find themselves in even more serious trouble. Finding talented players is only part of the job. That talent also needs to be nurtured. I don't know if the idea of an Academy along the lines of the Australian system is feasible, but they desperately need to put a junior cricket programme in place.

Some of the greatest players in the history of the game hailed from the West Indies, people of the calibre of Sir Viv Richards, Gordon Greenidge, Clive Lloyd, Desmond Haynes and Curtly Ambrose. The list is endless. It seems a waste of their knowledge and talent not to use them to coach and encourage the kids or the present team. These are proud people who take no pleasure in seeing the decline of a side they once graced and I'm sure they would do anything to help. At the same time I believe there is a responsibility on former players to offer encouragement, instead of sniping, to get in and help, rather than slag everybody off.

I am all for experimenting and embracing ideas that might make the game more attractive to the paying public. There is always room for improvement as long as common sense does not fall by the wayside and alterations are made one at a time, instead of confusing people by bringing in too many changes simultaneously just for the sake of it.

One of the most contentious areas is the growing influence of technology and how far that should go with assisting umpires. They have an unenviable job these days because decisions are being scrutinised like never before. Even the most clear-cut catch behind can start to look dubious after a dozen replays of shots from every conceivable angle.

As players we accept that umpires are human beings and will not get every decision right. All we want is consistency and to be able to have a rapport with them. David Shepherd and Steve Bucknor are the leaders in the world today because there is a regular dialogue. If you ask why an appeal has been turned down they will give an answer, even though they're not obliged to. The game will be the worse if that human element is removed.

The other side of the argument is that a bad decision can cost a player his Test career, but from experience I think the good and the bad even themselves out over time in most cases. There are areas, too, where I wonder how reliable the technology is.

In South Africa in 2000–01 they experimented with a 'carpet' which was superimposed on replays to assist with lbw decisions. Most networks have this and I think it is a good idea on replays, but not for actual decision-making.

I agree with the use of the third umpire and replays to help with runs outs, stumpings and catches when the ball looks as though it might have fallen short or been taken on the half-volley. If we go much further the umpire might as well be replaced with a computer and a clothes peg to hang our caps and sweaters on. If every lbw appeal was referred to the third umpire the over rates would come down to single figures because umpires would be afraid to make a decision. I can see with a run out that a camera bang in line with the crease gives a perfect view, but where lbws and bat-pad catches are concerned the umpire has the best seat in the house. Bat-pad catches especially are not always clear on the TV.

We have experimented in Australia with having three umpires used on a rotational basis, so each of them effectively operates for two sessions each day. It is hard to imagine just how tiring it can be to stand upright for hours on end, day after day, and to concentrate on every ball. It sounded like a good idea in principle, but I was surprised at the results. It just seemed that an umpire lost the feel for the game during the time he was away. I imagined that a couple of hours away to relax and maybe lie down would have energised them, but that was not really the case and I don't think the umpires themselves were convinced by the trials. Sometimes when an idea like that is introduced you realise how good the game is already, but it might be worth another try. I still think it could work.

Test cricket has worked well for years. There is no point tinkering for the sake of it, and the only major changes I think administrators need to consider are with the hours of play. One idea is a no ball or wide being punished with a free hit next ball. For Test cricket, I think the lunch and tea breaks should be altered to allow thirty minutes each time, instead of forty and twenty respectively. Then there is a case for starting in the afternoon and playing under floodlights, say from 2–9 pm.

This would immediately be attractive to cricket-lovers who go to work but would like to pop in – maybe after tea – to watch the final session when the temperatures are a bit cooler. It would also be a way of getting kids into the game after school. In Australia we have big grounds and plenty of seats waiting to be filled. Now that floodlights are used extensively in one-day cricket I think it is only a matter of time before Tests follow suit.

One question that would have to be overcome concerns the ball. Clearly you could not switch between red and white. The problem is that the white one loses its colour. It would last a bit longer in the five-day game because with fewer aggressive strokes there is less chance of it being hacked up. The answer would be to take a new white ball at night, say after 60 overs. That would really bring bowlers into the game and I expect one or two batsmen might want to have their say.

Where one-day cricket is concerned I see great scope for improvements. Even as a bowler I can understand why the game is stacked in favour of batsmen because crowds pay to see lots of big hitting. As well as the first 15 overs, I think there should be a flexible period of 5 overs when the same fielding restrictions apply with only two men allowed outside the circle. The captain of the batting side would decide when the 5 overs begins and a loud siren could be used to inform the crowd. I think that would be quite dramatic.

The options are enormous. If the first 15 overs have been profitable and two batsmen are well set the captain might decide to keep going from overs 16–20. Alternatively, he might wait until the hardest-hitting batsman comes out and then take the 5 overs. Can you imagine the excitement in the stands if Lance Klusener started to make his way to the crease to the screech of the siren? Another, intriguing possibility would be to call for the 5 overs if your side was behind the eight ball to try to swing the initiative. Then there would be questions for the fielding captain. Should he hold back his best bowler, perhaps even ending a good spell prematurely? The more I think, the more I am convinced this idea would add something different. I also believe there is a case for stipulating at least five rather than four fielders in the circle at all times and for keeping a catcher close to the wicket throughout the 50 overs.

One area which is sure to grow is the indoor game. Our matches in the Colonial Stadium in Melbourne against South Africa in 2000 were a massive success. The three matches attracted an average attendance of more than 30,000, even though they clashed with the AFL finals. I guess the crowd figures could be put down to the novelty value or the quality of the opponents. But my own opinion is that the Australian people simply enjoy watching cricket. There were teething problems – not least the cold – but the pitch which had been dropped into place was superb. I also like the way that batsmen walked to the wicket to the song of their choice. That added to the atmosphere and I don't think it made the contests any more of a gimmick. You are entitled to have some fun in one-day cricket. I expect a number of grounds, not just in Australia, to investigate retractable roofs.

I wonder how much of a global sport cricket can become. In theory it could be played anywhere the climate allows and I think it is important to spread the word. It is a fantastic game which helps to foster lasting friendship and genuinely enriches people's lives. Having said that, the ICC has a responsibility to make sure that when countries are granted full one-day or Test status they have the players and the structure to justify their elevation. A side being pummelled game after game inflates opposing team and individual records artificially and does nothing for the long-term future in the country concerned.

I am all for new countries playing international cricket, as long as they are good enough.

Sri Lanka have shown what is possible since joining the fold around twenty years ago. Whatever I think of Arjuna Ranatunga, I have enormous respect for their efforts and the way they held their own and gradually improved to the point where they won the World Cup in 1996. Zimbabwe, too, have become a strong one-day side who can be very dangerous. That has come through experience, but in the longer game, while they have not exactly struggled, they have not made the progress they would have anticipated. I cannot comment about Bangladesh because we have only played them once, in the 1999 World Cup. My gut feeling is that they will emerge as long as they are given regular fixtures to gain experience, because there is such an enthusiasm for the game in that part of the world. I hope they make a go of it.

A few years ago I came out in favour of a formal World Test Championship and I am pleased to say the ICC adopted something in 2001 along similar lines. The World Cup means there is a definite champion in one-day cricket and it was only a matter of time before something happened in the longer game.

The amount of cricket played is a topic guaranteed to provoke a few discussions. Realistically, we have to accept that the demands are only going to become greater as more countries join the Test fold and the respective Boards stage matches in June, July and August, traditionally the preserve of England or time off. We have to find the right balance between demand and rest and recovery.

Maybe selectors will adopt a rotational system over the next few years. Being a travelling cricketer is enough of a strain on family life as it is and the pressures will intensify as the schedule becomes busier. The rotation system is an interesting one. It is a delicate balancing act, but I can understand the selectors acting to extend the careers of the likes of Brett Lee and Jason Gillespie and to make sure they are right for upcoming series. Asking fast bowlers to fire day in, day out, for a whole campaign is extremely tough.

Boards have to maintain the right balance between Test and one-day cricket. For India and Pakistan the ratio is around three or four limited overs games to every Test, spread over the course of a year. England are at the other extreme, playing seven to eleven Tests and ten one-day internationals in a summer. In any twelve-month period I think a total of ten to twelve Tests and twenty to twenty-five one-day games is enough international cricket, and a good balance. Not everybody prefers the intensity of a 50-over match to the subtlety of the Test game. When a country goes into a Test match after a long series of one-day games they can be vulnerable if certain habits have crept into their game and I'm convinced the increase in limited overs games has contributed to the number of Tests finishing early.

We have to be careful to achieve and maintain the right ratio. Good players can adapt from one form of the game to another, but it may be that more specialists emerge. I don't particularly like the term 'separate teams' to describe Australia's Test and one-day sides. It should be thought of as the same team with a few changes. A player can make a good career in the limited overs game if he can improvise with bat and ball, score a few quick runs and maybe develop a good yorker and slow ball, but that same person might not have the patience for the longer form. Some other reasons why Test matches are finishing sooner is that the one-day game has meant some batters have lost the art of batting for a long time.

The general decline in the standard of pitches has not helped either and it has started to cause me concern. In the chapter about my season at Hampshire I said that groundsmen/curators should be left alone to prepare simply the best wicket they can, instead of having pressure put on them to cultivate something for their own bowlers. The wider good of the game is more important than the self-interest of any one side. Queensland and New South Wales tend to prepare surfaces to suit their own team and South Australia sometimes follows suit. As I have suggested for county cricket in England, maybe it is time that Australia considered doing away with the toss and letting the visiting team choose whether to bat or bowl. This would definitely be a good idea in Queensland and New South Wales.

In Australia, perhaps because the country is so vast and with varying climates, we are fortunate to have pitches with such different characteristics, so that young players learn to adapt. In most other countries they tend to be similar, either slow turners on the sub-continent or seamer-friendly in England, especially early in the season. In Melbourne you get a fast, bouncy pitch at the start which gets slower and then turns a little. In Queensland it does a bit early then flattens out and then turns – the perfect Test pitch – while Tasmania does a little bit early but then becomes harder for bowlers. Adelaide gives something for everybody – Adelaide Oval is probably the best batting track in the country for the first couple of days but by the end it can be the most spinner-friendly.

It will be interesting to pick up this chapter again in ten years or so and see whether any of my suggestions have been adopted and how many of my predictions have come true. These are only my opinions, and my crystal ball is unlikely to be any clearer than the next. It has been a very interesting journey so far and I hope it continues for a while yet!

SHANE WARNE IN TEST CRICKET

All records and statistics
up to and including Australia v. South Africa
6 January 2002

Compiled by Vic Isaacs

Test career series by series

	M	I	NO	Runs	HS	Avge	50	Ct	Overs	Mdns	Runs	Wkts	Avge	Best	SR	5wI	10wM
India in Australia, 1991/92 (Won 1, Drawn 1)	2	4	1	28	20	9.33	–	1	68	9	228	1	228.00	1/150	408.0	–	–
Australia in Sri Lanka, 1992/93 (Won 1, Drawn 1)	2	3	0	66	35	22.00	–	1	38.1	8	158	3	52.66	3/11	76.3	–	–
The Frank Worrell Trophy in Australia, 1992/93 (Won 1, Lost 2, Drawn 1)	4	7	0	42	14	6.00	–	3	108.2	23	313	10	31.30	7/52	65.0	1	–
Trans-Tasman Trophy in New Zealand, 1992/93 (Won 1, Lost 1, Drawn 1)	3	4	2	49	22*	24.50	–	1	159	73	256	17	15.05	4/8	56.1	–	–
The Ashes in England, 1993 (Won 4, Lost 1, Drawn 1)	6	5	2	113	37	37.66	–	4	439.5	158	877	34	25.79	5/82	77.6	1	–
Trans-Tasman Trophy in Australia, 1993/94 (Won 2, Drawn 1)	3	2	1	85	74*	85.00	1	4	151.3	49	305	18	16.94	6/31	50.5	1	–
South Africa in Australia, 1993/94 (Won 1, Lost 1, Drawn 1)	3	4	1	16	11	5.33	–	2	175.1	63	307	18	17.05	7/56	58.3	2	1
Australia in South Africa, 1993/94 (Won 1, Lost 1, Drawn 1)	3	5	0	41	15	8.20	–	–	190.5	69	336	15	22.40	4/86	76.3	–	–
Australia in Pakistan, 1994/95 (Lost 1, Drawn 2)	3	4	0	69	33	17.25	–	2	181.4	50	504	18	28.00	6/136	60.5	2	–
The Ashes in Australia, 1994/95 (Won 3, Lost 1, Drawn 1)	5	10	1	60	36*	6.66	–	5	256.1	84	549	27	20.33	8/71	56.9	2	1
The Frank Worrell Trophy in West Indies, 1994/95 (Won 2, Lost 1, Drawn 1)	4	5	0	28	11	5.60	–	2	138	35	406	15	27.06	4/70	55.2	–	–
Pakistan in Australia, 1995/96 (Won 2, Lost 1)	3	4	1	39	27*	13.00	–	–	115	52	198	19	10.42	7/23	36.3	1	1
Sri Lanka in Australia, 1995/96 (Won 3)	3	1	0	33	33	33.00	–	5	164.4	48	433	12	36.08	4/71	82.3	–	–

Test career series by series (continued)

	M	I	NO	Runs	HS	Avge	50	Ct	Overs	Mdns	Runs	Wkts	Avge	Best	SR	5wI	10wM
The Frank Worrell Trophy in Australia, 1996/97 (Won 3, Lost 2)	5	7	0	128	30	18.28	–	6	217.1	56	594	22	27.00	4/95	59.2	–	–
Australia in South Africa, 1996/97 (Won 2, Lost 1)	3	5	0	42	18	8.40	–	3	133	47	282	11	25.63	4/43	72.5	–	–
The Ashes in England, 1997 (Won 3, Lost 2, Drawn 1)	6	10	0	188	53	18.80	1	2	237.1	69	577	24	24.04	6/48	59.2	1	–
Trans-Tasman Trophy in Australia, 1997/98 (Won 2, Drawn 1)	3	3	0	71	36	23.66	–	–	170.4	36	476	19	25.05	5/88	53.8	1	–
South Africa in Australia, 1997/98 (Won 1, Drawn 2)	3	5	1	27	12	6.75	–	5	187.1	51	417	20	20.85	6/34	56.1	2	1
Border-Gavaskar Trophy in India, 1997/98 (Won 1, Lost 2)	3	5	0	105	35	21.00	–	–	167	37	540	10	54.00	4/85	100.2	–	–
The Ashes in Australia, 1998/99 (Won 1)	1	2	1	10	8	10.00	–	2	39	7	110	2	55.00	1/43	117.0	–	–
The Frank Worrell Trophy in West Indies, 1998/99 (Won 1, Lost 2)	3	6	0	138	32	23.00	–	3	83.5	18	268	2	134.00	1/70	134.0	–	–
Australia in Sri Lanka, 1999/2000 (Lost 1, Drawn 2)	3	4	0	6	6	1.50	–	2	56.1	20	115	8	14.37	5/52	42.1	1	–
Southern Cross Trophy in Zimbabwe, 1999/2000 (Won 1)	1	1	0	6	6	6.00	–	–	53.1	13	137	6	22.83	3/68	53.1	–	–
Pakistan in Australia, 1999/2000 (Won 3)	3	4	1	99	86	33.00	1	4	130	37	370	12	30.83	5/110	65.0	1	–
Border-Gavaskar Trophy in Australia, 1999/2000 (Won 3)	3	3	0	88	86	29.33	1	3	127	35	335	8	41.87	4/92	95.2	–	–
Trans-Tasman Trophy in New Zealand, 1999/2000 (Won 3)	3	4	0	36	12	9.00	–	4	129.2	33	414	15	27.60	4/68	51.7	–	–

Test career series by series (continued)

	M	I	NO	Runs	HS	Avge	50	Ct	Overs	Mdns	Runs	Wkts	Avge	Best	SR	5wI	10wM
Border-Gavaskar Trophy in India, 2000/01 (Won 1, Lost 2)	3	5	0	50	39	10.00	–	2	152.1	24	505	10	50.50	4/47	51.70	–	–
The Ashes in England, 2001 (Won 4, Lost 1)	5	4	0	13	8	3.25	–	6	195.2	33	580	31	18.70	7/165	37.80	3	1
Trans-Tasman Trophy in Australia, 2001/02 (Drawn 3)	3	4	0	201	99	50.25	–	2	124.2	19	430	6	71.66	3/89	124.30	–	–
South Africa in Australia, 2001/02 (Won 3)	3	4	0	85	41	21.25	–	–	173.3	35	473	17	27.82	5/113	61.20	1	–

Opponents

	M	I	NO	Runs	HS	Avge	50	Ct	Overs	Mdns	Runs	Wkts	Avge	BB	SR	5wI	10wM
England	23	31	4	384	53	14.22	1	19	1167.3	371	2693	118	22.82	8-71		7	2
India	11	17	1	271	86	16.93	1	6	514.1	105	1608	29	55.44	4-47		–	–
New Zealand	15	17	3	442	99	31.57	3	13	734.5	209	1881	75	25.08	6-31		2	–
Pakistan	9	12	2	207	86	20.70	1	6	426.3	138	1072	49	21.87	7-23		4	1
South Africa	15	23	2	211	41	10.05	–	12	859.4	265	1815	81	22.41	7-56		5	2
Sri Lanka	8	8	0	105	35	13.12	–	8	259	71	706	23	30.69	5-52		1	–
West Indies	16	25	0	336	32	13.44	–	14	547.2	132	1581	49	32.26	7-52		1	–
Zimbabwe	1	1	0	6	6	6.00	–	–	53.1	13	137	6	22.83	3-68		–	–
TOTAL	98	134	12	1962	99	16.08	6	78	4562.1	1320	11493	430	26.73	8-71		20	5

Wicket breakdown

	B	Ct	Ct(wk)	C&B	St	LBW
England	26	36	19	4	7	19
India	5	16	2	1	1	4
New Zealand	18	33	7	2	5	10
Pakistan	7	23	3	1	3	12
South Africa	16	35	6	4	2	18
Sri Lanka	1	14	4	1	2	1
West Indies	6	28	4	2	2	7
Zimbabwe	–	3	1	–	–	2
TOTAL for 430	**79**	**193**	**46**	**15**	**22**	**75**

5 wickets in an innings

7-52	v West Indies	Melbourne	1992–93
5-82	v England	Birmingham	1993
6-31	v New Zealand	Hobart	1993–94
7-56	v South Africa	Sydney	1993–94
5-72	v South Africa	Sydney	1993–94
5-89	v Pakistan	Karachi	1994–95
6-136	v Pakistan	Lahore	1994–95
8-71	v England	Brisbane	1994–95
6-64	v England	Melbourne	1994–95
7-23	v Pakistan	Brisbane	1995–96
6-48	v England	Manchester	1997
5-88	v New Zealand	Hobart	1997–98
5-75	v South Africa	Sydney	1997–98
6-34	v South Africa	Sydney	1997–98
5-52	v Sri Lanka	Kandy	1999–00
5-110	v Pakistan	Hobart	1999–00
5-71	v England	Birmingham	2001
6-33	v England	Nottingham	2001
7-165	v England	The Oval	2001
5-113	v South Africa	Adelaide	2001–02

10 wickets in a match

12-128	v South Africa	Sydney	1993–94
11-110	v England	Brisbane	1994–95
11-77	v Pakistan	Brisbane	1995–96
11-109	v South Africa	Sydney	1997–98
11-229	v England	The Oval	2001

Test record at each ground

	M	I	NO	Runs	HS	Avge	50	Ct	Overs	M	Runs	Wkts	Avge	BB	5wI	10wM
IN AUSTRALIA																
Adelaide	9	15	2	208	86	16.00	1	11	425.4	117	1059	34	31.14	5-113	1	–
Hobart	5	5	2	111	70	37.00	1	4	179	44	461	24	19.20	6-31	3	–
Brisbane	7	8	1	234	86	33.42	2	7	403.2	132	955	47	20.31	8-71	2	2
Melbourne	8	11	0	54	18	4.90	–	6	384.1	99	894	37	24.16	7-52	2	–
Sydney	10	14	3	177	37	16.09	–	7	520	143	1291	49	26.34	7-56	4	2
Perth	8	11	0	228	99	20.72	1	11	295.3	64	878	20	43.90	4-83	–	–
IN ENGLAND																
Edgbaston	3	4	0	97	47	24.25	–	3	141.4	46	382	15	25.46	5-71	2	–
Headingley	3	2	0	0	0	0.00	–	2	119.2	36	268	3	89.33	1-43	–	–
The Oval	3	4	0	86	37	21.50	–	4	175.2	52	466	20	23.30	7-165	1	1
Lord's	3	2	0	5	5	2.50	–	2	130.2	37	289	13	22.23	4-57	–	–
Old Trafford	2	3	1	71	53	35.50	1	1	133.4	58	248	17	14.58	6-48	1	–
Trent Bridge	3	4	1	55	35*	18.33	–	–	172	59	381	21	18.14	6-33	1	–
IN INDIA																
Calcutta	2	4	0	20	11	5.00	–	–	96.1	10	364	3	121.33	2-65	–	–
Bangalore	1	1	0	33	33	33.00	–	–	60	15	186	5	37.20	3-106	–	–
Chennai (formerly Madras)	2	4	0	63	35	15.75	–	1	113	25	388	7	55.42	4-85	–	–
Mumbai (formerly Bombay)	1	1	0	39	39	39.00	–	1	50	18	107	5	21.40	4-47	–	–

Test record at each ground (continued)

	M	I	NO	Runs	HS	Avge	50	Ct	Overs	M	Runs	Wkts	Avge	BB	5wI	10wM
IN NEW ZEALAND																
Wellington	2	2	0	29	22	14.50	–	2	110.5	42	268	11	24.36	4-68	–	–
Auckland	2	4	1	24	12	8.00	–	2	84.3	29	210	11	19.09	4-8	–	–
Christchurch	1	1	1	22	22*	–	–	–	48	19	86	7	12.28	4-63	–	–
Hamilton	1	1	0	10	10	10.00	–	1	45	16	106	3	35.33	2-61	–	–
IN PAKISTAN																
Lahore	1	1	0	33	33	33.00	–	–	71.5	14	240	9	26.66	6-136	1	–
Karachi	1	2	0	22	22	11.00	–	1	63.1	22	150	8	18.75	5-89	1	–
Rawalpindi	1	1	0	14	14	14.00	–	1	46.4	14	114	1	114.00	1-58	–	–
IN SOUTH AFRICA																
Durban	1	2	0	14	12	7.00	–	–	55	20	92	4	23.00	4-92	–	–
Johannesburg	2	3	0	25	15	8.33	–	–	114.3	42	239	11	21.72	4-43	–	–
Cape Town	1	1	0	11	11	11.00	–	–	77	31	116	6	19.33	3-38	–	–
Port Elizabeth	1	2	0	21	18	10.50	–	3	41.2	12	82	5	16.40	3-62	–	–
Centurion	1	2	0	12	12	6.00	–	–	36	11	89	0	2.47	–	–	–
IN SRI LANKA																
Kandy	1	2	0	6	6	3.00	–	–	22.5	7	70	5	14.00	5-52	1	–
Galle	1	1	0	0	0	0.00	–	1	28.2	12	34	3	11.33	3-29	–	–
Colombo (SSC)	2	3	0	59	35	19.66	–	2	32.1	6	129	3	43.00	3-11	–	–
Moratuwa	1	1	0	7	7	7.00	–	–	11	3	40	0	–	–	–	–

IN WEST INDIES

St John's	1	1	0	11	11	11.00	–	–	35	.9	101	3	33.66	3-83	–	–
Bridgetown	2	3	0	51	32	17.00	–	2	78.2	13	260	6	43.33	3-64	–	–
Port of Spain	2	4	0	57	25	14.25	–	2	29.5	9	77	1	77.00	1-16	–	–
Kingston	2	3	0	47	24	15.66	–	1	78.4	22	236	7	33.71	4-70	–	–

IN ZIMBABWE

Harare	1	1	0	6	6	6.00	–	–	53.1	13	137	6	22.83	3-68	–	–

Milestones

1st Wicket	RJ Shastri	c DM Jones	206 v India	Sydney	1991–92
50th Wicket	N Hussain	c DC Boon	71 v England	Nottingham	1993
100th Wicket	BM McMillan	lbw	4 v South Africa	Adelaide	1993–94
150th Wicket	SJ Rhodes	c ME Waugh	0 v England	Melbourne	1994–95
200th Wicket	HP Tillakaratne	c RT Ponting	119 v Sri Lanka	Perth	1995–96
250th Wicket	AJ Stewart	bowled	1 v England	Manchester	1997
300th Wicket	DJ Richardson	c & b	0 v South Africa	Sydney	1997–98
350th Wicket	HH Kanitkar	lbw	11 v India	Melbourne	1999–00
400th Wicket	AJ Stewart	c Gilchrist	29 v England	The Oval	2001

Leading batsmen dismissals

12	AJ Stewart	England
10	MA Atherton	England
9	N Hussain	England
9	GP Thorpe	England
8	WJ Cronje	South Africa
8	DJ Richardson	South Africa
7	R Dravid	India
7	D Gough	England

Fielders who assisted in dismissals

MA Taylor	51ct
IA Healy	34ct 15st
ME Waugh	32ct
AC Gilchrist	12ct 6st
RT Ponting	18ct
c & b	15ct
SR Waugh	14ct
GS Blewett	11ct
DC Boon	11ct

First-class career season by season

Season	Country	Team	M	I	NO	Runs	HS	Avge	50	Ct	Overs	M	Runs	Wkts	Avge	BB	5wI	10wM
1990/91	Australia	Victoria	1	1	0	20	20	20.00	–	–	37	13	102	1	102.00	1/41	–	–
1991/92	Australia	Victoria	9	11	4	120	30*	17.14	–	2	312	81	853	20	42.65	4/42	–	–
1991/92	Zimbabwe	Young Australia	2	3	2	53	35*	55.00	–	1	97.4	28	207	11	18.81	7/49	1	–
1992/93	Australia	Victoria	9	13	1	172	69	14.33	2	5	309.5	57	983	56	36.40	7/52	2	–
1992/93	New Zealand	Australia	4	5	2	51	22*	17.00	–	1	187.5	81	337	19	17.73	4/8	–	–
1992/93	Sri Lanka	Australia	3	4	0	67	35	16.75	–	1	38.1	8	158	3	52.66	3/11	–	–
1993	England	Australia	16	15	4	246	47	22.36	–	8	765.5	281	1698	280	22.64	5/61	2	–
1993/94	Australia	Victoria	10	12	2	151	74*	15.10	1	10	574.2	176	1255	63	19.92	7/56	5	1
1993/94	South Africa	Australia	5	8	1	84	34	12.00	–	1	278	96	552	24	23.00	4/86	–	–
1994/95	Australia	Victoria	7	14	1	101	36*	7.78	–	5	373.2	123	814	40	20.35	8/71	3	1
1994/95	Pakistan	Australia	4	5	0	73	33	14.60	–	2	210.4	59	598	23	26.00	6/136	2	–
1994/95	West Indies	Australia	6	6	0	51	23	8.50	–	5	178	46	553	23	24.04	4/70	–	–
1995/96	Australia	Victoria	9	9	2	132	36	18.85	–	9	449.5	131	1057	42	25.16	7/23	2	1
1996/97	South Africa	Australia	5	7	0	101	44	14.42	–	4	169	60	397	16	24.81	4/43	–	–
1996/97	Australia	Victoria	7	10	0	159	30	15.90	–	8	314.1	87	795	27	29.44	4/95	–	–

1997	England	Australia	12	17	1	293	53	18.31	1	–	5	433.4	111	1154	57	20.24	7/103	4	–
1997/98	Australia	Victoria	9	12	2	138	36	13.80	–	1	7	498.5	115	1381	47	29.38	6/34	3	1
1997/98	India	Australia	5	8	1	129	35	18.42	–	–	3	209	43	739	12	61.58	4/85	–	–
1998/99	Australia	Victoria	5	7	2	98	38	19.60	–	–	8	178.1	32	631	33	63.10	2/80	–	–
1998/99	West Indies	Australia	6	10	0	190	33	19.00	–	–	6	162.5	37	509	11	46.27	3/26	–	–
1999/00	Australia	Victoria	6	7	1	187	86	31.16	2	–	7	257	72	705	20	35.25	5/110	1	–
1999/00	New Zealand	Australia	4	5	0	60	24	12.00	–	–	6	158.2	38	519	17	30.52	4/68	–	–
1999/00	Sri Lanka	Australia	5	7	1	55	27	9.16	–	–	5	102.5	30	272	15	18.13	5/52	1	–
1999/00	Zimbabwe	Australia	2	3	1	8	6	4.00	–	–	0	92.1	27	238	10	23.80	3/50	–	–
2000	England	Hampshire	15	22	2	431	69	21.55	3	–	14	639.4	183	1620	70	23.14	6/34	5	–
2000/01	Australia	Victoria	2	2	0	39	27	19.50	–	–	2	47.5	8	140	9	15.55	5/49	1	–
2000/01	India	Australia	4	7	0	59	39	8.42	–	–	2	192.4	40	642	18	35.66	7/56	1	–
2000	England	Australia	8	10	2	237	69	29.62	2	–	13	263	56	784	42	18.66	7/165	3	1
2001/02	Australia	Victoria	8	11	1	296	99	29.60	2	–	8	373	63	1156	29	39.86	5/113	1	–
TOTALS			188	251	33	3801	99	17.43	13		148	7904.4	2181	20849	781	26.69	8/71	37	5

SHANE WARNE IN ONE-DAY INTERNATIONAL CRICKET

All records and statistics up to 24 February 2002

One-day international career series by series

	M	I	NO	Runs	HS	Avge	50	Ct	Overs	Mdns	Runs	Wkts	Avge	Best	SR	Econ	4wI
Australia in New Zealand, 1992/93 (Lost 1)	1	1	0	3	3	3.00	–	–	10	0	40	2	20.00	2/40	30.0	4.00	–
Benson and Hedges World Series in Australia, 1993/94 (Won 6, Lost 4)	10	6	1	15	9	3.00	–	4	90	5	301	22	13.68	4/19	24.5	3.34	2
Australia in South Africa, 1993/94 (Won 4, Lost 4)	8	3	0	87	55	29.00	1	3	69	3	285	11	25.90	4/36	37.6	4.13	1
Pepsi Austral-Asia Cup in Sharjah, 1993/94 (Won 2, Lost 1)	3	1	0	4	4	4.00	–	1	29	1	103	9	11.44	4/34	19.3	3.55	1
Singer World Series in Sri Lanka, 1994/95 (Won 1, Lost 2)	3	2	0	31	30	15.50	–	1	28	1	109	7	15.57	3/29	24.0	3.89	–
Wills Triangular Series in Pakistan, 1994/95 (Won 5, Lost 1)	6	3	2	39	15*	39.00	–	–	58.2	4	238	6	39.66	4/40	58.3	4.08	1
Benson and Hedges World Series in Australia, 1994/95 (Won 3, Lost 1)	4	2	0	26	21	13.00	–	2	39	1	133	6	22.16	2/27	39.0	3.41	–
New Zealand Centenary Tournament in New Zealand, 1994/95 (Won 3, Lost 1)	4	2	2	7	5*	–	–	2	40	6	140	5	28.00	2/18	48.0	3.50	–
Australia in West Indies, 1994/95 (Won 1, Lost 3)	4	3	2	22	12	22.00	–	1	39.1	5	204	4	51.00	2/33	58.7	5.20	–
Benson and Hedges World Series in Australia, 1995/96 (Won 7, Lost 2)	9	2	1	6	3*	6.00	–	3	80.1	7	317	15	21.13	3/20	32.0	3.95	–
Wills World Cup in India, Pakistan and Sri Lanka, 1995/96 (Won 5, Lost 2)	7	5	2	32	24	10.66	–	1	68.3	3	263	12	21.91	4/34	34.2	3.83	2
Carlton and United Series in Australia, 1996/97 (Won 3, Lost 5)	8	5	1	38	11	9.50	–	3	75.4	5	325	19	17.10	5/33	23.8	4.29	2
Australia in South Africa, 1996/97 (Won 4, Lost 2)	6	5	1	45	23	11.25	–	3	54.1	2	272	10	27.20	2/36	32.5	5.02	–

One-day international career series by series (continued)

	M	I	NO	Runs	HS	Avge	50	Ct	Overs	Mdns	Runs	Wkts	Avge	Best	SR	Econ	4wI
Texaco Trophy in England, 1997 (Lost 3)	3	3	1	20	11*	10.00	–	1	29	0	129	1	129.00	1/39	174.0	4.44	–
Carlton and United Series in Australia, 1997/98 (Won 5, Lost 5)	10	6	1	35	17	7.00	–	7	93.3	3	405	12	33.75	3/48	46.7	4.33	–
Pepsi Triangular Series in India, 1997/98 (Won 3, Lost 2)	5	4	1	27	14	9.00	–	2	49	0	219	5	43.80	2/45	58.8	4.46	–
Coca-Cola Cup in Sharjah, 1997/98 (Won 4, Lost 1)	5	3	2	32	19	32.00	–	–	47	2	221	4	55.25	2/28	70.5	4.70	–
Carlton and United Series in Australia, 1998/99 (Won 9, Lost 3)	12	8	2	43	11	7.16	–	6	112.5	2	532	19	28.00	3/16	35.6	4.71	–
Australia in West Indies, 1998/99 (Won 3, Lost 3, Tied 1)	7	5	2	84	29	28.00	–	–	63	10	254	13	19.53	3/28	29.0	4.03	–
ICC World Cup in England/Ireland/Scotland/Netherlands, 1999 (Won 7, Lost 2, Tied 1)	10	4	1	34	18	11.33	–	1	94.2	13	361	20	18.05	4/29	28.3	3.82	2
Aiwa Cup in Sri Lanka, 1999/2000 (Won 4, Lost 1)	5	4	0	43	21	10.75	–	1	40	1	214	6	35.66	2/36	40.0	5.35	–
Australia in Zimbabwe, 1999/2000 (Won 3)	3	–	–	–	–	–	–	2	19	1	82	4	20.50	2/40	28.5	4.31	–
Carlton and United Series in Australia, 1999/2000 (Won 3, Lost 1)	4	3	2	29	16*	29.00	–	4	36	4	170	4	42.50	2/52	54.0	4.72	–
Australia in New Zealand, 1999/2000 (Won 4, Lost 1, NR 1)	6	2	0	19	12	9.50	–	2	49	4	194	9	21.55	3/50	32.6	3.95	–
Australia in South Africa, 1999/2000 (Won 1, Lost 2)	3	2	0	32	32	16.00	–	2	28	3	98	3	32.66	2/30	56.0	3.50	–
South Africa in Australia, 2000/01 (Won 1, Lost 1, Tied 1)	3	2	1	16	9*	16.00	–	2	30	2	101	2	50.50	2/38	90.0	3.36	–

	M	I	NO	Runs	HS	Avge	50	Ct	Overs	Mdns	Runs	Wkts	Avge	Best	SR	Econ	4wI
Carlton Series in Australia, 2000/01 (Won 9)	9	1	0	7	7	7.00	–	–	84.5	5	377	18	20.94	4/48	28.2	4.44	1
Australia in India, 2000/01 (Won 2, Lost 2)	4	2	0	31	18	15.50	–	4	38	0	222	4	55.50	3/38	57.0	5.84	–
NatWest Series in England, 2001 (Won 4, Lost 1)	5	2	1	28	14*	28.00	–	5	45	3	232	10	23.20	3/52	27.0	5.15	–
VB Series in Australia, 2001/02 (Won 4, Lost 4)	8	6	0	72	29	12.00	–	2	75	4	324	6	54.00	2/65	75.0	4.32	–

Opponents

	M	I	NO	Runs	HS	Avge	50	Ct	Overs	M	Runs	Wkts	Avge	Best	4wI
Bangladesh	1	–	–	–	–	–	–	–	10	2	18	1	18.00	1/18	–
England	14	9	3	89	21	14.83	–	6	130.5	2	562	16	35.12	3/16	–
India	18	15	5	109	19	10.90	–	5	162.2	2	844	15	56.26	3/38	–
Kenya	1	1	1	0	0*	–	–	–	10	0	25	1	25.00	1/25	–
New Zealand	26	12	1	143	29	13.00	–	11	242.2	16	941	48	19.60	4/19	3
Pakistan	16	10	2	97	30	12.12	–	10	151.1	15	662	30	22.06	4/33	3
South Africa	42	27	5	268	55	12.18	1	18	385.4	23	1564	55	28.43	4/29	3
Scotland	1	–	–	–	–	–	–	–	10	0	39	3	13.00	3/39	–
Sri Lanka	17	9	2	53	21	7.57	–	4	156	7	721	28	25.75	3/20	–
West Indies	27	12	6	132	29	22.00	–	11	250.4	29	1045	50	20.90	5/33	2
Zimbabwe	12	2	1	16	11*	16.00	–	7	105.3	5	444	21	21.14	4/34	1
TOTAL	175	97	26	907	55	12.77	1	72	1614.3	101	6865	268	25.61	5/33	12

Wicket breakdown

	B	Ct	Ct(wk)	C&B	St	LBW	HW
Bangladesh	–	–	–	–	–	1	–
England	3	5	1	2	2	3	–
India	1	9	1	1	3	–	–
Kenya	–	–	–	–	1	–	–
New Zealand	5	22	1	3	7	10	–
Pakistan	5	8	3	2	7	5	–
Scotland	1	1	–	–	1	–	–
South Africa	10	20	2	1	12	10	–
Sri Lanka	5	15	2	–	4	2	–
West Indies	10	16	4	3	6	11	–
Zimbabwe	4	7	3	1	4	1	1
TOTAL for 268	44	103	17	13	47	43	1

4 wickets in an innings

4-25	v New Zealand	Adelaide	1993-94
4-10	v New Zealand	Melbourne	1993-94
4-36	v South Africa	Port Elizabeth	1993-94
4-34	v New Zealand	Sharjah	1993-94
4-40	v South Africa	Faisalabad	1994-95
4-34	v Zimbabwe	Nagpur	1995-96
4-36	v West Indies	Chandigarh	1995-96
5-33	v West Indies	Sydney	1996-97
4-52	v Pakistan	Adelaide	1996-97
4-37	v Pakistan	Sydney	1996-97
4-29	v South Africa	Birmingham	1999
4-33	v Pakistan	Lord's	1999
4-48	v West Indies	Melbourne	2000-01

One-day international record at each ground

	M	I	NO	Runs	HS	Avge	50	Ct	Overs	M	Runs	Wkts	Best	Avge	4wI
IN AUSTRALIA															
Adelaide	8	5	0	49	22	9.80	–	8	73.5	4	308	16	4/25	19.25	2
Brisbane	6	3	0	25	9	8.33	–	2	59	1	281	5	3/41	56.20	–
Hobart (Bellerive Oval)	4	2	0	9	5	4.50	–	–	35.2	0	154	8	3/45	19.25	–
Melbourne (Colonial Stadium)	3	2	1	16	9*	16.00	–	2	30	2	101	2	2/38	50.50	–
Melbourne	25	11	1	74	29	7.40	–	9	239.4	18	916	40	4/19	22.90	2
Perth	7	6	3	33	16*	11.00	–	5	69	2	317	11	3/53	28.81	–
Sydney	24	12	4	81	17	10.12	–	15	210.1	11	908	41	5/33	22.14	2
IN ENGLAND															
Birmingham	1	1	0	18	18	18.00	–	–	10	4	29	4	4/29	7.25	1
Bristol	1	–	–	–	–	–	–	1	9	0	48	0	–	–	–
Cardiff	2	1	0	15	15	15.00	–	2	20	1	96	4	3/52	24.00	–
Chester-le-Street	1	–	–	–	–	–	–	–	10	2	18	1	1/18	18.00	–
Leeds	3	2	0	5	4	2.50	–	1	30	1	129	3	2/33	43.00	–
Lord's	4	1	0	5	5	5.00	–	2	37	1	188	8	4/33	23.50	1
Manchester	2	1	1	14	14*	–	–	–	17	6	27	5	3/11	5.40	–
Nottingham	1	1	0	14	14	14.00	–	–	9	1	60	2	2/60	30.00	–
The Oval	2	2	2	11	11*	–	–	1	16.2	0	88	1	1/39	88.00	–
Worcester	1	–	–	–	–	–	–	–	10	0	39	3	3/39	13.00	–

One-day international record at each ground (continued)

	M	I	NO	Runs	HS	Avge	50	Ct	Overs	M	Runs	Wkts	Best	Avge	4wI
IN INDIA															
Ahmedabad (Sardar Patel Stadium)	1	1	1	11	11*	–	–	1	10	0	45	2	2/45	22.50	–
Bangalore	1	1	0	13	13	13.00	–	–	10	0	58	1	1/58	58.00	–
Chennai (formerly Madras)	1	1	0	24	24	24.00	–	–	10	0	52	2	2/52	26.00	–
Delhi	2	1	0	14	14	14.00	–	1	20	0	89	2	1/35	44.50	–
Indore	1	1	0	18	18	18.00	–	–	10	0	64	0	–	–	–
Jaipur	1	–	–	–	–	–	–	–	10	1	30	0	–	–	–
Kanpur	1	1	0	2	2	2.00	–	–	9	0	43	1	1/43	43.00	–
Kochi (formerly Indore)	1	1	0	0	0	0.00	–	–	10	0	42	0	–	–	–
Margoa	1	–	–	–	–	–	–	–	8	0	62	0	–	–	–
Mohali	1	1	1	6	6*	–	–	1	9	0	36	4	4/36	9.00	1
Mumbai (formerly Bombay)	1	1	0	0	0	0.00	–	–	10	1	28	1	1/28	28.00	–
Nagpur	1	–	–	–	–	–	–	–	9.3	1	34	4	4/34	8.50	1
Visakhapatnam	2	1	1	0	0*	–	–	3	20	0	63	4	3/38	15.75	–
IN NEW ZEALAND															
Auckland	4	1	0	7	7	7.00	–	–	40	4	121	6	2/21	20.16	–
Christchurch	1	–	–	–	–	–	–	–	9	0	50	3	3/50	16.66	–
Dunedin	2	1	1	5	5*	–	–	–	20	1	111	2	2/50	55.50	–

Napier	1	1	0	12	12	12.00	–	–	10	2	34	1	1/34	34.00	–
Wellington (Westpark Trust)	1	–	–	–	–	–	–	–	0	–	0	0	–	–	–
Wellington (Basin Reserve)	2	2	1	5	3	5.00	–	–	20	3	58	4	2/18	14.50	–
IN PAKISTAN															
Faisalabad	1	1	1	15	15*	–	–	–	9.2	0	40	4	4/40	10.00	1
Lahore	3	1	0	2	2	2.00	–	–	30	2	129	0	–	–	–
Multan	1	–	–	–	–	–	–	–	10	1	29	1	1/29	29.00	–
Peshawar	1	1	0	13	13	13.00	–	–	10	0	51	1	1/51	51.00	–
Rawalpindi	1	1	1	11	11*	–	–	–	9	1	47	0	–	–	–
IN SOUTH AFRICA															
Bloemfontein	1	–	–	–	–	–	–	–	10	0	37	1	1/37	37.00	–
Cape Town	3	1	0	23	23	23.00	–	–	30	1	116	6	3/31	19.33	–
Centurion	2	1	0	9	9	9.00	–	–	18	2	93	3	2/52	31.00	–
Durban	3	3	0	35	23	11.66	1	–	24.1	3	115	3	2/36	38.33	–
East London	2	1	0	4	4	4.00	–	–	20	0	70	3	2/36	23.33	–
Johannesburg	3	2	1	38	32	38.00	–	–	30	2	131	3	2/30	43.66	–
Port Elizabeth	3	2	0	55	55	27.50	1	–	119	0	93	5	4/36	18.60	1
IN SRI LANKA															
Colombo (PSS)	1	–	–	–	–	–	–	–	8	0	27	2	2/27	13.50	–

One-day international record at each ground (continued)

	M	I	NO	Runs	HS	Avge	50	Ct	Overs	M	Runs	Wkts	Best	Avge	4wI
Colombo (Khettarama)	3	3	0	37	21	12.33	–	–	27	0	151	4	2/52	37.75	–
Colombo (SSC)	2	2	0	34	30	17.00	–	–	17	1	70	3	3/29	23.33	–
Galle	2	1	0	3	3	3.00	–	–	16	1	75	4	2/36	18.75	–
IN UAE															
Sharjah	8	4	2	36	19	18.00	–	–	76	3	324	13	4/34	24.92	1
IN WEST INDIES															
Bridgetown	3	1	0	20	20	20.00	–	–	28	5	112	4	3/28	28.00	–
Georgetown	1	1	1	19	19*	–	–	–	6	0	35	2	2/35	17.50	–
Kingston (Arnos Vale)	2	2	1	17	11	17.00	–	–	19.1	6	63	4	2/30	15.75	–
Port of Spain	4	4	2	50	29	25.00	–	–	39	2	209	4	3/35	52.25	–
St John's	1	–	–	–	–	–	–	–	10	2	39	3	3/39	13.00	–
IN ZIMBABWE															
Bulawayo (Queens Sports Club)	1	–	–	–	–	–	–	–	9	1	40	2	2/40	20.00	–
Harare	2	–	–	–	–	–	–	–	10	0	42	2	2/42	21.00	–

Milestones

1st Wicket	AH Jones	st IA Healy	29	v New Zealand	Wellington	1992–93
50th Wicket	RS Mahanama	bowled	20	v Sri Lanka	Colombo (PSS)	1994–95
100th Wicket	JR Murray	c GS Blewett	24	v West Indies	Melbourne	1996–97
150th Wicket	CL Cairns	st AC Gilchrist	56	v New Zealand	Sharjah	1997–98
200th Wicket	Moin Khan	c AC Gilchrist	6	v Pakistan	Lord's	1999
250th Wicket	VVS Laxman	st AC Gilchrist	11	v India	Visakhapatnam	2000–01

Leading batsmen dismissals

8	DJ Cullinan	South Africa
7	WJ Cronje	South Africa
6	CD McMillan	New Zealand
6	JN Rhodes	South Africa
5	JC Adams	West Indies
5	Inzamam-ul-Haq	Pakistan

Fielders who assisted in dismissals

IA Healy	13ct 21st
AC Gilchrist	4ct 22st
ME Waugh	17ct
c & b	13ct
MG Bevan	11ct
DR Martyn	11ct

All one-day cricket (internationals and domestic) to 24 February 2002

M	I	NO	Runs	HS	Avge	50	Ct	Overs	Runs	Wkts	Avge	BB	4wI
229	141	32	1351	55	12.39	1	92	2077.2	8743	352	24.83	5/33	17

INDEX